FAST BOAT
NEKKID

An Escapade by Sea from
ALASKA to MEXICO

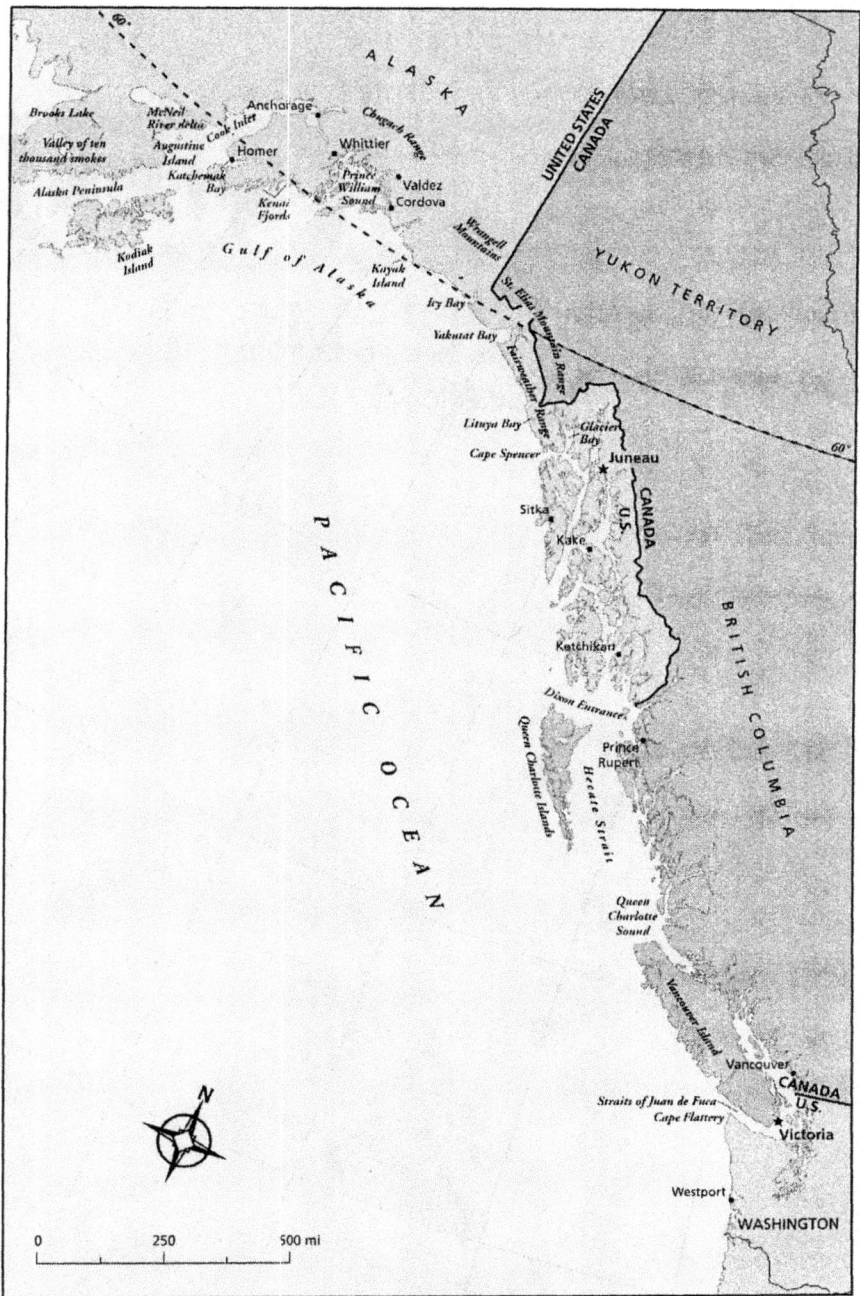

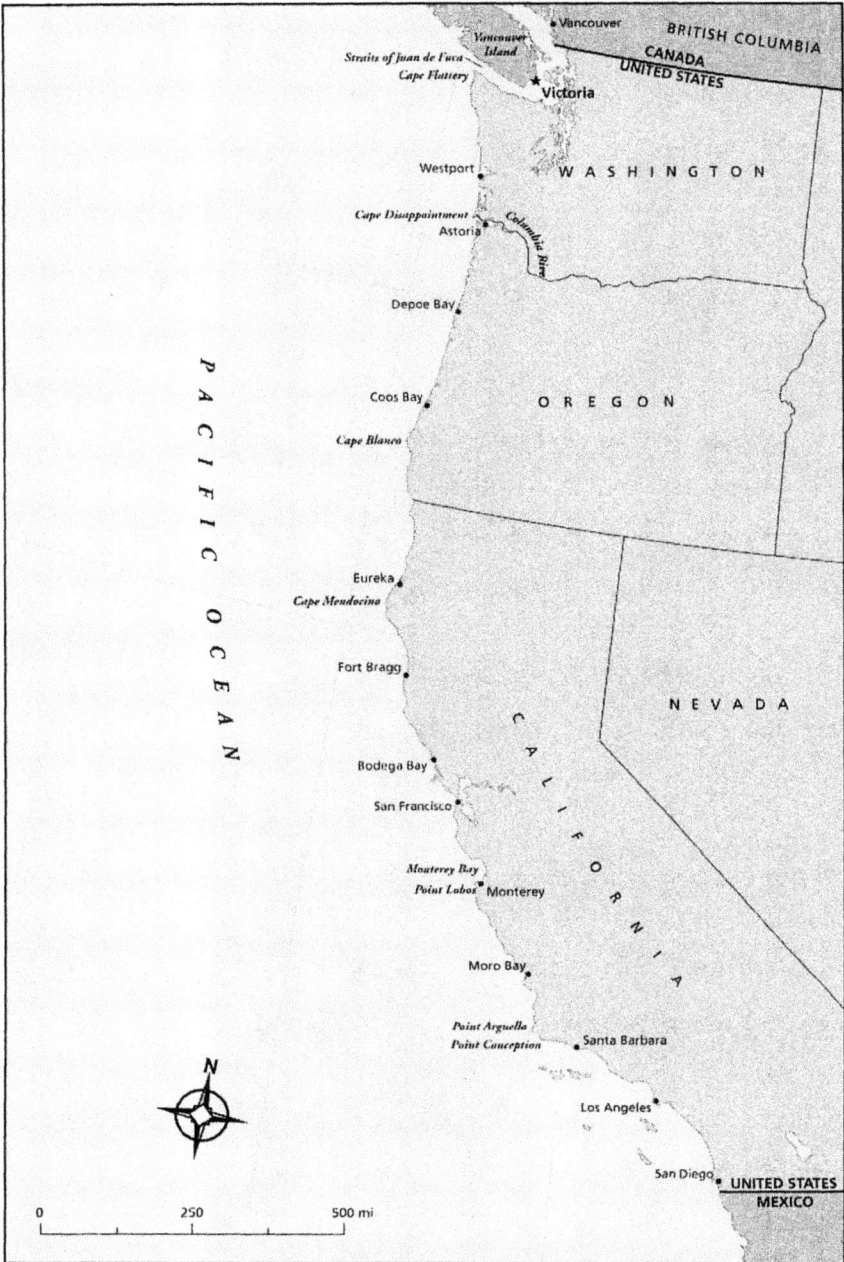

Vancouver

BRITISH COLUMBIA

Vancouver Island

CANADA

UNITED STATES

Straits of Juan de Fuca

Cape Flattery

★ Victoria

W A S H I N G T O N

Westport

Cape Disappointment

Astoria

Columbia River

Depoe Bay

P A C I F I C   O C E A N

Coos Bay

O R E G O N

Cape Blanco

Eureka

Cape Mendocino

Fort Bragg

N E V A D A

C A L I F O R N I A

Bodega Bay

San Francisco

Monterey Bay

Point Lobos Monterey

Moro Bay

Point Arguello

Point Conception Santa Barbara

Los Angeles

San Diego

UNITED STATES

MEXICO

N

0   250   500 mi

FAST BOAT
NEKKID

An Escapade by Sea from
ALASKA to MEXICO

Phil Phillips

Paperback ISBN: 978-0-578-97930-4
Originally published by Xlibris, 2005
ISBN 1-4134-5983-8 and 1-4134-5982-X
LCCN 2004094340 // V.2.0

Additional copies of this book and two more books by the author, *Rascal and Me* and *Slow Boat Nekkid*, are available from Amazon and other fine retailers.

Contents

Table of Costal Charts

To those who live at least a part of their lives
just for the sheer joy of it,
and to those who will, including
Grant Edward"Hot Rod' Phillips

Acknowledgments

FOR ALL OF this book that is eloquent, witty, brilliant, precise, concise, vivid, profound, refined, praiseworthy, I alone am responsible and accept the credit. For its deficiencies, others should be held to account. These include Tom Fryer, John Sefton, and Carol Bravo, who read early drafts and offered thoughtful advice, and Linda Stadtmiller, who turned my scribbles into processed words over and over again. Though they share the blame, I owe them grateful thanks. My parents, too, deserve a share of responsibility. It was they who encouraged me as a small child to run away from home, though I confounded them by returning.

A Note on Distances

THE TERM "MILES," as I use it in this book, means statute miles (one statute mile is 5,280 feet) when on land, such as the hauling of *Rascal* from Florida to Alaska. It means nautical miles (one of these is 6,076 feet) when at sea. In general, the greater the distance I refer to the less precise are its stated number of miles; for very long expanses the stated miles are only rough approximations.

All the intricate twists and turns of the U.S. and Canadian western coastlines make an accurate assessment of the length of the voyage's three main segments and its total length difficult to determine precisely; the meandering route I chose makes it nearly impossible. My conclusions as to these distances are approximations.

Introduction

*Yeah, youse at de mid-life awright. Youse halfway
tween de hospital and de cemetery. Jes hafded.
—Overheard at a beach front bar.*
- Guana Cay, Bahamas

THE LEXICON OF American English is indebted to the Southern humorist Lewis Grizzard (RIP) for making the important distinction between the word naked and its vernacular counterpart nekkid. "Naked," he said, "is when you ain't got no clothes on. Nekkid is when you ain't got no clothes on and you are up to somethin'. You are naked in the shower, but nekkid in a hot tub with a person of the other gender. Babies are naked, *Playboy* centerfolds are nekkid."

The simple declarative statement, "Darlene is naked," standing alone, is a bland fact, deprived of spirit. But if we say, "I wish Darlene were nekkid," another and livelier facet of mind is brought to life: sensations are invoked, vivid images appear, and beguiling prospects take us firmly in their grasp. Getting naked is just an everyday event, a mindless necessity. But getting nekkid… well, that's another matter altogether.

Nekkid suggests an escapade, spontaneity, passion, a zest for life. Naked people's faces wear the vapid flatline look of an accountant reading an IRS form. For a nekkid person, though, it's not hard to conjure the image of a wry, expectant smile or a smirk of eager anticipation or a twinkling eye and gleeful grin. Nekkid is just plain fun. It was the desire to get nekkid, in the metaphorical sense, that led to the solo adventure in a fast open boat that is the subject of this book.

Most of us go about our daily lives, from birth through maturity and beyond, in a lockstep performance as programmed as a computer's. We play, go to schools, have friends, love, marry, raise children, pursue a career, participate in sports and community, all the while making peer-approved, rather predictable choices along the way. Sociologists tell us we are, most of us anyway, bound rigidly by genetic command, social convention, class expectation, custom, and fashion.

We, in short, live out most of our lives naked, rarely or never breaking free of those subtle bonds that hold us to the established and routine, to the predictable and expected behavior that got us where we are. After long years of faithfully adhering to the norm, after we have arrived at and passed maturity and acquired the material necessities and luxuries we'd like, we come to realize it's high time for a lark; it's time to get nekkid. John Lee Hooker said it another way in his song, Boogie Chillen:

> "I heard papa tell mama,
> let that boy boogie-woogie,
> it's in him,
> and it's got to come out."

This story is about getting nekkid, or doing the boogie-woogie if you like.

Running around solo in a small, fast open boat is a common experience for people who live near the water. Nothing new there. But using it to travel long distances (my longest trip so far was 7,660 miles) over an extended period and doing it alone, well that's odd. Not exactly bizarre and not weird either, but certainly odd. It's just not done much, but it's one of the ways I break free of constraints and take on something for the sheer joy of it, just because it's fun

Why I do it is not really all that important. If you're lucky enough to find something you find exciting—reading Keats, bass fishing, playing bridge, or mud wrestling—it's utterly pointless to ask yourself why you like it. Yes I know this runs contrary to the feminine ideal that we should, as the cliché goes, get in touch with our feelings, but first I'm not a female, and second, I just don't care to know why. It's not important. All I know is I like it and that's enough, kind of like having a taste for Hank Williams over Pia Zadora.

Still, if I were backed into a corner and had no choice but to say why I came to this peculiar pastime, I would cite speed and the teenlike exhilaration from going fast, especially over the water with wind in my face. I'd also mention the elegant simplicity of an open outboard-powered fiberglass boat—not a lot of mechanical stuff to break—and it's easily hauled overland anywhere you may want to go.

But by a large measure the greatest appeal of my offbeat hobby is the nearly perfect sense of unconstrained personal freedom I get when flying along over a wide blue sea—like the feeling you got that fine day every June when school let out for the summer and you walked off the grounds a newly uncaged person, though merely on parole. As citizens of a country that today celebrates feminine and often repudiates masculine ideals, most of us have become far too risk averse—French, in a word. Avoiding injury, both economic and physical, and especially emotional, is among our highest priorities these days. The safety net, once a device for catching errant circus acrobats, has become an economic and social featherbed to cushion us from our follies and misfortunes, the government version of a hangover cure.

Governments at all three levels, responding to our concerns, impose silly rules to protect us from ourselves, implying thereby that we're too dumb to do so on our own. It's unlawful to buy or sell a new car, at first without seat belts, now without air bags. Of course it's also unlawful to decline to use them or to disable them. It's unlawful to take your child anywhere in a car without properly using a government-approved baby seat; to manufacture or distribute most consumer products without helpful warning labels like "Don't stick your hand under a running lawn mower"; to build an addition to your home without a government agency approving its design and inspecting its construction; to operate a boat without a list of required gear on board; to rent your home, or decline to rent it, to any person you choose—and the list goes on and on and on.

At the turn of the millennium, the Code of Federal Regulations, official repository for all federally made rules, the webbing of the safety net, comprised more than two hundred volumes and required nearly twenty feet of shelf space. Each of the states and most counties and municipalities have, in addition, their own versions of the Code. With each well-intended rule, a tiny grain of our freedom is lost. As the grains grow in number, they begin to bury us under a pile of suffocating restrictions and press the sweet breath of a free life from us.

As if government rules were not enough, a long list of fun stuff not yet unlawful is aggressively discouraged by preachy busybodies. Included are such gleeful events as: eating too much of anything, but especially high-fat foods; drinking to excess, which is at least half the fun; and driving fast cars or gas-slurping SUVs. Also dimly viewed is robust profanity; cussing as a rhetorical flourish is becoming a lost art. Even laughter itself suffers. Humor at the expense of one ethnic or gender or religious or other group and humor that is vulgar, tasteless, or profane, which together make up nearly all of the very best jokes, is a no-no. And whatever else, be sure not to smoke, dip, or chew or you'll have the pests telling you, with that gravely self-righteous look on their faces, just how awful *your* habit is, as though you gave a damn.

We're discouraged by law and by law-molded social convention from experimenting, from taking chances, from being impetuous, from acting inanely. From getting nekkid. What once was wild fun, reckless passion, and unrestrained exhilaration is now at least a taboo, maybe a misdemeanor, or even a felony. So we grow timorous. We get naked but too rarely nekkid, and the boogie-woogie that's in us never gets out.

But out on the vast plains of the open sea, one man in a boat will run up against few of those suffocating intrusions into private life imposed by the nanny state or hell-bent do-gooders. Those annoying idealists who would fence the asylum, who are devoted to protecting us from ourselves; making us the perfect citizens; or telling us just how we should live, work, and behave are, out on the ocean, nowhere to be seen.

Out there are no traffic lanes or traffic signals—or traffic for that matter. At sea there are no federal security guys commanding us to remove our shoes or groping us to find that lethal toothpick with which we might capture an airliner. We are not obliged to recycle, to refrain from riding in the bow of a boat or the back of a pickup truck, to wear a helmet while riding a motorcycle or a bicycle, or to talk in offend-nobody, sanitized blandspeak. We can cuss and tell dirty jokes and ethnic jokes. And we can smoke, dip, or chew, or drink as much of anything anywhere we have a mind to. Those freedom-robbing laws, rules, and regulations are few out there, and even these can be easily ignored, or only selectively obeyed if we like, because there are no cops—well, not many anyway.

In a masterful deception, bordering on delusion, we are, when at sea, returned to the precivilized state of nature, to the aboriginal man, where we actually face the very real consequences of our behavior, and the safety net is a mere abstraction. We are, in two words, magnificently free.

Well, almost. As if to underscore the delusion and crash the celebration of freedom, I was unknowingly destined to violate a few of the few rules there are, to encounter the cops as a result, and to pay a small fine. Nobody's perfect!

In ironic testament to our contemporary aversion to perceived risk, some may think my unusual hobby is too dangerous, foolhardy even. But it's neither, not even close, when seen from the perspective of, say, the amazing adventures of Joshua Slocum. Setting out from Boston in 1895 at the age of fifty-one, on his ninety-five-year-old, thirty-seven-foot, wood-hulled sloop, the *Spray,* he returned more than three years later, becoming the first person to sail alone around the world. For navigation, he had only charts, a sextant, and astronomic tables. For communication, he had only his voice. For weather forecasts, he had nothing on which to rely but his own skill at reading the skies. He had no VHF, cell phone, satellite phone, radar, fathometer, GPS, chart plotter, no survival suit, or strobe light. No motor powered the *Spray* upwind or through doldrums. Nor had Slocum any money, advertising sponsor, or insurance. He had no Social Security, disability, unemployment, minimum wage, Medicare, Medicaid, or other I'm-from-the-government-and-I'm-here-to-help-you benefits.

The wood hull of the *Spray*, unlike modern fiberglass, was prone to leak at its seams and its planks to separate under stress. Sea worms bored into it, weakening and eventually penetrating the hull with potentially disastrous consequences. Canvas sails, more so than modern nylon, would rot and rip and tear away in a gale. And, of course, no coast guard or marine patrol anywhere in the world could come to his aid or—more likely in their modern role—cite him for spilling oil (lamp oil in his case); for not having required safety gear, or this or that permit, license, certificate, or registration; or for not having a sanitation system that complied with environmental laws. (We can only imagine what Slocum's reaction would have been had he been told that discharging human waste into the sea could be a felony.) Yet for all these limitations, seen from the vantage point of coddled modernity, he made it. Now that was an adventure! And dangerous too. By sharp contrast, my travels are closer to the vagrancy of a Depression-era vagabond, except that *Rascal's* accommodations, spare as they are, are more luxurious than a railroad boxcar, and folding money for food, drink, and fun is not a significant constraint.

It wouldn't be an easy task to get past my wife the idea that after a life spent conforming to the programmed norm (excepting a few lapses here and there) I wished now to spend some time getting nekkid. In fact, this was going to be a pretty hard sell, especially if I used dumb, direct-guy talk like "Honey, I think I'll take a long boat trip." Instead, I decided to present the matter in the vernacular of pop psychobabble. I told her that I had earned a midlife crisis and, by God, I intended to have one.

She responded in a needlessly brutish way: "Mid life, huh? And how many men do you know who are 108 years old?"

A cheap shot. Unfazed, I continued, telling her that I had narrowed the possibilities to two: either a weeklong, wild house party with just me and a gaggle of nekkid girls or a long solo trip in a fast open boat. She replied, "Bon voyage."

The author, at Hachiman Shrine, Kamakura, Japan. Above, age seven, with brother. Below with father and brother.

Chapter One

*There is nothing—absolutely
nothing—half so much worth doing
as simply messing about in boats.*
- Kenneth Grahame

MY LOVE FOR rootless wandering, a turn of mind that so far has culminated in the voyage that is the subject of this book, had its earliest beginning, so far as I can tell, in the Pentagon. There, on the second floor, down one of the building's interminable corridors, was a large, windowless but noteworthy room. In this great space, a sea of government-issue wooden desks made of coarse-grained oak, stained to resemble varnished mahogany, were arranged in a grid of neat rows, perfectly spaced each from the other. At every desk was a slat-backed wood chair with armrests and a seat vaguely contoured to fit the anatomy of a sitting human. On every chair sat a man dressed in the distinctive white summer uniform of a U.S. Navy sailor. Clean-shaven and short-haired, these were the desk jockeys of the Bureau of Personnel, or BuPers as the unit was known in the Department of the Navy.

On one particular day, like most, the room was a din of clattering typewriter keys, intermingled with the ding of the bell that told the typist he had reached the right margin. At one desk, the Underwood upright held in its grip a five-part set of papers— original and four onionskin copies interspersed with sheets of carbon paper—stamp-signed by Dan A. Kimball, Secretary of the Navy. These official orders directed my then 36-year-old father,

Lieutenant Commander Philip B. Phillips, M.D., to proceed from his current duty station at the U.S. Naval Hospital, Pensacola, Florida, to the U.S. Naval Hospital, Yokosuka, Japan for a tour of duty as Assistant Chief of Psychiatry.

Two weeks later the orders arrived at our home with what would prove to be fateful consequences. Until that day, my world had been a place of enveloping arms, caressing voices, and the daily fun of tormenting my two younger brothers. Its outermost physical limits included our tiny bungalow and its miniature yard, the surrounding neighborhood perhaps three blocks square, a nearby wood, a railroad trestle over a saltwater lagoon, a white sand beach with an alluring islet an easy swim away (where I was sure pirate-buried treasure lay), the interior of the family car, and the elementary school on the Navy base. My world was enticing if miniature, and already I had explored it, wide-eyed and alert with every step. When those orders arrived, sent by the desk jockeys at BuPers, my little realm changed abruptly. Dad almost immediately left for Japan. A few months later, Mother loaded me, age six, and brothers Tom, four, and Mark, two, into her sun-faded blue 1947 Plymouth two-door sedan and set off across the country to San Francisco for the first leg of our trip to Japan.

As the oldest, I was privileged to sit in the right front seat, which was also closer—too close, if you had asked me—to Mom's disciplining slaps. There, wind blowing through the triangular vent window kept me cool, and there too, I propped my chin on the open window frame and watched as America unscrolled before me. On two-lane blacktop roads, we drove west across the bottom of the country, later called the Sunbelt, through farmland and forests, over arid hills, and across pool table-flat deserts. In late afternoons, Mother would stop at some family-owned local motel with a name like Kozy Kabin Motor Kourt having the all-important swimming pool. Our room, usually a separate cabin with walls of tongue-in-groove, stain-darkened knotty pine, served that night as our new home, but one with exotic surroundings.

After eight days of exploring the country from our windows, we reached San Francisco and there moved into a hotel in the heart of a beehive-busy place, where buildings blocked the sun, streams of odd people paraded along the sidewalks, and honking cars and trucks jammed the streets. Steep hills and trolley cars and Chinamen, peculiar accents, and the pungent smell of salt sea that rolled in each evening with the fog delighted my impressionable mind and revealed a world wondrously varied and textured, filled with sounds and aromas and scenes and people I had never imagined. The city had not yet gone wobbly, as it was to in the sixties. It, as yet, housed no potheads or flower children and, regrettably, the generous sharing of affection known as free love had not yet come into vogue, though at my age it would have had a limited appeal anyway.

At the docks in San Francisco Bay, we boarded the U.S.S. *Daniel Patrick* and began the long voyage to Japan. By the time we arrived two weeks later, I had ventured down every companionway, along every bulkhead, and through every hatch on the ship, and I had marveled for hours at a time at the vast emptiness of the Pacific Ocean. This trip was all youthful preparation for what I imagined would be an adult career devoted to piracy on the high seas. (As events ensued, I turned first to law then to real estate development, careers some would charge are the modem equivalents of my childhood fantasy.) My brothers were too young to be let out of sight, so I had done it alone or with new friends I met on board.

When we arrived in Japan, my father made another of those fateful decisions that would lead to the adventure described in this book. Instead of quartering his family in a bland American-style apartment on the fenced-in enclave that was the Yokosuka Navy base, he chose instead to rent a fine traditional Japanese home in the nearby village of Kamakura. Though I could speak not a word of Japanese, nor any of the village kids a word of English, I was in little-kid heaven. A block away was a Pacific beach, where I could watch the local fishermen at work. Nearby was a famous Buddhist temple and the town's commercial area. A mile away began the foothills that in the distance grew to the mountain range that farther on framed Mount Fuji, a perfectly symmetrical volcanic cone and mystical symbol for the Japanese.

In short order, I explored all these magical places and many more, each filled with mystery and the inner secret of discovery. With no brothers old enough and few neighborhood friends who spoke English or whose parents allowed them the idle pleasure of child's play, I often had no companions to join me. I went on foot and alone— or at rare times with Japanese kids from the neighborhood—always wide-eyed and awestruck at the places, sounds, and exotic scents that revealed themselves with nearly every footfall.

Though they spoke in hushed tones not meant to be overheard by children, I overheard my parents talk about the threat of violent Communists. I didn't know who the Communists were, but they sounded like a group of mean, butt-paddling teachers, or worse. My father drove me to school each day, not knowing that I knew he carried a loaded .38 special Smith & Wesson revolver in the glove compartment for our protection, which seemed about the right armament for defending against overly mean teachers. Each day, the ride to school was like a tense scene from a John Wayne western, and I reveled in it.

After a year, those sailors at their desks in BuPers interrupted my youthful roaming and sent my father a new set of orders, assigning him to Bethesda Naval Hospital in Maryland. By ship across the Pacific and car through the heartland, we traveled to a modest home in a leafy suburban neighborhood. By now a veteran explorer with confidence far beyond my years, I pushed out across the landscape and found ... well, not much. We were surrounded by other leafy neighborhoods, each like the last. Though here I experienced my first snowfall and first sled ride, an abandoned mica mine, a broken arm, and the grown-up sights of Washington, D.C., after the thrall of Kamakura, what I encountered was too predictable, not a place that held out the possibility of exciting discovery. I had happened upon the newly evolving suburbia, a place with all the goose-bump thrills of canasta games and P.T.A. meetings. This was where the Man in the Gray Flannel Suit lived.

A year later, however, those sailors and their Underwoods came to my rescue and now sent orders summoning my father back to Pensacola, Florida, back to the home port where my experiences of life all began. In yet one more of those fateful decisions, Dad rejected housing the family in another leafy suburb, maybe sensing the family had had enough of that. Instead, we moved out to the country, a rural area west of Pensacola, almost at the Alabama line. Horses and cows and chickens and hogs lived just up the street. Here were moonshine whiskey, drag strip cars, camping and fishing and hunting, and honky-tonk bars filled with the dulcet sounds of Jim Reeves and Patsy Cline, all a major improvement over suburbia. But Delores occupied most of my mind's time, at least she did after bestowing in the fifth grade coat room that first kiss upon my virgin lips. I knew she undressed each night in front of opened curtains just because she loved only me, even if her audience was a platoon of horny preteens like me. Somehow, even in the innocence of fifth grade, I knew that her stoplight-red lipstick, painted eyes, and slinky strides meant she was headed for a fun-filled life, sadly without me.

Just two blocks from our home began a wood that stretched for miles, seemingly to the ends of the earth. It had dark swamps, vast savannas, sand ridges covered in gnarled blackjack oaks, upland heads of ancient live oaks and towering pines, long-abandoned sand quarries and water-filled borrow pits. By foot and later on horse-back—John Wayne had replaced Blackbeard as my childhood idol—armed first with BB gun, then pellet rifle, and later rifle or shotgun, I spent afternoons during the school year and idle days of summer wandering its sandy paths.

Only the rhythmic clop of Fargo's sauntering gait, sounds of soft breezes whispering through boughs of Southern pine, and crickets chirruping in the heat of day could be heard. On each visit to the wood, I pushed out beyond the familiar, out into new thickets and untrammeled watery bogs, every step a sensory delight I wished would never end. That wish was not shared, however, by the woman whose dropped purse I recovered at a place I later learned was called

Lover's Lane. She, and especially her husband, seemed not to be adequately grateful for my act of chivalry in returning it to her, though just why I wasn't sure.

Then it ended. Not suddenly, as if I had just up and quit, or even noticeably at first, but gradually, imperceptibly, my attention shifted, like that of all young boys at such a place and time, to the newly discovered fun stuff: girls, cars, cold beer, and girls. And there my focus remained through the tribulations of public school and a brief bout with delinquency. After the juvenile court judge's patience wore thin from seeing me appear before him too many times as a result of colorful pranks and infractions, he arranged for me to take a guided tour of the state reform school—then called the School for Boys, though it could as easily have been called the School for Promising Criminals. I recall the event vividly, especially the part about the big wooden paddle used to blister the asses of particularly active miscreants. The whole tour had a this-will-be-your-life-if-you-don't-stop-screwing-up tone and produced the desired effect, more or less. Soon enough came college, military, graduate school, and law school. No matter how hard I might fight it, maturity began to seize me in its brow-knitting, hand-wringing, blue-suit-white-shirt-and-red-tie grip. Career and family soon followed.

Adventure, the secret inner thrill of discovering new places was no longer an important part of my life. Blackbeard, John Wayne, and Fargo had receded from memory, as had the fulgent glow of Delores's lipstick. All those years of discovery were now nearly forgotten. Yes I went new places, met new people, and learned, and I achieved goals and matured even further, but these were never the same as path-breaking journeys of new physical discovery. The secret thrill wasn't there (nor was Delores, all the pity). Intellectual pursuits had stifled the sensory, the mind had subdued the heart. I had grown from wide-eyed boy explorer to thrill-seeking hormone-driven delinquent to intermittently mature adult, and along the way I had lost some of my capacity for adventure.

Eventually, as the years went by, the success of my business, after its near collapse, grew more and more to depend on the valuable contributions of some key employees, which meant I had idle time to dream again. I came to realize that what I sought was the return of that wonderment at happening upon new places—but not places thronged with tourists, or jammed with traffic, or regulated by the National Park Service; or places with fine hotels, or rustic inns, or cute shops; and certainly not places that had been robbed of life by too many rules. After an involuntary stretch as a soldier—talk about too many rules!—hiking and camping in the wild had lost any appeal it ever had. What then? Where could I discover again that perfect rapture I had found as a boy wandering through the wood? Where, in the song of John Lee Hooker, could I boogie-woogie, or in the words of Lewis Grizzard, could I get nekkid?

Then the idea came to me. I could do it in a boat! It's one thing to drive around the country on its highways and back roads, staying at motels and seeing the sights through a car window, quite another to view the world from a boat, especially a small fast boat. Coming as an epiphany, the decision to embark on a travel adventure alone on a small boat drove me with unrelenting persistence from my home in northeast Florida to a fishermen's hotel at the end of a slender peninsula jutting into Kachemak Bay at Homer, Alaska. Let me explain.

Ten or so years before, I had bought my first boat powered by outboard motors. Unlike earlier and larger inboard-powered boats, she was light, nimble, and fast, able to cruise along comfortably at forty miles an hour for hours on end. The boat. which I named *Rascal*, after *Rascals in Paradise* by James A. Michener, was sleek, a thing of rare and perfect beauty, with defiant bowsprit, shiny fiberglass skin, and glistening superstructure supporting a small canvas tee-top to ward off the Florida sun. Those motors hung off her stern put out 450 horsepower of just plain old rip-roaring fun.

Designed for offshore fishing, the boat had an open cockpit partly shaded by the tee-top; an instrument console and helm located amidships; and racks on the interior side of her gunwales on which to store fishing rods. Even more obviously marking her as a sport fishing boat was the twenty-gallon live-bait tank on the aft deck. This is where fishermen more resolute than I could keep their shrimp or poagies swimming about until, plucked from the tank, they could be offered up as a tempting attraction to one of their larger predators, an attraction likely to result in the predator ending up in a sauté pan (something like the result of a young man's prolonged exposure to perfume and décolletage—bait of another sort). But I never used the boat for fishing.

The day she arrived, shipped from a dealer in Atlanta, I was at the marina to inspect her and approve final payment. To that day, I had not seen even a photograph of her. I only knew that she was a thirty-one-foot Fountain, center console, sport fishing model with twin Mercury outboards. Slightly used, she was warranted to be in flawless condition with few hours on the motors. When I first saw her, she was even more beautiful than I had imagined. Her long, torpedo-slender hull and that prominent bowsprit were accented by thin parallel stripes of coral and two shades of emerald green, and her white vinyl upholstery had subtle tasteful stripes of matching colors.

After equipping her with a few essentials, I started touring the waterways near my home where, just as I had done as a small boy, my rootless wandering began modestly. I first traveled upstream on the St. Johns River, which, because it is one of the few major rivers in the world with a northward flow means I went south. From the mouth of the St. Johns at the Atlantic Ocean, I took various trips all the way to Lake Monroe near Orlando, where for *Rascal* the river becomes unnavigable. Along the way I'd pass ships taking on containers of ocean-going freight, slide under high bridges through Jacksonville's downtown, and travel down a long lagoonlike stretch to a small bankside town, where I'd stay the night.

Early next morning, I'd continue south on a very different canal-narrow river. The route would take me through immense hardwood swamps—dark places of alligators and cottonmouth moccasins and deadheads lurking in the tannin-laden water. Soon the river opened into Lake George, where I'd head for Silver Glen Springs, a rupture of Florida's subterranean aquifer through which millions of gallons of clear cold water flow daily. Continuing south through viridescent swamps, I'd traverse the opaque waters of a still narrower river dotted here and there with more springs gushing torrents of icy water. There I'd spot families of lumbering manatees, turtles hitching a ride on drift logs, great blue herons and snowy egrets standing motionless in the shallows, and ospreys circling overhead alert for signs of prey. In moments of fanciful daydreaming, I'd imagine warriors of the pre-Columbian, now-extinct Timuquan or Aix or Ocalan tribes paddling dugout canoes, or early Spanish soldiers laboring along the jungle paths clad in clanking armor, poor substitutes for the swarthy pirate or swaggering cowboy of my youth. Finally, I'd arrive at Lake Monroe, stay the night, and make the return trip home still enthralled by it all.

These voyages led to others, always south. I'd travel out in the ocean or in the protected Intracoastal Waterway to St. Augustine, then Daytona, Stuart, Miami and the Florida Keys, eventually to Key West, known by its citizens as the Conch Republic because it once imagined itself seceding from the Union (a laudable idea perhaps, but one with an unfortunate history). I crossed Florida on the spectacular Okeechobee Waterway, went south through the mazelike Ten Thousand Islands, and passed along the primal Everglades to the Keys. I I don't know how many of these trips I made; there were many, but not nearly enough.

Venturing farther, I left the comforting and now familiar coast of Florida and crossed the Florida Straits from Ft. Lauderdale ninety miles east across a slender reed of the Atlantic Ocean to Grand Bahama Island. From there, I wandered among the Abaco chain in the Bahamas archipelago, a glorious place to be, especially in a boat like *Rascal*—a place of translucent waters, colorful reefs, and gleaming beaches, not to mention thong bikinis that could fit in a shot glass and rum that could fit there too.

With each trip, and especially those open ocean crossings, two in blackest stormy night, my seamanship skills and confidence grew.

I confronted all manner of weather, sea conditions, and mechanical problems, and made mistakes and learned, helpful stuff, such as when you see birds standing in it the water's too shallow for the boat. Not cautious by nature, impetuous even, I managed to overcome whatever I got myself into, mostly without serious consequence or excessive bail.

One day, with a map of North America in hand, I began to wonder about a still more adventuresome trip. Quickly I decided to go south from Jacksonville to Stuart, cross the Okeechobee Waterway, travel west on the Caloosahatchee River to Ft. Myers, then traverse the coastline of the Gulf of Mexico all the way to my boyhood home of Pensacola at the extreme west end of the Florida panhandle, the Redneck Riviera—which I did. With this voyage completed, my confidence in both the boat and her captain grew further.

This trip and those before it were parades of exhilaration. Along each mile was something new and fantastic, places I had never seen, seas and skies and shores, sights and smells, all new. Challenges of navigation, weather, and seamanship demanded skills I had not yet fully developed, which is a nice way to say I got lost and storm pummeled and ran aground a lot. I became for a short time that youthful explorer, though not the pirate, the ensuing years had left behind. I was learning all about nekkid and how much fun it could be.

Shortly after the Pensacola trip was completed, I thought to myself, well that was a fine adventure, so what's next? It was natural to conclude that I should extend what I had done before and travel along the entire U.S. coastline of the Gulf of Mexico, so I did this too. Following more or less the same route I had earlier taken to Pensacola, I continued west, crossing Mobile Bay at the place where Admiral David Farragut once said, "Damn the torpedoes. Full speed ahead!" There I yelled out, with nobody in earshot, "Damn maturity. Full speed ahead!" and pressed the throttles to their limit.

Along the coasts of Alabama and Mississippi, I came upon enormous barge strings, five barges wide and six long, pushed by powerful towboats (yes, they're called towboats even though they push).

Entering Lake Pontchartrain, I visited the beguiling city of New Orleans, the Big Easy, a voluptuous fleshpot and a swell place to get nekkid if you're so inclined; it's the local industry. From there, through locks, I went up the Mississippi River a short ways, and through more locks, entered into the exotic world of Louisiana bayou country. I traveled Bayou Teche and Bayou Lafourche and the broad shallow reaches of Vermillion Bay cloaked in dense swamps and great stands of Spanish moss-laden hardwoods standing root-wet in black water.

There, Cajuns fished from pirogues, these easily mistaken for the flat-bottomed dugout canoes of ancient Indians but for the outboard motors hung from their sterns. In a galvanizing moment, one of these famously hot-tempered guys became so irate when *Rascal's wake* inadvertently rocked him that he charged after me yelling obscenities, I suppose, in incomprehensible Cajunized French. Taken by a fit of mindless pique, the fisherman aimed his shotgun at me and fired! This book is a testament to his errant marksmanship.

Passing through more miles of glimmering waterways winding through blackwater swamp, I reached the Texas coast and stopped at Galveston. It was there that I saw being constructed on land what must have been the world's largest offshore oil platform. Nothing in my life's experience could have prepared me for the enormity of this freakish steel thing, this erector set gone berserk. It was as if all the skyscrapers of Manhattan had been gathered together in one place, taken apart, and their steel skeletons restacked higgledy-piggledy on the flat shores of Galveston Bay. Here too I learned about the tragic hurricane of 1901, this country's worst natural disaster—at least until disco music came along—claiming 6,000 lives and destroying much of the town.

Each morning I fired up the motors, and when the props turned and ruffled boils of water spat from *Rascal's* stern, I moved out, facing the new day with eager anticipation. Onward along the low scrubby coast, over brackish lagoons, their tidewaters languid under the summer sun, I continued for mile after glorious mile, enraptured by the strange new worlds I encountered, places that delighted all the senses (if you disregard the petroleum tank farms and pecking hen-like oil wells).

Though adventure still lay before me, the end of the voyage was growing near and, finally, on the Mexican border, at Brownsville, Texas, the parade of wonderment stopped (quite unlike the parade of illegals headed the other way). For a fabulous waterway that had for so many miles brought such delights, the end was inglorious. Up a narrow channel to a drab shipping pier clad in creosote is the south terminus of the Intracoastal Waterway. There I laid my hands upon the pier in silent reverence, not as if I had broken par or an Olympic record—these are personal achievements of athletic competition—it was more like the end of an idyll. Another fine adventure was completed, and largely without serious mishap, save the woolen tongue and alarming memory gap with which I awoke after a night of gallivanting in the French Quarter. My desire for still more adventure grew.

One spring day while seated on a beach near my home, I thought about this last trip and imagined a map of North America. It was then and there that I decided my next journey would be one of truly grand dimensions. What the hell! Why not? Traveling north, I would reach the northernmost tip of Maine, head east across the Bay of Fundy, run the length of Nova Scotia's east coast and round its northern tip at Cape Breton just fifty miles from Newfoundland. From there, I'd turn west through the Gulf of St. Lawrence, travel up the St. Lawrence River through Lake Ontario, cross part of Lake Huron, pass through the Straits of Mackinac, and run down Lake Michigan to Chicago. There, I'd take the Chicago River, Illinois River, the Mississippi, Ohio, and Tennessee Rivers, and the Tenn-Tom Waterway to Mobile, Alabama, turn hard left and run along Florida's panhandle and west coast to Key West and then north along Florida's east coast back to Jacksonville. I would, in short, circumnavigate the entire eastern United States and a part of Canada, which I did. The trip was memorable, filled with fun and high adventure, about which I wrote a book, *Rascal and Me* (Xlibris 1999), this story's prequel.

This last escapade was a few years ago, and at fifty-four advancing age has become my enemy, threatening to impose on me both the physical limitations of a creaky body and the mental constraints of diminished élan. I wanted to take on more adventures before my idea of a high time is eighteen holes of golf—in an electric cart of course—followed by a martini or two and a nap. Once again I imagined a map of North America, and there it was, right before my eyes: The map was cockeyed, hanging badly out of balance, its right side lower than its left. What was wrong, of course, was that I've traversed the Gulf and the Atlantic coasts, both on the right side of the mind's-eye map, but not the coasts washed by the Pacific Ocean or the Bering, Chukchi, or Beaufort Seas, all on the left side.

Having traveled only two out of the six U.S. coasts—and both of those on the right coast, none on the left—would not do. It was an incomplete picture, a partly done job. I was only half nekkid. So for the next trip I would voyage along the Pacific coast of Alaska, British Columbia, and the lower forty-eight states. I'd start or end somewhere along Alaska's southeast coast. The rest of the Alaska coast, up there in the tundra and polar ice cap, would have to wait.

~~~

Having never before set foot in Alaska, now prominent on my itinerary, I thought it would be prudent to learn something of the state. What I found was that it is, by almost any measure, the most profoundly unusual of the fifty states. It seems to be a land for which superlatives were invented. Among much else, Alaska has the country's largest: fresh water lake, concentration of bald eagles, state park, percentage of males in its population, carnivores, expanse of unpopulated wilderness, glacier, mountain, number of volcanoes and earthquakes, national forest. It is an enormous state, the largest in the U.S. by a wide margin, more than twice the size of Texas. Into its land area can be placed the next three largest states with room left over for Maryland and Delaware. If you began filling it starting with the smallest states, Alaska would accommodate twenty-one of these with enough room left for Pennsylvania.

Its land area, like that of all states, is calculated as though it were flat, not taking into account the slopes of its mountains, yet mountains it has in abundance. Seventeen of the twenty highest peaks in the U.S. are in Alaska. A square mile there is quite different from a square mile in, say, Kansas. To make the two equal, you would need to imagine all of those mountains being mashed flat, as a cube of Jell-O under a toddler's hand. The result would be a state about twice its reported size. Alaska is also expansive. From north to south it measures 1,420 miles, the distance from Miami to Mystic, Connecticut. East to west, Alaska measures 2,500 miles, the same distance from Savannah to Los Angeles, the entire width of the lower forty-eight.

Despite having a vast area, there are only a tiny number of humans living there. On average, the lower forty-eight has seventy-four people living in each square mile; Alaska has one. If you subtract the half of its population living in the three largest towns—calling them cities would be a stretch—density drops by half to one person per two square miles. That leaves enough room outside of town for every person, man, woman, and child, to sit alone in the middle of nearly a thousand football fields. Suburban sprawl has not yet come to Alaska.

For most of us, sitting alone in the midst of an area the size of a thousand football fields would be, well, let's call it peculiar, or perhaps eccentric. Not so for Alaskans. Much of the state's nonurban population lives on unpaved roads and most of these are not connected to the statewide road system. These people live out in the bush, and seem quite happy to do so.

Alaska is a hotbed, both in the figurative and quite literal senses of the term, of geologic activity. A part of its coast is the thousands of miles-long joint between the Pacific and North American tectonic plates, a joint with the stability of a St. Patrick's Day celebrant. Along the entire length of it occur earthquakes that result from the plates' grinding shifts, and from these also come tsunamis. There are volcanoes, the festers and boils of hot magma stewing just under the surface, some rising improbably from the sea. They belch fire and ash and cinder and bleed pyroclastic flows into the world above ground.

Fields of alluvial deposits, some with quicksand, others with arid sand perfect for fueling dust storms, dot the state.

Alaska's mountains, great sheaths of densely crinkled earth crust, harbor oozing glaciers and crevasse-ridden ice fields. Its bays and inlets and lakes are thick in winter with pack ice and calved bergs from the glaciers. Lying just below its surface, Alaska has deposits of oil, oil shale, natural gas, gold, diamonds, copper, and much else of value. In short, Alaska is, it could be concluded without a hint of exaggeration, geologically eventful.

If the state sounds as though it may be a nice place to "get away from it all," as the expression goes, the cautious adventurer will want to consider the unsettling fact that Alaska also has an astonishing array of ways to get yourself killed. Setting aside the everyday calamities like cancer, heart disease, car wrecks, and violent crime, Alaska offers premature death by, among many others, wild animal attack, and from an impressive assortment of deadly beasts. Chief among these are bears, grizzly, black, brown, and polar. Indeed, the state has the highest concentration of bears in the world and, given the frequency with which they attack humans, these are a particularly irritable lot. Even the prevalent moose—described as a horse designed by committee—becomes sufficiently hostile that it will charge, though in its distinctly waddle-gaited way, and maim people. Alaska also has wolves, elk, caribou, sea lions, orcas, and walruses, none suitable for a petting zoo.

Cold air is a popular contributor to early demise. Outdoorsmen are, as a rule, sufficiently prepared for frigid temperatures and not often its casualty. Those whose vehicle breaks down at an inopportune time and place and drunks wandering about in sub-zero weather, however, commonly freeze to death in Alaska.

At 33,000 miles, Alaska's coastline is longer than that of the entire lower forty-eight. All of this coast is washed by frigid water which, as we shall see, claims the lives of anyone so unfortunate as to be aboard a boat that sinks in it, something boats in Alaska seem to do in alarming numbers. The state's rate of work-related deaths, primarily those working on the water, is five times that of the other states. Boats there encounter some of the foulest weather in the world and thus the largest waves, run into icebergs or reefs or rocky shores as a result of equipment failure, dense fog, or williwaws, or they just ice up and roll over.

Falling, too, has terminal consequences in Alaska, though of a more dramatic sort than elsewhere. Tumbling from a mountain peak, dropping through thin ice, or plunging into a crevasse is nearly always fatal. As I will later reveal in some detail, Alaska's unstable geology produces deadly earthquakes, quake-caused land-and ice slides, volcanic eruptions, and most murderous of them all, tsunamis. Even a simple stroll in the woods can have an unpleasant ending, thanks to the abundance of quicksand.

Finally, an appropriate adverb for this subject, given a population that is decidedly more male, five years younger, and much more heavily armed than the rest of the U.S.—you can see where this is going— and add to this accident-waiting-to-happen concoction the amount of heavy drinking that goes on there, especially in winter, Alaska is home to some stupendously dumb, and humorous, examples of self-destruction. Indeed, its rate of what is charitably described as "unintentional injuries" and its rate of firearm-related deaths are both double that of the other states. It is safe to say that Alaska's gene pool is regularly cleansed by the terminal antics of some of its (formerly) colorful citizens.

Now, armed with at least an elementary grasp of the state where I am destined to spend many days and log many hundreds of miles in a boat, it's time to begin travel preparations in earnest.

Chapter Two

Ever wonder how "what the hell"
is always the right answer?
- Marilyn Monroe

I HAVE DECISIONS to make, and the most critical is to determine what kind of boat to take. Never did I give serious thought to making the voyage in a sailboat. Though I've sailed several thousand miles, hoisting stubborn mains, easing jib sheets, tacking and jibing, the whole business just never appealed to me much.

Then, too, sailboats, if they're to sail, require wind, and when the wind blows from anywhere along an arc of about ninety degrees around the desired direction of travel, a sailboat can't go there. It must instead tack back and forth in a tedious effort to insinuate itself into the wind, traveling forty miles to advance ten on the rhumb line. Just think how awkward driving anywhere would be if you could only go sideways. You'd be arrested before you got there. Of course the sailboat's captain can drop the pretense of travel by anachronism and just crank up the motor, something they do much of their time underway.

Sailboats are also ponderous: slow as a three-toed sloth and agile as the Postal Service. With a single motor and one puny propeller attached to the aft of a heaving blob of wood or fiberglass, a sailboat won't make more than about seven knots under power, less if tide or current is opposing. The world goes by unspooling before your eyes at the speed of a lugubrious Gregorian chant. I want to travel at the speed of pulsating rock 'n' roll.

When strong tidal flows oppose *Rascal*, as they commonly do in the labyrinth of channels that make up the Inside Passage, I just advance the throttles. Her powerful motors send the light hull skipping easily over the fiercest of currents, overfalls, and boils, even raging rapids—a fine example of nature subdued. A sailboat, with its underpowered motor, is brought to a toddler crawl in even wimpy tidal currents, and in the gushing torrents common twice a day in the Inside Passage, it's first slowed then brought to a dead stop. Hoping to escape the tide's grasp, its captain can rev the motor until the bearings rattle and smoke billows from the exhaust. But soon the boat will be overwhelmed and spun in a water-driven pirouette, completely out of control, the rudder a useless appendage. Knowing this certain result, sailboaters don't challenge strong currents, but lay up, cowering in some protected anchorage for hours while awaiting a more favorable tide. That's not for me.

Sailboats and large power yachts have some advantages. They sacrifice speed and power for sumptuous living, and aboard a boat in Alaska, sumptuous means warm and dry with hot food and coffee or an aged brandy at hand. Even when single-handed, a captain chugging along at six knots can just bring his vessel to a halt, drop the anchor, and go below to brew coffee or make lunch. He can take hot showers, cook full meals, and sleep comfortably after lounging with drinks and music. If it pours rain, a routine event in a land where annual rainfall can exceed two hundred inches, owners of large boats are perched in a dry, comfy wheelhouse, often with wholesome centerfolds tacked to the bulkheads.

Rascal has all the comfort of a pup tent made from fish net. If it rains, I get wet; if the weather is cold, so am I. My boat has no head, no galley, no running water, no heater, no lounge, no music, and no bulkhead room for centerfolds. If I want hot liquid, I have to pour it from a thermos, if brandy. from a flask. Passengers on large vessels live in opulence in contrast to life aboard *Rascal*.

The second advantage of large boats is that they're decked. In heavy seas, with hatches dogged, portholes secured, and scuppers cleared, they can take waves breaking over them, shed the water, and keep plowing ahead. *Rascal* is an open bucket. If a wave breaks over her, she fills with water and has only undersized bilge pumps for relief. Speed is her sole defense to swamping but, luckily. *Rascal* is blazingly fast. With a cruising speed of thirty-five knots, she is five times as fast as a sailboat and far more nimble. Her top speed of fifty knots is the nautical equivalent of supersonic. If it's cold or wet or seas are rough, I have a trying time of it for a while, but just for a while, because in short order *Rascal* will reach a calm refuge, leaving her corpulent cousins many hours behind. All boats are compromises, but for this voyage, *Rascal* is exactly the right boat.

The next important decision is the direction of travel. In the summer when I will go, the prevailing winds and thus the seas are north to south. A small power boat, given a choice between attacking rough seas by running bow first into the oncoming waves (called a head sea), or running in the same direction as the waves (a following sea), is more comfortable and safer in the latter. In a head sea, the bow of a light fast boat is forced upward by the steep leading face of a wave, causing the boat to launch off the crest and land in the trough with a jarring slam. This plays havoc with the boat, its fragile electronics, and its even more fragile captain's attitude—and, worse, it fizzes the beer supply something awful.

The hulls of lesser boats will crack under such severe stress, but *Rascal* is so strongly built that even protracted punishment won't damage her (though from personal experience, the same cannot be said of running into a reef at full tilt). Launching can be reduced by cutting back on the throttles near the crest or by attacking the wave at twenty to thirty degrees off perpendicular (called quartering) but the only way to stop it is to slow down, bringing her off plane. Even then, she will launch in extreme conditions.

In a following sea, the trick is to slow down some but remain on plane, climb the more gently sloped back of a wave and, just before launching over the crest, cut back slightly on the throttle, allowing the bow to settle back into the water on the face. Power is then increased to drive the boat down the face and up the back of the next wave. Active throttle management requires dexterity in demanding conditions but, with practice, results in a smoother ride, or at least a less gut-wrenching one.

Racing down the face of a large wave can be dangerous, and it's not the recommended strategy for most boats, unless the captain is eager for his boat to sink. If gravity drives a boat down the face at a speed greater than its props are driving it, control is diminished—something like doing the boogie woogie faster than your brain can tell your feet what to do. The boat will slew off course and, if unchecked, will continue to slew until it's broadside to the wave and vulnerable to rolling over, called broaching. With *Rascal's* long, narrow hull, broaching would be a serious risk, but her deep-vee hull design helps keep her on track, reducing but not eliminating the slewing.

Another danger in following seas is the risk of stuffing the bow into the back of the next wave, causing the boat to flip stern over bow, a nautical somersault called pitchpoling. With earlier errant helmsmanship, I too often stuffed the bow, but *Rascal's* hull design allowed her to dissipate the sudden deceleration by sliding off to one side rather than pitchpoling, thus saving me from considerable embarrassment, or worse. After carefully deliberating these issues, I become convinced that travel from north to south is the right call, though it is a direction with a checkered history. (Regrettably for my ancestors, it was favored by General Sherman.) I'll confront following seas—if prevailing winds actually prevail—in a boat reasonably well-suited to the conditions, if not to comfort.

The next decision to make is where to start. With a road atlas of Alaska and small-scale planning charts of its coastal waters, I at first focus on Juneau, which is near both Glacier Bay National Park and the northern end of the Inside Passage. But there are no roads to the place, a characteristic of many coastal Alaskan towns, so *Rascal* would have to be delivered onboard a ferry. I investigate the possibility of having the boat hauled behind a truck, which then would travel on the Alaska State Ferry Service. This promises to be too complicated, though it remains a possibility. Secondary roads do run through the mammoth coastal mountain range to Skagway and Haines, both at the north end of the Inside Passage, so these locations become an object of study, until it finally dawns on me that by starting the trip there, or at Juneau for that matter, I'd miss a lot of spectacular coastline farther north.

Looking at the atlas and chart more closely, and with a new objective firmly in mind, I now begin to consider Anchorage. The largest city in Alaska—actually the only place that could remotely be termed a city (population 257,000, forty-one percent of those living in the entire state)—it lies at the northern end of Cook Inlet at a place where three rivers cascade down from the surrounding mountain ranges into the inlet.

And therein lies the problem with Anchorage. All that water streaming out of the mountains brings with it tons of suspended alluvium. So much glacial silt has poured into the inlet over so many millions of years that its upper reaches are clogged with the stuff. At low tide, you could walk across an arm of Cook Inlet near Anchorage were it not for the discouraging fact that you'd sink into oblivion in the viscous goo—a fine place for a mud wrestling convention maybe, but no place for a walk.

Ships use caution entering or leaving Anchorage's harbor at low tide and, once there, stay in the dredged ship channel. Outside the channel, miles of mire are exposed to view, a prairie of quicksand. When the tide floods, as it does twice daily, the silt is stirred up, and the water becomes a granular mocha-chocolate milkshake. Outboard motors, like those on *Rascal*, suck in sea water for cooling, and when they do the suspended grit eats away at the water pumps, shortening their useful life dramatically and, when they fail, causing the motors to overheat.

Then there are the tides. With highs up to thirty-eight feet, these are not the little freshets common to my native Florida but are torrents reaching velocities of five knots or more. When they're low, the floating docks of Anchorage's only small craft facility sit on dry seabed. As a result of these extremes, Anchorage is not a place friendly to small boats like *Rascal*.

Nor will any place on Cook Inlet suffice. Its entire west shore is an unbroken, corrugated wall of frozen mountains reaching to the water's edge, and no roads lead there at all. The east shore, rather inhospitable itself, is a high, steep bank with only a few places where a boat could be launched easily at a marina with dockside fuel. One location, the town of Kenai (keen-eye), was a possibility, but a glance at a nautical chart of Cook Inlet reveals that this may not be such a good idea after all. The inlet, I learn, is a natural wind tunnel. With mountains lining one shore and steep cliffs the other, and aligned on a north-south axis, the inlet receives Aleutian-bred storm winds that, channeled and concentrated, whip up enormous seas. Worse, if a small boat is caught in one of these howlers, there are few refuges. I decide to avoid Cook Inlet entirely.

=================================

It all began innocently enough. Four Army buddies, bored with the deadening routine of Fort Richardson, decided to shoot some birds on their day off. So, early on a brisk fall morning, the feel of approaching winter brushing their exposed faces, Roger Cashin and his three friends headed out of Anchorage to Knik Arm off Cook Inlet. Here, on ancient plains of glacial silt washed down out of the Chugach and Talkeetna mountains, are the Palmer Hay Flats, a fine place to hunt ducks in early fall. These flats are the final resting place of densely packed, fine-particle alluvium, glacial silt once attached to mountainsides, now washed into Knik Arm. So much of it has settled here, piled so high over the millennia that the silt has filled the Pleistocene valleys at the confluence of the Knik and Matanuska Rivers. When the tide is out, the alluvial flats are dry—but not receptive to heavy footfalls.

To position himself for the day's hunt, Roger Cashin walked out onto a dry stream bed, a place where Wasilla Creek feeds out of the lower end of Palmer Slough. Standing there amid a crazy-quilt of meanders and sloughs, 200 yards from either shore, he peered off into the early morning sun in search of ducks. His three companions took up positions along the banks of the creek and waited, motionless lest they give themselves away and spoil the hunt.

As Cashin stood there in silence, the dutiful hunter awaiting his prey, he was ever so slowly, imperceptibly at first, succumbing to one of Alaska's many natural treacheries. The sand on which he took up his post looked harmless enough when seen through the inexperienced eyes of a young soldier far from home. It was dry and a little gooey to the step but not threatening. As he stood there, however, he could sense every so often that his government-issue boots were sinking gently, quietly into the mire. Now and then, with hardly a thought about it, he plucked first one boot then the other from the grasping muck. Each time he did so, the effort required increased ever so slightly. This went on for some time, as Cashin shifted his weight back and forth, until he tried once again to unstick himself, just as he had done moments before. This time, his boot would not lift. He had stood quietly just a moment too long, he had sunk just a little too deep.

Slowly, in dim recognition, he began to know that he was trapped. As he struggled to lift one leg, the other became the platform for his effort, receiving all of his weight, magnified by the power of straining muscle, and it sank farther. The other leg, yielding to the same forces, sank too. Soon he was up to both knees in the mire. Calling to his three friends for help, he abandoned any pretense of a duck hunt. In a fleeting, unknowing moment, he had gone from animal hunter to trapped animal. His friends, not yet sensing he was in danger, laughed and hooted at him. They threw rocks and howled at his predicament. Wait 'til they got back to the base and told everybody how Roger got himself stuck in the goo. It was all good fun—until they looked up and saw the incoming tide.

Tides in Cook Inlet run to thirty feet and more, and tidal bores can be torrents of water charging wildly back up the ancient basins from whence they ebbed hours before. But on this morning what they saw was a sluggish crawl of aqueous murk slithering up Knik Arm. It came at them, and at Roger Cashin, as melted butter flows over hot pancakes. They had plenty of time, no cause for panic.

One friend ran off to phone for help. The others, too little too late, stood by to light a signal fire and shout encouraging words to Roger. Soon enough a bush pilot in a single-engine plane, having heard of Cashin's plight, went in search of help. Spotting a group of hunters nearby, he flew as low over them as he dared, opened his door, and shouted above the noise of his thrumming motor, "Man stuck in mud." He had yelled at Doc Puddicombe, who was hunting geese with his strapping young sons, Lany, Lynn, and Joe.

Doc and his boys promptly got to the scene in their fourteen-foot airboat, skimming easily over the still ankle-shallow water. When they arrived, they could see that what had been ankle-deep to them was now waist-deep to Roger Cashin; he had sunk up to his groin. Worse, much worse, he was wearing Army boots laced up tight against his calves. Locals who knew the dangers of the flats wore only loose fitting hip boots so their legs could be extracted easily, leaving the boots behind in the muck.

Doc and his boys tried to slip a machete down Cashin's leg hoping to cut the laces, but he had sunk too deep. The machete wouldn't reach. They tried pulling him out with the power of the airboat. Cashin hung on while Doc revved the motor, but it didn't work. Doc's boys tried to pull him straight up using the boat for purchase; that didn't work either. The boys got in the water with hip boots on and tried to dig Roger out. Frigid water flooded their boots, numbed their bodies, and continued rising; digging would never work. Growing frantic now, the boys used an oar slipped through Cashin's belt to try to pry him out—no luck. And still the tide came on, sinister and relentless.

When Puddicombe and his sons had hunted the flats in years past, they had seen wounded ducks fall onto its glue-like surface. The birds would flap their wings in a futile attempt to escape, only to be sucked under as though by a demon from below. They had seen moose become entrapped, animals that appeared strong enough to escape. After a pathetic struggle, they too slipped beneath the surface. Now the trapped creature was a man, and they could see that his end was growing near, just like the ducks, just like the moose.

At this dark moment, when all seemed lost, a ray of hope appeared: The tide turned. That day was supposed to be a small tide, at least by Cook Inlet standards. Now, just as the cold, turgid water reached Cashin's upper chest, it began to recede, flowing back out of the flats, out of Knik Arm, through Cook Inlet and into the ocean beyond. Cashin grinned with the joy that came from thinking his life might be spared after all. It was just not his time. The Puddicombes said to themselves. *This guy is gonna make it.* They were overjoyed at Cashin's good fortune—until the wind changed and began to blow across the fetch of Knik Arm right toward the flats. The Puddicombes could feel it as the gusts blew at their faces when just minutes before it had been at their backs. In Cook Inlet, the wind amplifies the tide. If there is to be a normal thirty-foot tide, and the wind blows with it, the tide grows to thirty-five feet. If the tide normally runs at four knots, the wind will speed it to six.

On this day, at this tragic moment, Roger Cashin's life hung in the balance; his survival depended on the wind that until now had kept the icy waters at bay. When the wind shifted, Cashin and the Puddicombes realized the glimmer of hope the receding waters had offered was just a cruel hoax. Nature was playing a ghoulish trick, frittering away a fragile life as if a worthless gimcrack. The shifted wind blew and the receding waters stopped, then reversed. Water that had dropped to Cashin's mid-chest rose to his neck.

Seeing what was coming, the Puddicombes disassembled a shot-gun and told Cashin that when the water got too high he should pinch his nose and breathe through the barrel. It might be enough to save him until the tide ran out or the wind shifted again. Near shock from being submerged in the glacier-cold water so long, Cashin refused. With calm reserve, he removed his wallet, handed it to one of the boys and said, "Give that to my wife. Tell her I love her." As the water rose, Roger Cashin tilted back his head and died.

=================================

If not Juneau or Skagway or elsewhere on the Inside Passage, and not Anchorage or Kenai, then where should this voyage begin? Only three places in Alaska north of the Inside Passage can be reached by a truck pulling a boat trailer and have a launching facility and gas supply at dockside: Valdez, Seward, and Homer. A glance at the charts eliminates the first two. Using either would mean missing a significant part of some of the most spectacular coastal scenery in the world, the same reason not to use Juneau or Skagway. Lying at the extreme south end of the Kenai Peninsula and just north of Kodiak Island, Homer, Alaska is where this adventure will begin.

Now that I know where to start, I face the question of when to go. At first thought that seems an easy matter to decide: summer, of course. But there's a little more to it than that. Apart from the obvious problem of cold—both air and water—Alaska offers two principle weather challenges during the summer months: fog and rain. It has lots of both. Roughly, and with exceptions for variable local conditions (a huge exception as I was to learn), both get worse later in the summer. The best time to go and have a chance to avoid as much of both as possible is middle to late May, when the air masses that pass over the area aren't yet warm enough to cause convection fog or rainy summer lows.

The tradeoff is that May can be cold, particularly for a Florida native traveling at forty miles an hour in an open boat over forty-two degree water. Not me. May is too early. However, July and August, I learn, can get densely fog-shrouded most places and drizzle-wet along the Inside Passage, so that's too late. June seems to offer the best chance, and only a chance, of favorable weather. That I could manage to consider both coastal Alaska and favorable weather in the same train of more or less coherent thoughts betrays a talent for self-delusion, as I would learn. My fantasy stems from the same talent both Napoleon and Hitler displayed when they considered Russia and favorable weather. I select June 5th as the date I'll cast off from Homer.

Now that the preliminary decisions are made, I confront the matter of how to get *Rascal* from her home port in northeast Florida all the way to Homer—a distance of 5,000 miles—and from Mexico back to Florida—another 2,300 miles. After investigating flatbed rail cars, ocean shipping, and semi-tractor trailers, I reject them all for one reason or another, mostly that they are too costly or complicated.

With a few more phone calls, I begin to learn about an entire industry of people who haul boats all over North America for a price. Driving diesel-powered, heavy-duty pickup trucks, they pull triple-axle, conventional boat trailers on which they load boats of every description. These entrepreneurs travel hundreds of thousands of miles a year providing a valuable service at a modest price, and a lot of them crisscross the continent every day. They usually work through the services of boat transportation brokers who have a fixed place of business and are found in the Yellow Pages of most cities and on the Internet. After getting competing prices from three brokers, I hire Ken Burch, who agrees to pick up *Rascal* in Jacksonville on May 25 and deliver her ten days later to Homer, on June 5, a fine plan that, on reflection, bears the hallmark of genius, at least it does until put into effect. Only then do flaws begin to appear.

~~~

I started considering what gear would be needed for the trip the moment the initial planning began. I prepared two lists, one for personal gear and another for boat gear, and continually revised them as I learned more. At the top of the boat gear list was *Rascal*, my trusted and proven craft in which I had built up enormous confidence. That confidence did not extend to her U.S.-made outboard motors, which had often been troublesome, so these were traded before the trip for two new Yamaha 250-horsepower, fuel-injected outboard motors— far more reliable. The new motors, with fifty more horsepower than their predecessors, are slightly less fuel efficient. This, however, is offset by their much wider power band that allows the boat to cruise along happily at forty knots and, when conditions require it, also to cruise at much slower speeds and still remain on plane.

The Yamaha motors idle more smoothly, emit less smoke, and are quieter too. With the earlier motors, mixing two brands of outboard oil resulted in the oil intake clogging, causing the motors to overheat and the heat alarms to sound. Ordinarily, this was only a nuisance, requiring that I carry on board large quantities of a single brand of oil (the engine maker recommends its own brand, naturally) or that I periodically unclog the intake. Should the motors overheat at a precarious moment, however, the consequences could be dire. Happily, the new motors easily gulp down any mixture of oil brands whatsoever, and the heat alarms never sound from a clogged oil intake. I will have dire moments on this trip, for sure, but the new motors will never falter.

When traveling by boat over long distances in unfamiliar waters, it's helpful to know not only how much fuel is remaining—which any fuel gauge displays—but the rate at which fuel is being consumed. Yamaha offers as an option a gauge that displays this useful information and more and does so with a high degree of accuracy. On one particularly wild stretch of the Alaska coastline, the new gauge led me to a decision that almost certainly prevented disaster. Buying it turned out to be a prudent investment.

Rascal carries in her main fuel tank 207 gallons of gas, giving her a range of between 150 and 280 nautical miles, while setting aside twenty gallons as a minimum safety reserve. The variation in range results from variation in conditions: current, tide, wind, and seas all affect fuel consumption and thus range. Under ideal conditions, running along on a flat sea at 3,600 RPM with trim tabs fully retracted, *Rascal* gets a maximum of 1.5 miles per gallon, while under extreme conditions, she gets as low as .8. Both extremes are unusual though, and most commonly she gets about 1.3 miles per gallon in the mild conditions of a light chop, resulting in a range of 240 miles with a safety reserve.

I know from a careful study of planning charts that a particularly notorious stretch of Alaska's coastline is approximately 250 miles across the open Gulf of Alaska between fuel stops, without allowing for detours to explore along the way. Unless I add fuel capacity, that stretch cannot be prudently run in the rough seas I am likely to encounter.

More fuel will be needed, and I debate several ways to add it. Ripping out the decks and installing a larger tank would be too costly and time consuming, even if the bilge had adequate space to accommodate a larger tank. As another option, rigid polyethylene auxiliary tanks can be set on deck, strapped down, and plumbed into the fuel system—but these would sit too high above the waterline and might adversely change the boat's stability. They'd also use up too much of the already cramped deck area.

Flexible, rubber-like fuel bladders could also be set on the deck and likewise plumbed. These, too, would still sit above the waterline, but would have a lower profile and so exert less effect on stability. They'd offer the additional advantage that they can be stowed when otherwise not needed. In a decision that is to have potentially serious consequences (i.e., injury of the personal sort), I elect to buy and have installed four fifteen-gallon flexible fuel bladders, which would provide adequate range with a comfortable safety margin and even allow some exploring along the 250-mile stretch.

An anchor, while a useful addition to a sack of house cats, is nevertheless underappreciated as a safety feature on a boat. If a small boat with a planing hull should lose power in heavy seas, it will promptly turn crosswise to the waves and capsize, thus pretty much spoiling a cocktail cruise and giving one's female companion a subject for everlasting commentary on the captain's seamanship. To prevent this, an anchor is deployed to hold the bow into the seas. *Rascal* is equipped with two heavy-duty anchors, one primary and the other spare, and ten feet of heavy anchor chain.

I decide that 200 feet of anchor line, "rode" in nautical lingo, will be sufficient. The anchor locker doesn't have adequate room to carry much more and, in most of the area where I'll be, the depths are so great I can't carry enough anyway. Two hundred feet seems reasonable and is a widely accepted compromise for boats of *Rascal's* size. The decision to carry a spare anchor will prove to be wise. In depths over thirty feet, without enough rode to maintain an adequate ratio of depth-to-rode length, the solution is a sea anchor, a parachute-like bag that fills with sea water and holds the bow into the seas. In a pinch, a Dolly-size bra might work, but its inadvertent discovery in a storage locker by one's wife might result in personal injury more serious than drowning. To conserve scarce storage space, I elect not to buy a sea anchor and, to avoid having to explain why I have one on board, not to bring along a large bra.

After the boat and its motors, the most important and useful item for the entire voyage is a piece of advanced technology called a chart plotter, specifically a Northstar 951 XD chart plotter. This machine, smaller than a shoebox, performed flawlessly and helped me avoid numerous opportunities to become impaled on submerged rocks, or hard water as they're called in Alaska. The plotter operates by cleverly combining and processing at literally lightning speed the data it gathers from three sources. The first is a radio signal emitted by a set of twenty-four satellites circling the globe in six orbital planes. At any time, a minimum of four are observable from any position on earth, and the signal from these is picked up by global positioning system (GPS) receivers, of which the Northstar is one. The other two sources of data for the chart plotter are a differential beacon received from land-based transmitters and a collection of nautical charts reduced to digital impulses embedded in a cartridge just larger than a postage stamp.

GPS units have been around for some years and today are found on all commercial and recreational vessels that sail the ocean. The signal the units receive from the satellites is controlled by the U.S. military and, until the past few years, was intentionally degraded for public use, presumably in the interest of national security. The degraded signal resulted in GPS readings of a geographic position, or fix as it's called, accurate to about 300 feet. By comparison with the years before accurate chronometers (shipboard clocks) and extensive lunar tables came along, when latitudes were known roughly but longitudes were wild guesses, this seemed to be perfection in marine navigation, virtually pinpoint in an enormous ocean.

The fix wasn't really perfection, however, so competitors in this competitive marketplace, driven to offer improved products, did so. They combined the degraded GPS signal with another land-based signal also available to the public, called a differential beacon, and got a machine that gives fixes accurate to fifteen feet. One of these, the Northstar, works its magic aboard *Rascal*. GPS units with the radio signal no longer degraded, but without the differential beacon, improved their accuracy to fifty feet and better, while units with the differential beacon became still more accurate, often providing accurate positions down to six feet. (As this is written, further advances in technology have led to GPS units accurate to a virtual spot-on. Perfection is at hand.)

The other source of data for the chart plotter, the nautical chart, is itself the subject of wondrous technological invention. A collection of charts for a specific part of a coastline, including large-scale harbor charts with detail down to the smallest dock, and small-scale planning charts showing miles of vacant ocean with only depth-contour lines, is reduced to digital impulses embedded in a tiny plastic cartridge. These impulses are joined in such a way that when the captain views the chart plotter screen, the many separate paper charts, in varying size and scale, appear as one unified electronic chart. Information imprinted on the paper version can be manipulated on the electronic. If I want to zoom in to see a dock or zoom out to see a wide area, or to eliminate or add some detail, all I need do is hit various buttons and, presto! The area I wish to see, in the scale and detail I select, unfolds before me.

All this is swell stuff, but the chart plotter would be just another gee-whiz gadget were it not for its most compelling feature. When the right mode is invoked, the video monitor, about five inches square, displays a selected chart overlaid by an electronic icon of a boat representing *Rascal's* exact location. The icon appears even with its bow pointed in the same direction as the bow of the boat. Now I can know where *Rascal* is on the chart to an accuracy of six feet, and I can see what geographic and fixed man-made obstacles are lurking about in the dark or the fog or just under the surface waiting to do me in. Marine navigation has never had it so good, and it's hard to imagine how things might get better.

On prior voyages, I had only paper charts, and on long voyages I needed stacks of them, all too large to handle easily on the bedside table-size console at *Rascal's* helm. Though the charts were accurate and nicely detailed with all the information I could ever want, they couldn't tell me quickly at a glance where I was on their surface. The small stand-alone GPS unit that I used at the time could give a highly accurate latitude and longitude, but the thing had no charting capability. While traveling along in an open boat at forty miles an hour, keeping watch for obstacles, maybe with one eye on a radar screen, I would try, emphasize try, to locate my position on the paper chart, using only the lines of latitude and longitude imprinted on its perimeter. The accurate GPS readings became, when so transposed to paper charts in such a haphazard way, of little use and no comfort at all. The result was a propensity for calamity that caused many hours of nervous tension and one nearly ruinous collision with a reef.

Though the chart plotter allows me to avoid known charted obstacles, it is of no help in avoiding uncharted objects, like other boats, rare in Alaska, but still dangerous, and floating logs, surprisingly numerous and hard to spot—so I have on board a small radar. Boats and, especially, ships can be seen by radar, but not always. Small boats more than a few miles distant, and boats with no steel structure or adequate reflector to return the radar's searching radio beams, can't be seen on the radar screen with any degree of reliability. Moreover, in rough seas, the radar dome mounted on top of *Rascal's* aluminum tee-top at amidships bounces wildly, both on a vertical and horizontal axis, making accurate radar readings impossible for all but large steel-hulled boats and ships.

The radar I carry aboard *Rascal* is technically capable of reflecting objects as far as seventeen miles away but, when mounted only eight feet above the water, it can achieve no more than about eight miles of effective range. It is of no use whatever in spotting floating logs. Despite these limitations, however, *Rascal's* radar will prove to be the most useful of the electronics gear, second only to the chart plotter, and it continued to function well despite cold, rough seas, and an inexpert operator.

Also among *Rascal's* modern array of electronics is a very high frequency radio, or VHF, with separate banks of channels for international, Canadian, and U.S. frequencies, and channels dedicated to receiving weather broadcasts. Its range, limited by the low elevation of its eight-foot antenna, is ten to fifteen miles under good conditions without intervening land masses, such as the numerous and enormous Alaskan mountains. Finally, *Rascal* is outfitted with a digital depth gauge that also registers water temperature as well as an autopilot that steers the boat on a course set by the captain or on a pre-set course entered into the chart plotter and fed into the autopilot.

I choose not to use the autopilot in Alaskan or Canadian waters, even on long passages, because of the abundance of floating obstacles lurking just above or just under the surface. Obstacles like logs, spars, and assorted debris that collect along the coastline, often carried clear across the Pacific by storms and currents, are far too abundant. In Alaskan waters, there's always danger from icebergs, which come in sizes from football to bungalow. I will see thousands of these and avoid hitting all but one, and that one without harmful result. Then there are the many persistent dockside rumors of steel cargo containers dropped by freighters caught in violent seas, littering the oceans ready to damage seriously any hapless boat that should encounter one. The only protection against these obstacles, especially for a small, fast boat, is a watchful eye on the water ahead and a quick hand at the helm and throttles. Alaska is no place for an autopilot.

When skimming along over the reassuringly calm waters of Florida or the Bahamas, it's easy to become relaxed about the dead-serious matters of safety and survival. Avoiding complacency and maintaining focus on life-and-death issues comes naturally in Alaska. Its frigid black waters, seabeds overlain with heaping piles of granite, and icebergs floating about, to name just a few of a small boat's scourges, are enough to encourage a boat's captain to prepare well for emergencies, and I certainly do so.

Into a waterproof survival gear bag, I stow first and most importantly a device with the ungainly name of Emergency Position Indicating Radio Beacon, or EPIRB. The size of a champagne bottle with a ten-inch antenna attached, this device emits a radio signal on both the 406 and 121.5 megahertz frequencies. Sent automatically when the unit is submerged or a switch is snapped on, its signal is picked up by a system of satellites circling the globe, transmitted to one of many ground stations located all over the world, and finally routed to the nearest Rescue Coordination Center, which begins a search for the distressed vessel and its occupants.

Early models of EPIRBs transmit on two world-recognized emergency frequencies in the VHF band: 121.5 MHz (monitored by commercial aircraft) and 243 MHz (monitored by military aircraft). When satellites receive one of these signals, they are unable to store it, but must retransmit immediately, operating as a so-called bent pipe receiver. If no ground receiver is available at that moment in the satellite's orbit, the return signal is lost in the void. To be useful, the signal of these early EPIRBs must be received by a satellite that is at that moment able to transmit to a receiver on the ground, called mutual visibility. Since most ground receivers are in the Northern Hemisphere, an EPIRB signal transmitted from the Southern Hemisphere may go unheard. For a mariner in trouble floating off the Galapagos Islands, that's not good news.

Another serious flaw in these early models is that they lack precision. Their signal allows a position fix on the transmitting unit within a circle twelve miles in diameter, which leaves a very large search area and gives new meaning to the expression needle in a hay-stack. One final disadvantage is that because the signal is the same for all vessels, the receiver can't tell what type of vessel is transmitting, or even if it is a vessel, and has no way to confirm the signal isn't a false alarm. These models experience a ninety-nine percent false alarm rate! So naturally enough, rescue agencies receiving a signal from one of these early models require confirmation of an emergency before they'll deploy and, as a result, six hours pass on average before the rescue agency commences operations. That long, floating in Alaskan waters without a survival suit is too long. All they will find, if they find anything at all, is the frozen body.

With these limitations, inevitably technology would come to the rescue and develop improvements. The answer to all these shortcomings is the 406 MHz EPIRB, which I buy and stow in the survival bag. The satellite receives and stores the 406 signal until it passes over a ground station, thus allowing worldwide coverage. Within the signal my 406 would send is embedded a code that, based on a simple registration form I filed with a government agency, identifies who I am and what vessel I'm aboard, and tells the rescue agency whom to call to be sure I am truly at risk, thus significantly reducing the false alarm rate. When I'm bobbing around in the Gulf of Alaska hoping to be found, I can know with assurance that the Coast Guard will be notified of the EPIRB alert within forty-five minutes and that the search area will be less than a four-mile diameter. Better still, the 406 also transmits a homing signal at 121.5 MHz that further will help rescuers find me quickly.

Yet another advancement in EPIRB technology is now available. It combines GPS locational precision with EPIRB alert signals. The signal broadcast by the EPIRB unit and received by a geostationary satellite contains, in addition to personal and vessel identification, a constantly updated GPS fix on the EPIRB's location, reliable down to a search radius of sixty feet, and rescue units are notified within four minutes. On future voyages. I'll replace my standard 406 with a GPS/ EPIRB unit. To justify the slight extra cost (about $200), I reason that while floating in the freezing waters off Alaska, I don't want to imagine myself thinking. *If only I had spent the extra bucks and bought the GPS/EPIRB.*

The survival gear bag also contains a handheld backup VHF in a waterproof pouch, a small backup GPS unit, parachute flares, marker flares, fifteen-hour floating strobe light, strobe light mounted on an arm band, foghorn, knife, flashlight, extra batteries, waterproof matches, and a basic first aid kit. These, with the survival suit stuffed into its own carry bag and set on the open deck, constitute my defenses in the event of trouble.

Rascal's cocoonlike cabin is equipped in minimalist simplicity. It has no hot water, indeed no running water at all. Four plastic one-gallon jugs carried in a deck locker are all the supply I have. Her galley consists of what cold foods I bring aboard, like sandwiches, fruit, and the like, and thanks to Alaska's weather, no ice is needed for refrigeration. I also don't carry a propane heater or a stove. There is no head, and I leave the boat's Port-A-Potty (a tradename that suggests a mobile hygiene device from kindergarten which, come to think of it, it resembles) at home to provide more storage space.

=================================

When a person finds himself floating in the ocean as a result of, say, a capsized vessel, his body will immediately begin to lose heat, extracted by the enveloping colder water. This will happen in even the most tropical of oceans, because all open waters are cooler than the body's normal operating temperature of 98.6 degrees Fahrenheit. The greater the difference between water and body temperature, the faster the heat loss. When the core temperature (that of the brain, spinal cord, heart, and lungs) begins to drop, arms and legs become first numb, then useless. At ninety degrees, cardiac arrest is possible.

Below eighty degrees, the brain shuts down and unconsciousness results, often followed by drowning.

In the very cold waters of Alaska (the Gulf of Alaska along the Kenai Peninsula is mid-forties in summer, mid-thirties in winter), hypothermia progresses especially fast. A fifty-year old person—that's just younger than I—has a fifty-fifty chance of surviving fifty minutes in fifty-degree water. Make it thirty-five degree water, and survival time plummets to under half an hour. These slim prospects can be improved by using any of several techniques, like swimming slowly, treading water, holding still, using the Heat Escape Lessening Position (essentially the fetal position) and huddling with others. But in remote Alaska where help, if it's available at all, can be many hours away, these only delay the inevitable. As the locals put it with mordicant wit, the only reason to wear a life jacket is so the Coast Guard can find the body. Happily, one device is available that allows a person to survive in cold water for an extended period, long enough for help to arrive. That device is the survival suit.

Made of bright orange, heavy gauge, closed cell neoprene, a survival suit resembles a diver's wetsuit, with the important difference that it's designed to keep the wearer dry. Attached to it are water-tight gloves and shoes and a head cover with flaps that fold across the neck and chin, leaving only a small part of the face exposed. An inflatable pouch across the back of the shoulders, with its inflating hose secured at the left breast, allows the wearer to float on his back and keep his head out of the water. A signal whistle is in easy reach. The suit zips up the front using a heavy-duty waterproof zipper that has a strap attached to allow the zipper to be grasped with the awkward fingers of the glove. It is not an exaggeration to say that a man fully clothed in a survival suit closely resembles an oversized Gummy Bear.

The survival suit comes in a carrying bag that can be opened quickly in time of need. Properly donned, it allows the wearer to survive up to a maximum of thirty-six hours, though the manufacturers claim, no doubt on the cautious advice of lawyers, just three to five hours, and the longest known survival time is twenty-seven.

Even if the garment is a great improvement over floating in cold water unaided, the survival suit has two deficiencies, both related to its design, and they substantially erode the suit's efficacy as a lifesaving device. An example of the sort of event that might occur illustrates both fatal flaws. A 100-foot steel hulled, seaworthy vessel is working its line of king crab pots in December in the Gulf of Alaska. At this time of year, frequent violent storms brew in the Bering Sea and come howling into the Gulf, bringing high winds, sleet, snow, and monster waves. These conditions are routine and, for the crew, just part of the dangerous but sometimes lucrative business of crabbing. In one particularly bad gale, the ship begins to roll violently under the relentless pounding of the seas. Ominously, its superstructure and rigging, exposed to salt spray, become encrusted with ice, adding tons of weight above the waterline and increasing the ship's roll. Disaster is now, without doubt, at hand.

The captain faces a life or death decision. He can order his men to climb into the ship's superstructure and rigging and dislodge the ice with bats, possibly saving ship and crew. Doing this is a common tactic in these nearly routine yet dangerous conditions. If, however, he orders his men up, an entirely sensible choice, and the ice builds faster than it can be removed, or if a rogue wave hits, or if the ship loses power or steerage and turns beam to the waves, it will almost certainly exceed its maximum roll angle and capsize with no warning. If the captain chooses to battle the ice rather than order his crew to don their survival suits, all aboard will perish in the icy waters.

Here then is the captain's dilemma: If he orders the crew to don their suits, he will in effect be giving up trying to save the ship, because the suits are so clumsy no meaningful work can be accomplished with them on. The ship would continue to ice up, and the crew, rendered largely ineffectual by the suits, could only stand by until it rolled, or they could abandon ship, jumping from a floating, if wildly rolling, deck into storm-roiled icy water, something crews are wisely reluctant to do.

This harrowing dilemma is made far worse by the second deficiency of the survival suit: It's a bitch to put on properly and more so in extreme conditions. The thing is so inflexible and bulky that it's nearly impossible to put on by yourself without lying down or standing with back against a convenient bulkhead. The recommended technique, regularly practiced by fishermen, drilled and timed, is to place the suit on the deck faceup, wriggle into it as if it were a pair of coveralls, stand, zip it up, close the neck flaps, and waddle off. All very well in a practice drill but quite difficult in the panic of impending disaster on a rolling deck in frigid, storm-tossed seas. If a crewman tries to put it on after he's in the water, he's doomed; it can't be done. And once the suit is on, as we've seen, the wearer is so clumsy that most dexterity is lost, so little lifesaving work can be accomplished, such as radioing for help or operating electronic controls or climbing about to chop away ice.

So the critical decision for the captain is at what point in a developing crisis does he order suits to be donned. Since survival suits became required standard equipment on commercial fishing vessels (in 1988), they have undoubtedly saved lives; but many Alaskan fishermen still perish every year because they find themselves floating in near-freezing water without their survival suit on, or with them on but leaking. The suits are, in other words, not nearly as effective as their name implies.

================================

Homer Spit is a six-mile long, several hundred yards wide whippet of low graveled land left over from one of the many geologic cataclysms that regularly rock the Alaska coast. With its ramshackle cargo of teetering sheds and tumbledown commercial shacks—happily including the Salty Dog, Alaska's oldest saloon—it extends obnoxiously from the shoreline into the otherwise pristine Kachemak Bay. It is at the extreme end of Homer Spit, standing in front of the fishermen's hotel where I have stayed too many nights, that I see *Rascal* for the first time in Alaska, at the end of her lengthy overland haul. She is a long awaited and welcomed but not a handsome sight. Miles of travel over highways under construction have left her covered in the dust and grime of several Western states, a significant part of British Columbia, and much of southeast Alaska. After a thorough scrubbing, she is launched, her main fuel tank and all four fuel cells filled, a total of 267 gallons, and her oil tank topped off. At long last, after months of preparation, we're ready to begin our great adventure. *Rascal* and I.

Until this very moment, my first on Alaskan water, things have not gone well. I arrive in Homer on the evening of June 2 to make final preparations, expecting to meet up with Ken Burch and the boat on June 4 and launch on the fifth. This is the date we projected he would arrive and, after several phone calls while en route, it appears this date is still a good estimate, barring the unexpected. What neither Ken nor I expect to happen, of course, happens: Ken's new truck blows its clutch in Denver. Murphy, author of the eponymous law—when things can go wrong they will—has chosen to become an unwanted passenger on my carefully planned trip.

Not content simply to throw at me a mere first order snafu, Murphy on this occasion hits me with his First Corollary: When things go wrong, they will do so at the worst possible time. Ken's clutch goes out on a Friday afternoon, when it is impossible to get replacement parts or a mechanic until the following Monday. Neither Ken nor I can do a thing but sit and wait, he in Denver and I at the end of Homer Spit.

On Monday, we're rudely introduced to Murphy's Second Corollary: When things go wrong, repairs will take longer and cost more than expected. Parts to complete the truck's repairs will take three to five days to obtain and the work to install them another two days, if all goes well, longer, if not. The entire clutch must be replaced, and neither the parts nor labor are covered by warranty. Now a pessimistic person, one who sees every turn of bad luck as an omen of more to come, might be getting spooked by these several mildly annoying setbacks. But not me.

With rosy optimism. I'm sure all will go well. Sure, that is, until once again Murphy intervenes, this time with his Law of Momentum: When things go wrong, they will tend to continue going wrong. Ken's repairs completed in Denver, he arrives in Casper, Wyoming, only to lose his transmission. In keeping with both the First and Second Corollaries, his is a transmission that's particularly rare, hard to find, and costly to replace. And, once again, misfortune strikes on a Friday afternoon. The result is at least another week of delay, courtesy of my now seemingly constant companion, the redoubtable Murphy. Events, it seems, have begun to approach that black hole of error, the condition known as fubar. I haven't yet begun to burn incense and recite incantations to the gods of Fate, but the idea has crossed my mind. Instead, I head for the bar in the firm conviction that no prospect is so bleak that it can't be improved by good whiskey.

Growing restless, I decide that while waiting for Ken's arrival in Homer I'll roam around Alaska and see a few sights not on my nautical itinerary. Over the course of the next twelve days, using car, train, plane, and bus, I visit Seward, Kenai, Anchorage, Fairbanks, and Juneau and, it's fair to say, none is a memorable place to which I might one day wish to return. This isn't because I have a jaded taste in places to visit or judge with unfairly high standards. These are just forlorn, tourist-infested towns that invade the periphery of a wild and stunning countryside. The land is fortunately of such monumental scale that the obscure towns are only tiny imperfections, nearly invisible from a distance.

Two places are uncommonly beautiful and without nearby towns—the Katmai Range and Mount McKinley. To see the first, I hire Jose de Creeft in Homer to fly me there in his Bird Dog, a World War II vintage, former artillery spotter plane. With its two seats arranged fore-and-aft rather than the conventional side-by-side, I can raise the windows on both right and left and lean my head out for a better look, as spotters once did, directing fire for the long-range guns of the U.S. Army.

On a magnificent day, we fly north and west across a radiant sub-arctic sky, over the mouth of the Cook Inlet to Augustine Island, an active volcano jutting from the glittering sea, still smoldering acrid fumes from its last eruption in 1986; it seems as if it may erupt again at any moment. Jose steers the tiny plane along valleys and through canyons among the vast fields of ice-covered massifs that make up the unearthly Katmai Range. From copses of alder along the banks of alpine tarns still frozen in June, brown bears, recently out of hibernation and in foul humor, emerge, then scurry away in a vain attempt to escape our noisy intrusion.

Jose sets the plane's floats gently onto Lake Brooks, causing flumes of white spray to paint the emerald waters, then vaporize, leaving only a faint trail from touchdown to shoreline. Here, deep in remote wilderness, is the Brooks Falls Ranger Station, where tourists will soon flock by float plane to watch bears feast on migrating salmon. It seems not to occur to the bears that all those spectators would make a fine entree, lined up along a viewing stand like a Sunday buffet.

Of the two types of bears common in this part of Alaska, black and brown, it is a charmless fact that only the black will consume human flesh. Brooks Falls has mostly brown bears, but I didn't find this knowledge particularly reassuring, since they're known to maim, maul, and kill humans with slight provocation. Walking in the forest around here, whatever the color of the nearby bears, I feel like an appetizer on the hoof. Singing aloud is supposed to avoid surprising the critters and thus provoking an attack, but my notes are off-key and more likely to offend than alert. So I talk loudly. Other people hearing you talking to yourself in the forest may suspect, with some reason, that the cheese has slid off your cracker. Better that than being consumed by a black bear or shredded by a brown.

On the flight back to Homer, Jose flies low and slow over the delta of the McNeil River, where brown bears are cavorting. From there, he takes us over one of the world's most active volcanic regions, including part of the Ring of Fire, a line of inactive and active (but for the moment quiet) volcanoes, and lands the Bird Dog on pea-green Crater Lake amid a moonscape of geologic destruction. There in the Valley of Ten Thousand Smokes are the latently sinister remnants of a 1912 eruption of Novarupta volcano, the greatest of such explosions in history. The ground still festers and steams, betraying the suppressed violence just below the surface. Seemingly to make the point that catastrophic eruptions are not merely a thing of the distant past, nearby Mount Redoubt exploded in 1993, its ash cloud shutting down air transportation for days. Wandering on foot through this netherworld of smoldering desolation is, I imagine, like walking the streets of Nagasaki just a few days after the atomic bomb exploded.

We return to the plane, take off, and fly over Cook Inlet, where four pods of Orcas, four to six in each, frolic in the calm sea. These killer whales, as they are aptly called, are objects of affection for eco-tourists, but they decimate the fish stocks and so are not loved by the fishermen here. That they are reminiscent of lawyers, in dark suits and white shirts, doesn't do their reputation any good either.

The Indians, or Native Americans if you like, call the mountain Denali, an Athabascan Indian name meaning, accurately enough, the Big One. (Reputedly, the name is also widely used by priapicly delusional men grown dissatisfied with Mr. Happy, a commonplace that lacks any hint of grand scale.) To see Denali, known to most of us as Mount McKinley, I take a four-hour train ride through dense, nearly uninhabited wilderness to Denali National Park. Though a stunningly beautiful place, it's far too thronged with tourists, tour buses, tour jeeps, hikers, gawkers, and oohers and aahers for my taste.

To escape it all, I charter a powerful twin-engine plane whose pilot flies me deep into the Alaska Range where McKinley, at 20,320 feet, is the largest among giants. Standing in chiseled relief against a cloudless blue sky, the Range is a tangled mass of crenellated earth, painted over in twinkling white luminance. At an altitude of 2,000 feet, we weave through a maze of jagged spires and gray battlements, over moraines, glacier fields, and deep crevasses, and around stolid peaks still draped in last winter's record snowfall. As we pass through a deep valley, its walls block out the sky on both sides of the plane. The pilot banks into a turn around a steep granite cliff at the valley's head, and there it is! In a riveting moment, we are confronted by nature's most pretentious monument to its earth-wrecking power. Looming high over the puny aircraft, shielding from view all that lies beyond, is the world's highest mountain.

Well, sort of. The people who decide these things long ago decided to measure mountain heights from sea level to peak. This convenient calculation eliminates what would otherwise be the world's highest mountain: At 32,000 feet, Mauna Loa in Hawaii rises from the ocean floor 18,000 feet before it gets to sea level and continues skyward another 14,000 feet. Using the conventional measure, it's thus said to be only 14,000-feet high. Mount Everest, which starts out sitting plumply on the Tibetan Plateau, a mesa already 18,000 feet above sea level, is therefore calculated to be 29,035-feet high, and McKinley is said to be at 20,320 feet. The same quirky convention of measurement is true of the many other mountains of Nepal and the Andes claimed to be higher than McKinley. Yet using this calculus leads to the patently ludicrous conclusion that all the buildings in Denver, even one-story shacks, are taller than any buildings in Miami.

The better method is to measure based on what we see in front of us, that is to measure from base to peak. Only in this way can we gauge the relative enormity of nature's rocky monoliths, or man-made buildings for that matter. Using this method, Everest is a mere 11,035 feet, an insignificant pimple on the earth's surface, while McKinley is the highest land-based mountain in the world at 18,000 feet above the ground, and Mauna Loa is the highest mountain in the world. And some buildings in Miami are taller than some in Denver too.

The plane has climbed to 10,000 feet (you need an oxygen mask or pressurized cabin at 12,000 feet), and still the highest peak of McKinley is nearly two miles above, sitting there imperiously as if looking down its granite nose at us. As we circle the mountain, passing close above its muscular shoulders, steeples and parapets and random outcrops of stone reach upward from a sea of glistening white. Extending to the horizon, miles upon desolate miles of mountains, bathed in iridescent snow, sparkle like a field of broken glass in the sunlight. The smaller stepchildren of McKinley, at up to 14,000-feet high, are only the tailings left over from nature's monumental sculpture.

On one face of McKinley, an antlike, filamented line, parted intermittently by the snow, becomes a series of hyphens and dashes unevenly spaced and on the move. This strange sight, I learn, is a single file of mountain climbers come to tackle the Big One, surprised to find hundreds of others going about the same business as they. Stand in line, wait your turn, the queue is greater than World Series ticket office proportions but barely detectable from the air, a mere hairline on the colossal mountain. After circling a few times on this blissful day, we work our way back down to lower altitudes and weave once again through raw peaks and saw-edged ridges, passing so close they seem to be at arm's reach. Mountain goats bounding among perilous footholds stare with craned necks at our intrusion into their icy world. At tour's end, utterly depleted by the sensory wonderland of Mount McKinley, I stand on the tarmac drained of all capacity to be awed.

~~~

One morning while eating breakfast at a cafe in Homer, the building and its contents begin to shake alarmingly with results both audible and visible. The building vibrates, dishes rattle, chairs scoot over the wood floor, and coffee in a full cup on my table forms tiny wavelets that slosh over the rim, filling the saucer.

Thus am I introduced to two of the many naturally occurring depredations that persistently plague Alaska: earthquakes and their waterborne consequences, tsunamis, though of the saltwater, not hot coffee, variety. If you're a student of hurricanes or thong bikinis, Florida is the place to be. For seismologists, nirvana is Alaska.

Of all the earthquakes that occur in the world, eleven percent take place in Alaska. Over half of all earthquakes in the U.S. occur here, and these are not just little shimmies either. Three of the six largest earthquakes in recorded history, and seven of the ten largest in the U.S., were in Alaska. They're numerous too. On average, the state gets 5,000 earthquakes a year. So common are they that none of the locals, including nobody in the Homer cafe but me, bothers to stop talking or look up from his morning paper when the quake hits and my coffee sloshes. Ho-Hum.

It seems not to have occurred to anybody in the cafe that this might be another Great Alaska Earthquake, like the monster shaker that struck in Prince William Sound on Good Friday, March 27, 1964. At 9.2 on the Richter scale, it was one to remember. (The Richter scale increases at an exponential, not a linear, rate. Thus a quake of 8.3 magnitude is 50 times stronger than one of 7.3 and 2,500 times stronger than one of 6.3.)

Instead of lasting a few seconds, like my coffee slosher, it lasted three minutes, and in that brief time wreaked geologic havoc and human devastation of monumental and tragic dimension. Vertical displacement over the affected area, 325,000 square miles, ranged from thirty-five feet of uplift to seven feet of subsidence. Anchorage, seventy-five miles from the epicenter, was devastated. Thirty blocks of buildings and roads were damaged or destroyed; landslides buried homes, many with people hovering inside.

A line roughly following the south coast of Alaska from the Aleutian Islands northeast to Prince William Sound and southeast to the Queen Charlotte Islands in British Columbia has the unfortunate distinction of serving as the unstable joint between two massive sections of the earth's crust, the Pacific and North American plates. Its instability results from the dense, ocean-covered, north-creeping Pacific plate trying to slide under the lighter North American plate. The fitful, herky-jerky movements of these colossal blocks of earth are what cause the quakes.

On a more personal and therefore rather more distressing level, the planned path of my nautical adventure includes a significant length of the unstable joint. Four of the nine largest earthquakes in Alaska occurred along the coast from Cordova to Cape Spencer, a segment of the seismic joint and an area in which, as we shall see, I was destined to spend more time than planned. One spot along this route, the Yakataga seismic gap, is described on a seismicity map as having a "very high probability of a major earthquake in the near future (emphasis added)." It is nearly on top of this fun spot that I was to sit at anchor for three eventful days, blissfully unaware of the inchoate disaster in the ocean floor beneath me.

Earthquakes are bad enough. They destroy buildings, alter the landscape, and kill human beings. They also are readily measured in TV sound byte-friendly numbers thanks to a handy scale developed in 1934 by one Charles F. Richter. But by far the most serious damage and loss of life comes from tsunamis, ocean waves generated by earthquakes or by undersea landslides caused by the earthquakes. No TV-friendly scale, like the Richter, exists by which tsunamis are measured; only grim statistics tell the story.

In the infamous 1964 quake, more than ninety percent of deaths were a result of tsunamis, some as far away as California and Oregon! The maximum recorded wave height was 217 feet. Waves struck Valdez, located on Prince William Sound near the quake's epicenter, obliterating the town's waterfront and killing thirty-three people. Minor damage from seiche action occurred along the U.S. coast in the Gulf of Mexico. Tide gauges as far away as Cuba and Puerto Rico recorded effects of the waves.

Following this devastation, the Alaska Tsunami Warning Center was established to provide early warning of the giant waves. But, not to put a damper on what seems like a good idea, the ATWC admits it can't provide adequate warning against locally caused tsunamis. Only a rapid ascent of the nearest hill promptly following a tremor offers any hope of survival on shore. Aboard a boat, the ATWC recommends quickly heading out to open ocean where the wave's power is more diffused and a vessel has a chance to ride up and over the crest. With nontsunami quakes a routine, almost daily event, the land-based populace understandably is lulled into inaction. Nobody goes running up the nearest hill when the earth shakes and dishes rattle. Those at sea, fatalists to begin with, know they'd have little chance of survival should a major tsunami hit. The attitude of Alaskans, both ashore and at sea, is one of blasé indifference, so the potential for a repeat of the disastrous 1964 event remains, and it could happen at any moment.

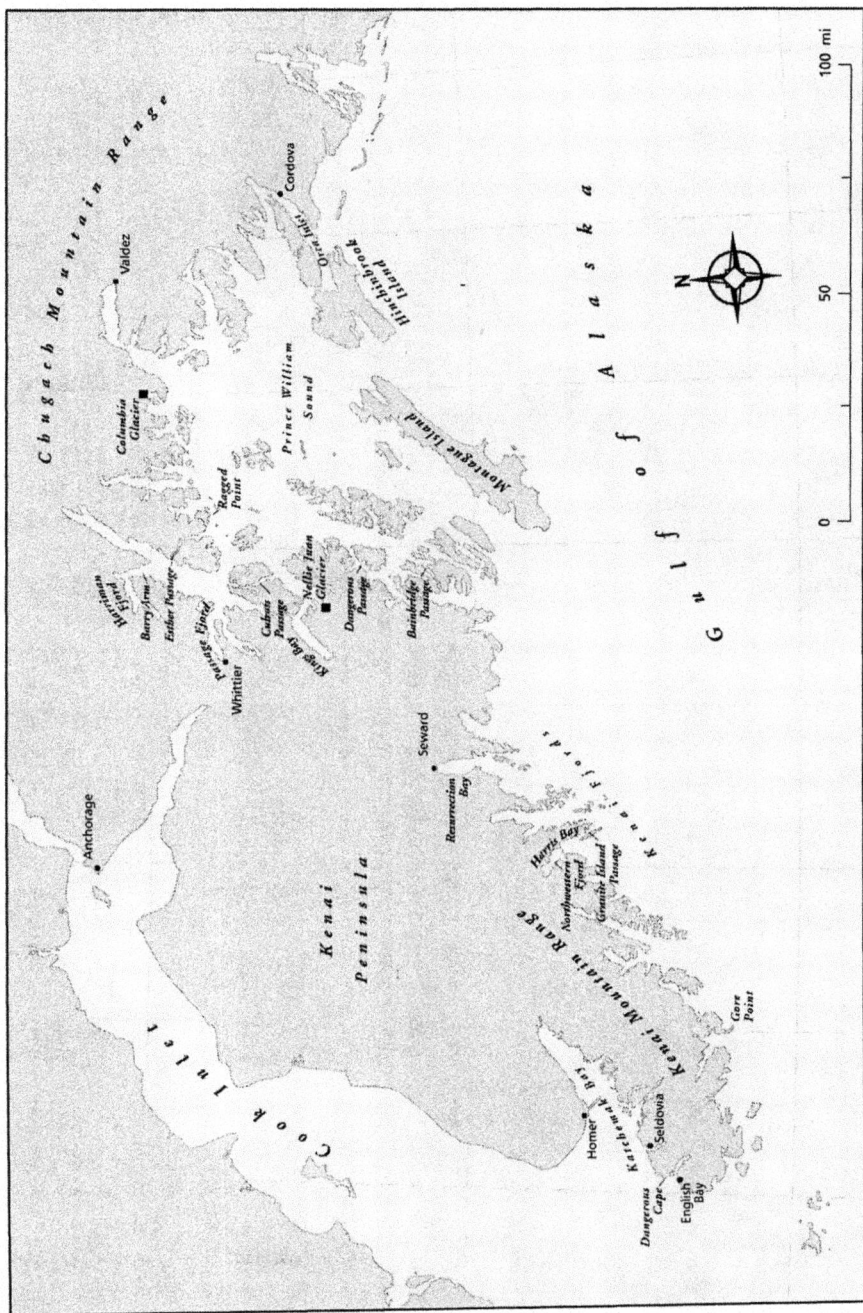

Chugach Mountain Range
Valdez
Cordova
Orca Inlet
Hinchinbrook
Columbia Glacier
Prince William Sound
Ragged Point
Harriman Fjord
Barry Arm
Esther Passage
Nellie Juan Glacier
Culross Passage
Dangerous Passage
Bainbridge Passage
Montague Island
Portage Fjord
Whittier
Kings Bay
Seward
Resurrection Bay
Anchorage
Kenai Peninsula
Harris Bay
Northwestern Fjord
Granite Island Passage
Kenai Mountain Range
Kenai Fjords
Gore Point
Cook Inlet
Homer
Kachemak Bay
Seldovia
Dangerous Cape
English Bay

Gulf of Alaska

N

0   50   100 mi

Anchorage, Alaska.

Cook Inlet, Alaska.
Augustine Volcano, Cook Inlet, Alaska.

Augustine Volcano, Cook Inlet, Alaska.
Brooks Lake, Alaska.

Kachemak Bay, Alaska.

Jose de Creeft's plane at Brooks Lake, Alaska.
Mt. McKinley, Alaska Range.

Chapter Three

Oh, Lord, thy sea is so great
And my boat so small.
- Fisherman's Prayer

- On a sign along the boardwalk,
Pelican, Alaska

IT'S EARLY AFTERNOON as I, at last, leave the harbor at Homer fully sixteen days after the planned departure date. The tiny speck on the earth's surface occupied by *Rascal* at Homer lies on a meridian of longitude that is some 2,100 miles west of the meridian on which the U.S.-Mexico border rests at San Diego, closer to Russia's nearest meridian than to San Diego's. More importantly, that border at San Diego, my destination, is something on the order of 4,200 adventure-filled miles away. If all goes well, this nekkid escapade will take six weeks' time, more or less. Whether the trip will require more time or less is not really all that important; this is an excursion that will not be constrained by time. It'll take as long as it takes.

At forty-six degrees, the water is cold. I am, after all, on the same latitude as Stockholm, Oslo, and the south tip of Greenland. Though the sun is out, the sky gin-clear, and the temperature in the mid-50s, the combination of cold water and blowing wind from *Rascal's* thirty-five knot speed quickly has me shivering.

Before leaving Homer, I bought rubberized, insulated work gloves and rubber boots with a felt sole pad for added warmth. The rest of my nautical wardrobe includes long johns, fleece shirt, fleece-lined jacket with collar zipped around the neck, wool socks, and wool pants. These are cheerfully encased in bright yellow foul weather pants and jacket stippled with colonies of black mold left over from a rainy Bahamas cruise, causing me to resemble nothing so much as an overripe banana. Still, I'm cold, especially my feet. *Rascal's* fiberglass hull and open deck are poor protection from the discomforts of Alaska's seas.

Crossing Kachemak Bay, I pass slowly by the quaint village of Halibut Cove, said to be an artist colony then, still in the bay, to Seldovia, of Russian heritage, where I stay the night. Both communities are sited on the south shore of the bay, and sit precariously in the shadows of the snow-covered (even in mid-June) Kenai Mountain Range. Neither can be reached by car or train, thought to be a virtue.

At five o'clock in the morning, nearly trembling with barely restrained excitement at what lies ahead (or is it the cold?), I'm aboard *Rascal*, gliding at idle speed over the waters of Seldovia's protecting cove. The props tear a jagged saw cut and the bow furrows soft waves, disfiguring the polished onyx surface and marking my path to the sea. The predawn air is crisp and bracing, the sky stark and cloudless. At this time of year in these high latitudes, the sun lights the sky nearly twenty hours each day, so already at this early hour the world has begun to color. As I leave the cove, pass English Bay, and make for the arrestingly named Dangerous Cape, the lights of a tiny Indian village twinkle like close-by stars as its occupants rise to prepare for a day of commercial fishing. Its backyards jammed hard against towering peaks, this tiny speck of a place is man's barest foothold in a harsh environment.

Off in the distance, rising grandly from a calm and vacant sea, is Augustine Island, an active 4,300-foot volcanic cone draped in a mantle of gleaming snow. This is the same island I flew over just a few weeks ago in the vintage spotter plane. Reflecting the earliest rays of a subarctic sun, its white sheath is burnished Dreamsicle pale-orange, set against a limpid sky and tarnished silver sea. Its soft pastel hues are a carnival of colors for a world usually painted in black and white and gloomy shades of gray. The scene is of such surpassing beauty that I'm moved to bring *Rascal* to a stop, turn off her motors, and drift amid beguiling splendor.

The coastal waters of the Kenai Peninsula are dotted with blobs of guano-covered stone, rumpled islets, stout pinnacles, and columnar shards rising from the depths—stony ziggurats from the Pleistocene newly sculpted in the calculus of geologic time. Weaving among these requires a careful watch ahead and a constant check of the chart plotter to avoid collision.

Complete reliance on the nautical charts, even my nifty electronic version, would be foolhardy. The 1964 earthquake so thoroughly jumbled the seabed that much of what the charts show is inaccurate, in some places wildly so. *The United States Coast Pilot*, a nine-volume set of sailing directions published by the National Oceanic and Atmospheric Administration, cautions that the quake caused bottom changes ranging from a subsidence of seven feet to a rise of thirty-five feet. Many of the depths, it warns, may be considerably different from those represented on nautical charts! This unnerving warning places greater than usual demands on vigilance. Rocks once sitting on the seabed far below may be still invisible but barely submerged and poised to rip a hole through *Rascal's* thin hull.

Organic obstacles present themselves too. Squatting in great noisy blankets across the blessedly flat ocean, numbering into the thousands, are sea birds of all kinds, most self-segregated by species: puffins, murres, cormorants, auklets, guillemots, petrels, shearwaters, gulls, terns, and kittiwakes. Here and there, barely visible on the surface, kelp roots thick as an arm, shorn from undersea beds, lay coiled in prop-fouling thickets. Some gather in wide serpentine swaths, joined by fields of brown tobaccolike leaves that undulate in the gentle swells. Nearer shore, fields of living kelp growing from submerged rock gardens wave eerily in the ocean backwash.

Ranking just after Canada's Bay of Fundy, this part of Alaska has tidal ranges that are among the world's highest. At up to thirty-eight feet, they present a challenge to coastal navigation, not so much because of their effect on depth—the waters are so deep as to be only minimally changed by tides—but because their surface speed and power drive them into opposing wind, waves, and swell with menacing result. These forces are nowhere more dramatically at odds than at Gore Point, locally called the Cape Horn of Alaska. Here, coastal ocean currents, lumbering swells, ebbing tide rips, and powerful winds crash headlong into each other, turning flat water into tumultuous sea. Happily, on this glorious morning, I encounter no wind, not the faintest zephyr, and I've purposely timed my arrival to coincide with the benign conditions of slack tide. Only gentle ocean swells and a mild chop ruffle the surface.

Beyond Gore Point, the sky is obscured by a slab of dead-gray rock rising 1,500 feet from the sea and spanning the horizon. This impressive edifice is the sheared side of a Kenai mountain, sliced deli meat-cutter clean by nature's lapidary. Barely detectable, moving beside its base, is a bobbing speck that on closer inspection turns out to be a sixty-foot, two-masted sailboat—such is the outsize scale of coastal Alaska.

On I cruise, up deep fjords, over marble-flat bays, through keyhole narrow passages, and alongside ancient glaciers, faces pockmarked from early summer calving of its iceberg offspring. The vista is a chaotic wonderland of fjords, islands, waterways, and bays, its foreshore lined with stands of Sitka spruce or red cedar or western hemlock, or barricaded with boulders pushed into place by ancient glaciers long since melted away. This once sulphuric wasteland of molten rock is today a shimmering garden of flamboyant forms, hammered, chiseled, scraped, and eroded by convulsive forces still at work. The coast is a racked and gnarled result of nature's power to deform, softened only by the sea that washes its base.

Formed eons ago by glaciation, the remnants of which are the tidewater glaciers of today, the fjords of the Kenai Peninsula are deep gouges in the earth's crust, backfilled with sea. Their steep sides rise from the depths to alpine peaks, craggy and granitic, revealing their relative youth. The imbroglio of islands, islets, lonely slabs of salt-washed stone and rock spires are just the splinters from the wreck of a once-shattered world. This is the coastal outskirts of the Kenai Mountain Range, a vast field of gaunt peaks overlain by an eons-old carpet of ice, the Harding Ice Field, still oozing glaciers into the sea.

Of all the magnificent fjords that furrow the coastline of Alaska, none are as audacious as those along the seaward approach to Harris Bay. Along the bay's west shore stands a miles-long colossal palisade of wet, gray rock splotched by tousled patches of moss and lichen. High up the wrinkled face of these storm-battered cliffs, murres and guillemots dive and wheel in noisy aerobatics, seeming unable to climb more than halfway to the top. Blackstone Bay, Thunder Bay, and Two Arm Bay are ice-carved pockets riven into the stone walls here, offering a besieged vessel quiet refuge. At the head of Harris Bay, sitting imperiously behind a protective barrier of calved bergs, is the Northwestern Fjord, ribbons of ice flowing from its every crevice and surrounded on three sides by barricades of granite. Making a sweeping turn to starboard, I head for Granite Island Passage on the way to Seward.

The Kenai Fjords, like all geologic worlds, is a place devoid of humanity, without emotion or intellect. It does not think or feel, argue or seduce. Here there is no corruption, indifference, cynicism, anger, regret, religion, love or hate, and no joy or elation. The place simply *is*. It exists, and only humans vainly attempt to give it humanity. We speak of it as cruel, unforgiving, angry, relentless, pastoral, but it is none of these. It is not a colorless world on the few days when the sun brings to life the deep green of the conifer forests, the cobalt blue of the sea, and the multihued sheets of wildflowers. But on most days, when scudding blankets of flinty cloud block the warmth and light, this is a world of black and white and shades of gray. Tiny, powerless humans float on flimsy craft along the edge of it all, and they are awed, overwhelmed and, in the end, captivated. This world returns them nothing. It is only a place.

Suddenly, commotion on the water surface! An enormous humpback whale is being harassed by a school of Dall's porpoises, a Boeing 747 attacked by a squadron of F-16s. Black with white markings similar to an orca's, but much smaller, the Dall's porpoise is very fast. Distracted from strafing the hapless, lumbering whale, they begin to frolic with *Rascal*, mistaking her shiny hull for a new playmate, I suppose. Like out-of-control torpedoes, they run under her hull, surface, dive, and resurface, dart up and down, flit about this way and that in a frenzy of unrestrained play. The show goes on for nearly half an hour while the harassed humpback swims away from its tormentors.

Running low on fuel, I head up the glorious emerald-watered fjord that is Resurrection Bay to the small town of Seward, nestled in the bay's deepest corner and dwarfed by steep-sided mountains looming over it. At nearly a thousand-feet deep, the bay is ice-free year-round, and that fact, unusual among Alaska's coastal towns, is the reason for Seward's founding. After fitful starts and stops, a rail line connecting the port at Seward with Anchorage was completed, making the town the main port for virtually all supplies entering Alaska. It remained so and might still be today were it not for that fateful three minutes on March 27, 1964, the day the Great Alaska Earthquake hit.

The same quake that wrecked Anchorage and jumbled the undersea floor nearly destroyed Seward. When it hit, a mile-long stretch of the town's waterfront shook violently, broke away from the mountainside, and slid into Resurrection Bay, a name that at that moment must have seemed tragically ironic. The resulting wave, thousands of tons of raging ice water, crossed the narrow bay in seconds, slammed into the enclosing mountain wall, bounced off, and headed straight for what remained of the town. The wave lifted a diesel locomotive from the rail yard, raised it into the air and tossed it, toylike, 200 feet. A fuel storage depot erupted in giant sheets of flame igniting the bay, now a boiling inferno surely sent up from the depths of Hell.

When the quake at last subsided, eleven people had perished and eighty-six houses had been destroyed, with 269 homes heavily damaged. Seward's days as an important port and railhead were over. Today, the town serves as a port for coal transport ships and in the summer months for cruise ships.

After refueling at the Seward docks and just as I'm about to cast off, I discover that one of the fuel bladders is leaking gas all over *Rascal's* aft deck and into the bilge where the electric bilge pumps are found. Fire is now possible, even an explosion from trapped fumes. The leak comes from two small nicks in the rubberized outer layer of the material used to make the bladders. I don't know how the nicks got there or when, but I'm fairly sure they only recently began to leak. The bladder is now useless, and I have no way to stop the leak. Part of the fuel reserve I was counting on to get me through the longest leg of the trip, the 250 miles from Cordova to Yakutat, is now gone, and the odds of successfully completing this long passage have just dropped a full notch.

<center>~~~</center>

Two hundred feet astern of *Rascal* at Seward's fuel dock, secured to the same dock with neatly deployed black-braided nylon lines, is a 120-foot sleek, Italian-designed motor yacht, elegantly but immodestly named *Elegante*. Its white hull and stainless steel trim polished to spot-free perfection, the yacht glistens in the bright rays of Alaskan sun. Its crew of eight, smartly attired in matching starched white uniforms, has just finished their morning duties and retired to their burl wood-lined quarters for lunch. After a half-hour has passed, a ninety-foot steel hulled juggernaut, the *Pacific Queen*, chugs into the harbor, its high sturdy prow, Baltic-type wheelhouse and deck gear describing an ocean trawler perhaps on the way home to Seattle from the Bering Sea. Its dented, paint-scraped, and rust-stained hull also describes the depressed state of the Alaskan fishing industry.

Needing a place to tie up while awaiting his turn at the cannery docks, the *Pacific Queen's* captain maneuvers the boat into dock space immediately forward of and bow on to *Elegante*. And there they sit nose to nose, as different as two vessels could be, just ten yards apart, seeming to stare—or is it glare?—at one another. *Elegante* stretches in grand repose. *Pacific Queen* squats in sullen anger. The one, whose tailored crew awaits wealthy owner and guests, pampered visitors to this raw world, the other whose denimed and flannelled crew struggles to eke out a living from the harsh Alaskan seas. As the guttural rumble of *Pacific Queen's* idling diesel engine reverberates across the harbor, deckhands in fish-slimed slickers prepare to make her fast to heavy dock cleats.

At this moment, in the midst of the dull routine of docking, and so without a hint of what is to come, it happens: The *Pacific Queen* charges at *Elegante*, fairly leaping through the harbor waters. The heavy steel brute rams the graceful yacht, strikes it a violent blow, then, just as quickly, jerks away. The jolt shakes the yacht to its keel and stresses its docking lines to the breakpoint, but it's the hull that absorbs the damage. The lightning fast jab punched a raw-edged, ten-foot hole in the forward bulwark of the yacht and added another scratch to a vast field of scratches on the sturdy trawler.

Rudely interrupted from their lunch, the yacht's crew comes streaming out of their quarters and onto the weather deck, stunned, eyes bulging, urgent alarm showing across their faces. The trawler's crew, half aboard, half dockside, stare quietly in embarrassed disbelief. When both crews realize neither vessel will sink right there at the dock and begin to assess the damage, the drama of the moment settles into the routine of a fender bender: Call the cops (the Coast Guard, who sit fifty yards away on the cutter *Mustang*), swap insurance cards. It appears the trawler's captain inadvertently caused its transmission to slip into gear while its engines idled too fast. The primary damage, apart from the physical, is to the *Pacific Queen's* captain's ego, reputation and, one supposes, his future employment prospects.

~~~

After cleaning up the mess from the leaked fuel, I cast off and head out across the shimmering waters of Resurrection Bay into the Gulf of Alaska, turn hard left and make for Prince William Sound eighty miles away. The seas are smooth, and the day is still dazzling and sunny as I pass just offshore of the Kenai Range and its fingers of granite peninsulas jutting into the ocean. Entering the sound through the Bainbridge Passage, itself a narrow, open-ended fjord, I pass among forested islands, through wind-rippled waterways and past sinewy glaciers flowing out of the high ice fields into nearly every crevice in the rocky coast. Patches of snowpack left over from winter dot the shoreline.

At Dangerous Passage, an unexpected obstacle blocks the way. The entire waterway is choked by thousands of fragments of pack ice left over from the spring thaw and by the shattered remains of shards calved from nearby glaciers. Weaving at idle speed, I'm soon brought to a stop, ensnared by sharp-edged ice. Seawater freezes at 28.6 degrees Fahrenheit, and most of the water I have passed over today has been forty-two. Hidden in the cold shadows of high mountains and shielded from warming winds and currents, this place has not yet welcomed summer and its ice-melting warmth. Unperturbed by the seasonal anomaly, a humpback whale feeds in the midst of it all, rolling languidly through the field of broken ice.

Though nearly ninety percent of their mass lies below the surface, icebergs float in a precarious equilibrium. They are dangerously tipsy and roll with no warning. Slowly, I alter course away from Dangerous Passage, weaving cautiously among the bergs in search of open water until, finding a fairlead, I am able to break free and head for the nearest port. Ending a perfect day that covered 400 miles and lasted a blissful fifteen hours, I arrive at the grim village of Whittier, lying in stark juxtaposition at the end of the scenic Passage Fjord.

The people of Whittier are all excited these days. Since its inception, the town has been reachable only by the Alaska Railroad from Anchorage, plane, or boat. Now a road, complete with tunnel, links the place to the outside world, though just why anyone would want to drive here—or get here any other way—is hard to imagine (I'm here because I didn't know any better).

The place began life as a military installation built during World War II When the military pulled out, its buildings were turned over to the town, which today consists of the same, now quite old, buildings adapted to civilian use, some repainted—most not. A few flimsy burger joints and the like, a rail yard in the middle of town close to the waterfront, and a petroleum tank farm at its outskirts comprise the town's main features. All of these are overwhelmed by what may be the most badly sited building anywhere in the non-Communist world: a fifteen-story former Army barracks—a kind of vertical trailer park—reborn as apartments, hotel, time share, grocery store, and post office. Imagine a squalid, Bulgarian high-rise workers' apartment building set in, say, Yellowstone Park.

As I tie up for the night, I encounter an unpleasant surprise. Another fuel bladder is leaking badly, this one from a rip in the underside of the bag. I surmise this tear occurred when I dragged the full bag a foot across the rough surface of *Rascal's* aft deck, a stress it should easily have sustained. Turning the bladder upside down to stop fuel from leaking out, I set it on *Rascal's* aft deck, again clean up the mess, and retire for the night to a room at June's Bread and Butter Fishing Charters and B & B, an unlikely combination of services to say the least. The term B & B evokes homey images of hearth, sideboard, and chintz, quite at odds with the tiny one-bedroom condo/time share on the fourteenth floor of the old Army barracks. In similar contrast, the majestic Passage Fjord and its mountains grace the world just beyond this ugly building.

Early next morning as I walk out across the dock preparing to leave, I'm startled by a strong petrochemical odor that penetrates the cold air. I reason the smell must be from a resin used by somebody working on fiberglass or maybe using some kind of paint stripper. No such luck. The bladder I set upon the deck last night is leaking profusely and has done so most of the night, with the result that its fifteen gallons has been reduced to a remaining two. The bladder has sprung a second leak, this one beneath a label and so not visible. Colorful gasoline stains float over the surface of *Rascal's* bilge water, though no gas has been pumped into the harbor by the bilge pumps, an event that, had it happened, would have resulted in about the same legal consequences as serial homicide.

Again, fire risk is at hand. After taking the nearly empty bladder ashore, I pump the raw fuel out of the bilge into buckets, haul these ashore for disposal, spray fresh water on the stains and dissipate them into oblivion, then flush out the bilge and, finally, cast off. I'm now down to just two fifteen-gallon reserve tanks, my confidence in these severely diminished.

~~~

In Prince William Sound, wild geologic upheaval has been caught in stop action. Sheer-sided fjords and dense ice pack, tangles of gnarled islands, and grotesque rock piles float in a moody sea encircled by hills carpeted in green shag and mountains armored in ice. Nothing about it is pastoral or bucolic.

It was ice that carved the sound I roam today. About six million years ago, the world got a whole lot colder. Snow and rain fell, turned to ice, became glaciers, and these pushed and churned and scoured their way through the mountains. Then, a million or so years later, it got warm, the ice melted, and new rivers cascaded out of the highlands. Great torrents of muddy meltwater carried fine silt and rasping pebbles down steep valleys, tumbled over waterfalls, and washed its detritus into broad, shallow plains. A few million years later, it all froze again in a new ice age, then melted again and froze again in a rhythm of destruction. Glaciers up to 2,000 feet high advanced, pushing before them broad fields of boulders and pebbles and sand that formed terminal moraines, marking forever the glaciers' tracks across the land. They retreated and advanced again. In the past 2.5 million years, there have been at least seventeen severe glacial episodes.

All this glacial movement—forming, advancing, melting, retreating—worked on the landscape like a million backhoes and road graders and bulldozers, shaping, cutting, and filling. Prince William Sound, the place where *Rascal* drifts on a vast blue field, is the magnificent result. The work still goes on today with all the industrial noise of a major construction project. Loud reports of bergs calving, like jackhammers at work opening pavement, and the constant crunch and grind of floating ice create a din in the otherwise serene fjords.

Cruising through the northwestern part of the sound, I visit Nellie Juan Glacier and Kings Bay, tour Barry Arm and Harriman Fjord, called the Glacier Bay of the Sound, and its collateral glaciers. Dense fields of chair-to house-size icebergs block the approaches to the glaciers' steep faces. After transiting the magnificent Culross and Esther Passages, timid sea otters curiously eyeing the loud intruder, I weave among rocks, islets, and gill nets set by salmon fishermen.

A truck-size iceberg with a pair of spindle-legged kittiwakes perched on its peak floats amid a dispersed field of bergs calved from the Columbia Glacier. A fine ice sculpture, the berg's once craggy features have been softened by a warm sun, giving it the voluptuous proportions of a Henry Moore nude. Yet here the sculpture is not the dark bronze of an aging statue, but a sky-lit translucent blend of pale shades of turquoise. Beneath its surface, the colors grow paler until lost in fields of arctic white, tinted the faintest blue. Rather than set in a museum on a pedestal illumined by a spotlight, this work drifts in natural splendor on a reflecting pool of cobalt sea surrounded by the ice-covered mountains from which it arose. No work of art was ever so gracefully displayed.

Encircled by distant walls of snow-drenched mountains, floating gently on the unruffled surface of wide blue water, I am alone in the midst of a beguiling tableau, a place of quiet and perfect splendor. I pass close by gamboling sea otters and harbor seals and drifting flocks of puffins and terns. In the distance, orcas patrol their domain. The pungent smell of the sea, moderated by the cold, comes to me on faint cat's paws as spangles of sunlight dance across the sound's gently crinkled surface. All around is lonely romantic vastness and profound beauty.

In fading light, I find Ragged Point and near it locate a tiny cove the entry to which I gain only by snaking through a rock-lined channel barely wider than *Rascal's* beam. Entering the cove, I am in a sanctuary of solitary stillness. The nearby adjoining shore gives way to a spruce forest from which not a sound emerges, much as if it were snow blanketed. A stone's throw away, a black bear cub turns his head, puzzled by this strange intruder, too young to be wary. The temperature colder now, a drizzle falls from the once clear sky, scaring the cove water's perfect sheen. I drop anchor and settle back on the stern seat, light rain running off my foul weather suit as I marvel at the serene world that envelopes me.

Following a night in a rain-drizzled fiberglass cocoon, snug in a dry sleeping bag, I awake to a quiet dawn, lift anchor, and head off into the remote wilderness. After a day spent wandering among fjords, islets, bays, and fields of bergs, I set course for Cordova, the last town before hitting the Gulf of Alaska. Carefully, I pass over Bligh Reef, the undersea pile of sharp-edged rocks that, like a can opener, easily opened the heavy steel hull of the *Exxon Valdez*, spilling eleven million gallons of oil into the sound. That was ten years ago. Today, the area affected by the spill is nearly completely recovered from the environmental effects and still reaps rewards from the economic impact of all those billions that flowed into the local economy in the aftermath. When I arrive in Cordova, deep in the southeast corner of the sound, it's 7:00 p.m., and the harbormaster's office is closed. Early in the morning, I'll leave the harbor and make way along the coast of the Gulf of Alaska. This is the leg of the voyage that has been my focus of concern since the early planning began, and it's the leg for which I had intended to use the four fuel bladders, now down to two.

~~~

The 400-mile stretch of North American coast from Cordova, at the southeastern foot of Prince William Sound, to Cape Spencer, the northernmost entry into the Inside Passage, is called both Coffin Corner and the Dangerous Coast, names not likely chosen by the Chamber of Commerce. Thus far I've encountered a Dangerous Cape, Dangerous Passage, and now Dangerous Coast, and I still have a lot of coastline remaining ahead.

The frequency with which the word "dangerous" appears in Alaskan names hints at the power of its waters to visit personal injury on the incautious mariner. This coast gets its ominous epithets from the number of lives its horrific weather has claimed, weather ranking with that of the Aleutian Islands as among the worst and least predictable in the world.

The Saint Elias Mountains, one of the world's highest coastal

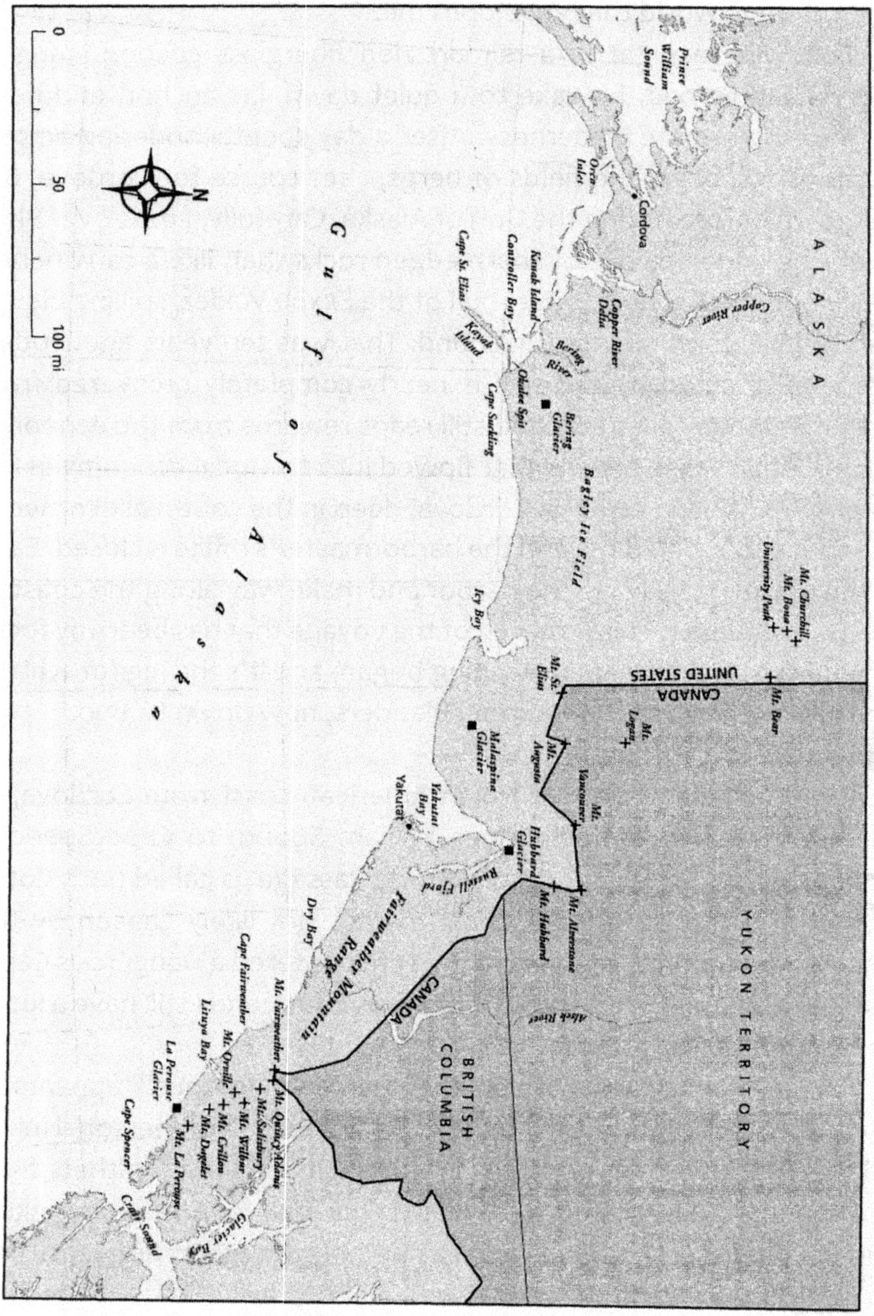
ALASKA
YUKON TERRITORY
BRITISH COLUMBIA
UNITED STATES
CANADA
CANADA
Gulf of Alaska
Prince William Sound
Orca Inlet
Cordova
Copper River
Copper River Delta
Controller Bay
Kanak Island
Cape St. Elias
Kayak Island
Bering River
Okalee Spit
Cape Suckling
Bering Glacier
Bagley Ice Field
Mt. Churchill
Mt. Bona
University Peak
Icy Bay
Mt. St. Elias
Mt. Bear
Mt. Logan
Mt. Augusta
Malaspina Glacier
Mt. Vancouver
Yakutat Bay
Yakutat
Hubbard Glacier
Russell Fjord
Mt. Hubbard
Mt. Alverstone
Alsek River
Dry Bay
Fairweather Range
Cape Fairweather
Mt. Fairweather
Lituya Bay
Mt. Quincy Adams
Mt. Salisbury
Mt. Orville
Mt. Wilbur
Mt. Crillon
Mt. Dagelet
La Perouse Glacier
Mt. La Perouse
Cape Spencer
Cross Sound
Glacier Bay
N
0
50
100 mi

ranges, traps storms in the Gulf of Alaska, allowing them to build internal pressure and thus especially fierce winds. Even without the storms, less common in summer months, sea conditions are influenced by natural forces often working in opposition. Tides here set parallel to, rather than against, the shore, thus acting like an ocean current, though one that reverses direction every six hours. To this is added a true ocean current, setting northwest at 1.5 knots, and the ever-changing and often fierce winds. Finally, ocean swells of varying heights and period roll in from as far away as the Sea of Japan, attacking from oblique to perpendicular angles to the wind, tide, and current. The result is wildly unpredictable weather that, with little warning, turns the sea from impassive to treacherous.

The first leg of the Dangerous Coast, at 250 nautical miles, is the longest and most desolate stretch of subpolar coastline in the United States, save those of the Bering, Chukchi, and Beaufort Seas along Alaska's northwest and north coasts. This section of shoreline is almost completely people free. A remote logging camp and a few vacant cabins are the only human habitations along its entire length. At the end of this stretch is the tiny hamlet of Yakutat (population six hundred, fifty percent of whom are Tlingit Indian), with an airport, left over from another World War II military installation, offering regularly scheduled, but infrequent, commercial air service, and a port capable of handling small ships, though it rarely does. Otherwise, access to this remote coast is available only in chartered aircraft flown by intrepid bush pilots to remote landing strips or sand beaches—though the high fatality rate among these pilots discourages the cautious traveler. For small boats with shallow draft, only Controller, Icy, Yakutat, and Lituya bays offer refuge, but the last of these can be entered solely under the rare conditions of slack tide and no onshore breakers. Yakutat alone offers fuel and supplies.

At the south end of Orca Inlet, from which the Cordova fishing fleet emerges into the Gulf of Alaska, stretching eastward along the shore for eighty miles, is the bewildering complex of shallow streams, meanders, sloughs, and glacial bars that form the 700,000-acre delta of the glacier-fed Copper River. This is North America's largest wetland, and each spring it hosts the continent's single largest concentration of migrating birds. Salmon run up the delta's waterways, some into the waiting gill- and seine nets of local fishermen. Sockeye, king, and coho salmon taken from this area are reputed to be among the tastiest in the world. The quality of salmon meat is said to be directly related to the length of the river up which nature compels the fish to swim in order to spawn, and the Copper River, reaching some 300 miles through the Chugach Mountains into the Alaskan interior, is among the longest anywhere.

East of the Copper River Delta is the smaller Bering River Delta, fed by meltwater from both the enormous Bagley Ice Field and the 2,300-square-mile Bering Glacier, the world's largest glacier outside of Greenland and the polar ice caps. Inland along this shore lies a tangle of white-clothed granite massifs, 4,000- to 6,000-feet high, their valleys filled with a crazy-quilt jumble of glaciers and ice fields, some advancing, others retreating, still gouging their eternal marks across the land. In the foreground are low dunes of gray sand and pewter silt.

Just offshore of the Bering Delta, sitting in grand repose but oddly out of place, is the seventeen-mile long, knifelike Kayak Island, lying atop the most active earthquake zone in North America. The seaward end of the island is the place where in 1741 the explorer Vitus Bering landed on the Russian Orthodox holiday of Saint Elias Day and claimed Alaska for the czar. In honor of the occasion, he named its western tip Cape Saint Elias—though it's the tip of an island and not technically a cape—a place with which I will soon become overly familiar.

Set deep into the coastal contour, is the remote and astonishingly beautiful Icy Bay. Rightly named, its shoreline is partly girded by the Guyot, Yahtse, and Tyndall Glaciers and by the western edge of the colossal Malaspina Glacier, which covers in dense ice pack most of the coastal plain from Icy Bay to Yakutat, some eighty miles.

But the real drama of the bay is Mount Saint Elias, at 18,008 feet, the third highest peak in North America. Just inland from the bay's shores, it reaches to the heavens, whiting out a vast part of the Alaskan sky. Only twenty-five miles distant from it, just beyond the Canadian border, is Mount Logan, at 19,850 feet, the second highest of the continent. But these elevation rankings are based on the same convention that has Everest higher than McKinley. Properly judged, these are, after McKinley, the third and second highest land-based mountains and the second highest and highest coastal mountains in the world!

From Icy Bay to Yakutat Bay, the shoreline is high glacial dune, backed by the Malaspina Glacier—North America's largest piedmont glacier at 1,500 square miles—and behind that looms a tapestry of nature at its most ostentatious. Just beyond the glacier and near the head of Yakutat Bay are Mount Augusta (14,070 feet), Mount Vancouver (15,700 feet), Mount Alverstone (14,500 feet), and Mount Hubbard (14,950 feet). Then comes Mount Fairweather (15,300 feet) and, just down the coast from Yakutat, Mount Bona (16,421 feet), Mount Churchill (15,678 feet), University Peak (14,470 feet), and Mount Bear (14,831 feet). Along this shore are ten of the twenty highest peaks in the United States (properly measured, these are among the highest mountains in the world). This stretch of coast is to mountains what Manhattan is to skyscrapers, and in *Rascal* I intend to cruise along the equivalent of the Hudson River, dwarfed and awed by it all.

~~~

Before leaving the dock in Cordova, I call my wife and tell her I expect the trip to Yakutat will require eight hours and that I'll leave the dock at 7:00 a.m. to catch the peak flood tide. The day promises to be cloudless and calm, a repeat of the first two days, as the high pressure center that caused this rare spate is expected to stay in the area all day. If, however, I don't call her from Yakutat by 7:00 p.m., twelve hours later, she should call the Coast Guard in Cordova and report me missing, a highly unlikely event, or so I think. This precautionary trip wire is a measure of the deep concern I've long harbored about the Dangerous Coast. Never before in all my travels have I undertaken a coastal segment so fraught with risk and without radio contact or nearby assistance should I need it.

Rascal carries 207 gallons of gas in her main tank, and the remaining two bladder tanks carry fifteen gallons each—assuming they too don't spring leaks—for a total of 237 gallons. To complete the leg to Yakutat, average fuel consumption, including the bladder tanks and with no safety reserve at all, has to be no worse than 1.05 miles per gallon. This figure assumes that the fuel in all three tanks will be fully consumed, though I know some residual fuel at the bottom of a tank never gets to the motors. How much I don't know. Moreover, rough seas, wind, tide, and current exert drag on the hull and increase fuel consumption. Lowering the trim tabs increases drag too, something like flaps on an airplane. In the worst conditions, consumption can drop well under 1.0 miles per gallon resulting in a range short of what is required to reach Yakutat. Clearly, to complete this leg, I'll need all the onboard fuel as well as generally favorable conditions.

My confidence in the integrity of the two fuel bladders is not high. What will I do if they begin to leak? Will I be able to detect it in time to save the fuel? How will I get fuel from the leaking, heavy, and awkward bladders into the main tank while stopped in the midst of stormy seas? Another unknown and unknowable fact on which the success of this leg depends is sea conditions. If seas are benign, I can make Yakutat safely, though with no room to spare for exploring. But if they turn rough, a common event along the Dangerous Coast, the rate of consumption will increase, along with the risk of coming up short on fuel.

Leaving Cordova harbor, I head out through the marked channel in Orca Inlet, home to the world's largest concentration of sea otters even after the depredations of the *Exxon Valdez*. Fifteen miles from the harbor, the inlet reaches into the Gulf of Alaska where, among a maze of dead-end channels and shallow bars of black glacial silt, I slip warily between parallel lines of breaking swells, as instructed by a fisherman the night before. While navigating among these breakers without help from the chart plotter (it can't tell me where the surf

breaks), I recall that his instructions were scribbled on a cocktail nap-
kin while we were seated at a bar; that we were both half toasted;
and that his scribbles, now my homemade chart, were as intricate and
incoherent as a tie-dye pattern. This seemed like an awkward time
to remember such things, and it didn't help that already I had run
aground on a submerged silt bar, though I had managed to back off
without any damage. At last, breaking free of the maze and in open
ocean, I set course for the sea buoy off Cape Saint Elias on Kayak
Island, seventy miles distant and some twenty miles offshore.

Almost at once, things begin to go awry. Winds kick up sharply
and seas over the shallow bottom grow choppy, requiring that I lower
the trim tabs to stabilize the boat. The rough seas and lowered tabs
reduce speed from the planned thirty knots to twenty-eight, and fuel
consumption stands at twenty-five gallons per hour, a rate already
eating into the reserve supply. Not good. If the seas lay down soon,
I'll have a chance to improve consumption in calmer water; after all,
I'm only in the first hour of an eight-hour trip.

Because I won't lower the trim tabs as far as I normally would, for
fear of increasing consumption still more, *Rascal* is pounding badly. As
she flies over the crest of each wave, she lands with a jarring crash,
and I face eight lonely hours of this. Though uncomfortable, I console
myself by thinking that instead of cruising along in the Gulf of Alaska,
I could be stuck sitting through a Wagner opera. By that contrast, this
ain't so bad after all. I could greatly improve the ride just by slowing
down but, unlike the economy achieved by slowing down in a car, a
planing boat actually increases the rate of fuel consumption as more
of its hull settles into the sea. Nervously, I watch the fuel consumption gauge read out its bad news.

Plowing along through the increasingly grisly seas, I perform
long division in my head to figure the rate of consumption and
double-check the gauge, but it proves accurate. Forty miles out of
Cordova, I can make out on the horizon the faint image of Cape Saint
Elias, the 1,600-foot high promontory weighting down the seaward

end of Kayak Island, rising improbably from the ocean, a vision akin to that of finding the Sears Tower in a Kansas wheat field.

After the pounding I've taken and worried about excessive fuel consumption in the heavy seas, I decide to anchor in the lee of the cape behind its high granite wall and wait for the wind to drop. It's 10:00 a.m., and I'm completely alone. The air is eerily silent except for the chuffing of a passing sea lion and later the gentle splashes of a few harbor seals frolicking around the boat. From gusts that reach me over the cape's high palisade, I know the wind is still howling. At the 520-foot-high Pinnacle Rock standing alone in the Gulf just a few miles seaward of the cape, great billows of sea spray erupt into the air like clouds of talc as waves dash themselves against its base. The temperature has dropped sharply, signaling that a front has arrived, as if I didn't already know.

After a few hours, it seems as though the seas may be calming and the winds subsiding. But I am growing concerned that I may not make Yakutat in time to stop my wife from alerting the Coast Guard, so I hoist anchor and head out. No longer protected by the lee, the boat is again attacked by the tormented seas that throw it around with ease and jerk me about as though I were on a rodeo bronco. Promptly surrendering, I scamper back to the haven behind Kayak Island.

A few hours later, I try again, still to no avail and, to make matters worse, I've used ten gallons of precious fuel in the two aborted escape attempts. I can't reach the Coast Guard or anybody else on the VHF. I call and call again, but the only answer is dead silence. Rarely in modern, hurly-burly life are we utterly alone, secluded beyond all the powers of technology, unable to touch someone, or hear the voice of another, or the familiar sounds of civilization. Now I am alone.

It's nearly 9:00 at night, cold and raining. By now Kitty has called the Coast Guard, and I'm sure they must be going into action; any minute I expect to hear a search plane. With the remaining fuel and no safety reserve, I need to eke out at least 1.06 miles per gallon if I'm to reach Yakutat. Still possible, but tight. To get here, I've averaged 1.15 miles per gallon. If I continue the same average, I can travel 180 miles, just thirteen more than needed to arrive in port, with no reserve. That is too damn close. So far, rough as the seas have been, I've managed to run on plane, on top of the water surface, thus reducing drag and getting a better rate of consumption. Should the seas become so rough that running on plane would be impossible, consumption would increase sharply, and I'd never make it. The Gulf of Alaska is no place to run out of fuel.

All through the night, the wind blows and rain falls in a thick, miserable drizzle. Though in the lee of Cape Saint Elias, I'm still anchored out in the Gulf of Alaska more than twenty miles off the coast, so the water is anything but calm and sleep is impossible. Even the gentlest lapping wave striking *Rascal's* drumskin fiberglass hull reverberates through the cabin like ten kids banging patty-cake. In the cold air, I break out a sleeping bag and crawl in, but sleep won't come. During the night, the winds shift from east to southwest partly robbing me of lee, and *Rascal* begins to dance around on her anchor line. The line saws noisily against the fairleads and wrenches at the cleats, so I check frequently to be sure it's secure.

The sun never completely sets at twilight during an Alaskan summer, as if to extend its luminance to a world badly in need of it. Along the coastal horizon, a dense veil of grim cloud reaches down from the heavens, but stops short of the horizon, leaving between the two an eerie ribbon of light, colored nuclear tangerine by the setting sun. Morning finally comes, and still the sky is ominous. Wind blows in gusts and gray drapes of rain fall intermittently. Many times I've tried to raise someone, anyone, on the VHF with no luck.

As I walk around *Rascal* in the dawn's light, checking the weather, the deck doesn't feel right underfoot. The subtle rise and fall of sea swells, followed by sharp tugs at the anchor line, a pattern to which I'd become accustomed, isn't there. My sleep-starved mind vaguely detects a harmony of boat and sea that I shouldn't feel from a deck securely tethered to the bottom. Something's wrong. Only slowly do I begin to comprehend that *Rascal* is drifting out to sea with the ebbing tide. Awakened from numb fatigue, I rush to the anchor rode secured at the bow and begin to haul it in, but it comes too easily, and I soon discover why. A steel shackle that secured anchor chain to rode is gone; its locking bolt has worked loose under the constant strain through the past many hours. All I pull up is rode. Anchor and chain are gone.

Now circumstances are beginning to cascade out of control and, as they famously do, at an awkward time. *Murphy, you son of a bitch, go away and leave me alone!* Defective fuel bladders, bad weather, excessive fuel consumption, no VHF contact, rough seas, and now lost anchor and chain. The odds in my favor are moving in the wrong direction, and the Gulf of Alaska is an unforgiving place to be on long odds.

I have a spare anchor, a large plow-type, but no chain. I can tie the rode directly to the anchor, but without a chain to hold it close to the sea floor, the rode will tend to pull the anchor upward and dislodge it. A chain would also protect the rode from chafing on rocks near the imbedded anchor. Without the steel shackle to connect rode to anchor, the rode could chafe and part at the connection. Lose the last anchor and I'll be deeper in the succotash than I am already.

It's time to forget about making Yakutat and return to Cordova before anything else goes wrong. I've been watching the seas, and in the past hour they seem to have calmed some. Wind speed has diminished, and the gusts are less robust. The massive breakers crashing onto Pinnacle Rock at the end of the cape seem smaller. The Gulf on the lee side of the cape looks calm. What I see could be an optical illusion; heavy seas seen from upwind look flatter than they are. Still, the signs calling me to leave look promising.

Desperate to be free again and bone weary, I take the bait and head out for Cordova, but in just a mile I know I've made a mistake. Nasty rollers and a stiff, formless chop, stirred up by gusting bellows of wind blowing over the cape quickly bring me off plane. Turning back for the security and calm of the cape's lee, I'm thoroughly chastened, tense, and anxious from the brief but sound beating I've just taken. That's the third and last time I'll attempt to leave without clear and windless skies and a calm sea, no matter how long I have to wait. A dense white fog joins the wind, rain, and cold, adds to my discomfort, and wraps Cape Saint Elias in a ghostly blanket.

In rigging the second anchor, I attach to the back of it a trip line and float so I can recover it if the rode parts, a second line of defense. With the outboard motors tilted up so the props are just barely in the water and out of the way of protruding rocks, I inch *Rascal* in as close to the shore as I dare, keeping a close eye on the depth gauge. The tide gauge on the chart plotter, using a tide reporting station just ten miles from here, shows the tide now at five feet above dead low. That means that if I anchor at any depth now less than five feet, *Rascal* would sit on the bottom at dead low tide. I find a secure spot with a depth of eight feet for a margin of error and toss overboard the anchor, trip line, and float; the anchor catches and holds immediately.

I run the rode through the fairleads in a bridle, spreading the stress between two bow cleats, rather than concentrating it on one, then crawl into the cabin, shed the foul weather gear and collapse, utterly spent. Enclosed within the thin walls of *Rascal's* tiny cabin. I'm at least protected from the still howling gusts of wind and rain, but not from the cold and not from exhaustion.

It's nearly 1:00 p.m., and I've been gone from Cordova thirty hours, much of it spent inside the cabin. Powerful gusts buffet the boat's aluminum tee-top, causing a droning sound I often mistake for the motors of a Coast Guard C-130 search and rescue plane. I don't need to be rescued, at least not yet, and I don't want the Coast Guard or anybody else endangering themselves to find me. Though I face potential problems—the anchor being foremost among them—I can endure here until this weather passes. My greatest concern is for my wife, our son, and friends, who must be severely distraught, by now believing I'm lost, and that thought anguishes me deeply. If I could be granted just one wish, it would be to tell them I'm okay.

Food may become an issue. I left Cordova with two turkey sandwiches and two cookies bought earlier in Whittier. The cookies and one sandwich I ate yesterday, and I'll eat half the remaining sandwich this afternoon and the other half late tonight or tomorrow. Then I'll just go hungry until I can get back to Cordova, a mild inconvenience, provided the weather breaks soon. I have four gallons of drinking water on board, and I begin to ration these severely.

At 4:00 p.m. I hear the unmistakable droning of a multi-engine, propeller-driven plane, probably the Coast Guard flying a search pattern. I leap to the VHF radio, grab the mike, press the talk key, and begin transmitting. No response. I keep transmitting. Still no response. The C-130 has powerful receivers on board and should be hearing me; something's wrong.

Then I spot the problem. The digital display on the radio shows a TX symbol indicating that the radio is transmitting properly when the talk key is depressed, but the display also shows an ANT symbol I haven't seen before. From the owner's manual stored in the cabin, I learn the symbol means there is a problem with the antenna, probably a connection that jarred loose in the heavy seas. No wonder they can't hear me.

Opening the survival bag, I pull out the handheld, backup VHF and on the first call raise the search plane. I report that *Rascal* is seaworthy and in good mechanical condition, that I've lost the primary anchor but have deployed the secondary, and that I plan to ride out the weather. With the coordinates I give them, they overfly me, but without a sighting; the gray ceiling is too thick and low. My only concern is when the weather will improve enough to return to Cordova and whether I have enough food—one turkey sandwich—to keep up body heat and energy in the wet, cold climate.

The Coast Guard Cutter *Mustang* and a distant fishing vessel, *Shadow Dancer*, on a course that will pass near the cape, offer assistance, and a ship far offshore with high-powered communications gear offers to serve as the primary communications base. The C-130, based in Kodiak, says that *Shadow Dancer* will arrive at my location in about two hours and will deliver a supply of food along with a weather report and forecast provided by the ship. The C-130 then returns to its base, and the *Mustang* returns to its port in Seward.

As I write this, I'm overcome with gratitude, but not the kind you feel when someone has saved your life; mine doesn't need saving. I'm grateful for the selflessness of all these people prepared to help another person, a stranger, in what they perceive to be a time of need. It's an experience that reaches into the soul and warms the heart even if, in the case of the Coast Guard, they're paid for this kind of work. As a C-130 crewman said facetiously in response to my thanks, "That's why they pay us the big bucks." My greatest concern all along has been the emotional distress that I know my wife and young son and friends must be suffering, and I still have no way of telling them I'm okay. The C-130 crew will call my home when they get back to Kodiak, but that will still be several more hours of grief for family and friends.

I raise *Shadow Dancer* on the radio, but keep it short; the VHF's batteries are low, and I have no way to recharge them, another of those cascading events. After arranging how and where we'll rendezvous, I hoist anchor and go out into the deeper water *Shadow Dancer* will need. Using my radar (oddly, *Shadow Dancer* has none), we find each other in the driving wind, cold, rain, and dense fog. Her first mate, crouched on the bow pulpit and heavily clad against the weather, hands me a bag of food and receives my thanks. He also delivers the latest updated forecast: The storm will worsen tonight, not at all what I wanted to hear.

I return to the shallow anchorage fifty yards off Kayak Island and prepare for worsening weather. I reset the anchor with trip line, feed out more rode than normal to make sure the anchor stays stuck, then fashion a piece of rubber hose into antichafing gear that I affix to the rode where it passes through a fairlead on the bow. Set for the night and ready for more storm, I turn in nearly forty hours after leaving Cordova in fine weather.

The rain and gusting wind strengthens through the night as waves pound the hull and *Rascal* heaves at the end of her tether. Worried about chafing the anchor rode, I get up in the night to rerig the bow attachment, going back to a bridle that avoids stressing the line at a single point. The anchor is holding well, as is the bowline knot I used to attach the rode to the anchor stock.

It's now 7:00 a.m., and I've been gone from Cordova forty-eight hours, forty more than originally planned. Throughout the previous day and into the night the wind, rain, cold, and fog continue. The sound of waves battering the hull and the anchor rode sliding across the deck and twisting at the cleats reverberates through the tiny cabin. Though uncomfortable and exhausted, I know I can easily survive, provided the winds don't clock around and attack the anchorage. My biggest concerns—whether the anchor will hold or the rode will chafe through at the stock—keep me alert through the day and awake all night checking and rechecking. An anchor alarm on the GPS will sound if the boat moves outside the rode's radius, but the alarm is mounted at the helm, and I couldn't possibly hear it from the cabin. I'll just have to keep checking.

More of the same: rain, wind, cold, fog. Intermittently, the wind subsides and the rain stops, and all about me in the cold wispy fog is silence, broken only by the cry of a gull or the snuffing of a surfacing sea lion. Out to the west, toward Cordova, the sea appears calm, a gently lolling surface of textured glass. But I remind myself it seems benign because what I can see is in the lee behind Kayak Island's blockade. Throughout my time at anchor here, I have witnessed these too brief calms that are only followed by winds of increased power, as if the layoff has reinvigorated the storm. Crashing surf just across the island and exploding breakers out to sea just off the cape remind me that to leave now would be foolish. Better to sit tight and bide my time waiting for the storm to pass.

Unsteady and sloe-eyed from lack of sleep, I prepare to check the anchor once again, donning foul weather pants and jacket, insulated rubber gloves, fleece-lined waterproof hat, and rubber boots. All night I've thought about my position, well anchored but only in a lee, not a snug harbor, and still twenty miles out in the Gulf of Alaska. Should the winds and seas come from the west, or even north or south, I'll be exposed. Though lack of sleep from the tossing boat and noisy cabin has dulled my senses, I'm tired of sitting and doing nothing. I want to devise a new strategy to improve my condition. Summoning energy from a dwindling supply, I locate on the chart plotter three potential new anchorages, one of which, my first choice, is north of Okalee Spit in a place I was told local fishing boats often go to wait out the weather. Though groggy, I study the charts, carefully taking note of rocks, depth contours, and sea bottom where I'd anchor.

Reluctantly, I decide to hoist anchor and make for the new haven, where my chances will be improved. As I pick my way from the Kayak Island shore through submerged rocks and out to safe water, the sea is placid, the result of a break in the storm. Farther out into exposed waters it remains so, and I think this may be the chance to escape my storm-bound prison and flee to Cordova. A check of the tides tells me that if I leave at this moment I'll hit the shallow and tortuous entrance into Orca Inlet at high slack tide, the perfect time; that's all I need—I'm off. After two hours of fairly smooth running, I hit Orca Inlet, weave cautiously between lines of thundering breakers stirred up by the storm, find the channel, and return safely to Cordova harbor at 7:00 a.m., seventy-two hours after I left.

Kenai Fjords, Seward, Alaska.
Rascal *in repose at Cordova, Alaska harbor.*

Resurrection Bay, Kenai Peninsula, Seward, Alaska.

Thunder Bay, Kenai Fjords.
Esther Passage, Prince William Sound, Alaska.

Prince William Sound, Alaska.
Glacier Ice Field, Harriman Fjord.

Culross Passage, Prince William Sound, Alaska.
The author in Culross Passage, Prince William Sound.

Bagley Ice Field, Chugach Mountains, Alaska.
Icy Bay, Alaska.

Icy Bay, Alaska.

Cordova, Alaska.

Kayak Island, Gulf of Alaska.

Chapter Four

COMMERCIAL FISHING IS, by a large margin, the most dangerous occupation in the U.S., its fatality rate twenty times the national average. Prior to 1988, each year on average twenty-four people died while fishing for a living, and thirty-four boats sank. In that year, Congress enacted the Commercial Fishing Industry Vessel Safety Act, which for the first time required fishing vessels working in cold waters to carry survival suits, life rafts, and emergency flotation devices for their crew members. Since then, the number of sinkings has remained about the same but with fewer fatalities recorded. Whether the reduced fatalities are a consequence of the new law or of heightened awareness and changed behavior among the fishermen remains to be seen. But it was not a spontaneous paroxysm of government compassion for dying fishermen that prompted this law. The statute was enacted in part as a consequence of a tragedy aboard the F/V *Saint Patrick*, a gripping story told by Spike Walker in *Working on the Edge* (St. Martin's Press 1991), from which the following is excerpted.

If the deaths of men off the fishing vessels *Vestjjord, Golden Pisces*, and *Cougar* hadn't been enough to shake up the fleet during the 1981 fall season, the dramatic incidents involving the crew of the "ghost ship" scalloper *St. Patrick* were.

On the gray and wintry morning of November 29, 1981, the 158-foot fishing vessel *St. Patrick* slipped her Kodiak moorings and slid east through the narrow passage of Near Island channel and moved out into the Gulf of Alaska. For the majority of the ten men and one woman on board, it would be a journey of no return.

On board was twenty-three-year-old Wallace Thomas. A few weeks earlier, he had ventured north to Alaska from his home in balmy St. Augustine, Florida. Like thousands of naïve and adventurous hopefuls before him, he'd come in search of a berth on one of the fleet's high-paying crab boats. Unlike most, he had managed to land a job as a full-share deckhand on the *St. Patrick*, a scalloper that had arrived several months before from the East Coast by way of the Panama Canal.

That night, Thomas lay uneasily in one of the crew bunks housed forward in the bow of the ship. The *St. Patrick* had begun to plunge and leap beneath him. He could hear heavy seas crashing across the deck overhead, and each time the ship's bow buried itself in a wave, Thomas felt himself being pressed heavily into his mattress. Then as the bow rebounded, soaring high over the crest of the next wave, he would float upward, entirely free of his bedding.

Sensing that the storm was building, Thomas left his bunk, slipped into his rain gear, and in the chilling spray and darkness made his way across the deck to the wheelhouse mounted astern.

It was nearly midnight when Thomas entered the comforting warmth and light of the galley. What he saw stunned him. The kitchen was in shambles. The new, tightly secured microwave oven had broken free and lay smashed on the floor. The cupboard doors were swinging open and a combination of catsup, pickles, grape juice, strawberry jam, buttermilk, and sugar was sliding this way and that with the G forces of the rolling ship, in a sticky, scrambled, flowing mass. Arthur "Art" Simonton, a former logger from the state of Washington (the most experienced deckhand on board), was standing with his back to the sink, clutching its edges, as he stared at the demolished kitchen. Other crewmembers were leaving as Simonton turned white-faced to Thomas. "We're going to put on our survival suits. This storm is getting out of hand."

Thomas felt sick with fright. He didn't own a survival suit! And he knew he didn't stand a chance in the thirty-nine degree seas without one. Though he had never worn one in his short career at sea, he knew about their buoyant, heat saving qualities.

The life raft! remembered Thomas. If the ship went down, it would be his only chance! He grabbed a flashlight and ran out on the back deck, where he managed to locate the tightly packaged, self-inflating raft. He read the instructions.

Looks simple enough, he thought.

Thomas made his way back inside, where he ran into the ship's newly hired cook, twenty-three-year-old Vanessa Sandin. The blonde-haired, green-eyed daughter of a Kodiak salmon fisherman was carrying her survival suit, an older variety that looked in poor shape. It didn't have a built-in flotation device or life vest attached. The normally cheerful Vanessa was terrified. "Wally! What should I do?" she asked.

"The wheelhouse would be the best place to be if the ship was to get in trouble," he told her. "I'll take you up there."

Thomas climbed the stairs into the wheelhouse, then jerked to a stop. Nearly the entire crew stood before him. Most were wearing survival suits.

There was thirty-four-year-old Jack Taylor and thirty-three year-old Curt Nelson, both from the state of Virginia. It was only Taylor's second trip out as a skipper of the *St. Patrick*. Nelson was his engineer. Then there was John Blessing, a hardworking youngster from Oregon. He'd come north to help finance his college education. And there was Harold Avery, Jim Harvey, and Ben Pruitt. All three of these tough, scrappy crewmen were from Virginia. Also there at the time was Robert Kidd. This incredibly strong and sinewy deckhand was from Rhode Island. And there was Paul Ferguson, a husky lad and former football player from Nebraska. Not in the room, but also on board at the time, was a youngster named Larry Sanders, as well as Arthur "Art" Simonton.

When Thomas looked out the wheelhouse window, he saw a mountainous wave rise out of the darkness and slam heavily into the *St. Patrick's* port side, lifting and shaking the entire ship. Wave after wave broke over the tall handrailings and collapsed across the deck below him with a thundering crash.

The black, foam-streaked waves looked mammoth in the far-reaching beams of the mast lights. Some of the waves towered above the wheelhouse windows, more than twenty five feet above the deck below.

To aid vision, the light at night in the wheelhouse was always kept to a minimum. In the near darkness, Thomas turned and looked at the others. Their wide eyes were filled with fear. The faces peering out from the sealed openings of the hoods of their survival suits looked bloated.

If anything happens to the *St. Patrick*, he thought, I'll have only the life raft to save me. Back inside, Wallace Thomas helped Vanessa Sandin slip her legs into her survival suit. Then he rushed below to look for a suit for himself. The knot in the pit of his stomach continued to tighten. As he searched below, he felt a monstrous wave strike the *St. Patrick*. The boat shifted sharply and Thomas staggered against the wall.

Thomas crossed the floor at the bottom of the stairs and started down the next gangway into the engine room. He had gone only a few steps when another wave drove into the ship. In a steady motion, the engine room rotated before him, and suddenly he found himself lying on his back on what had been the wall. Stored canned goods, oil filters, tools, and supplies fell noisily from their shelves. Several fuel lines broke and diesel fuel began to spew everywhere. Then the *St. Patrick* partially righted herself.

Thomas struggled to his feet and raced back toward the wheelhouse. His heart pounded as he crossed the sloping galley floor. The entrance to the wheelhouse stairway was marked by two full-length swinging doors. As he approached, the doors burst open and were ripped from their hinges as a wall of rushing seawater exploded through them. The broad and powerful current carried with it charts and navigational equipment. The seawater slammed Thomas against the wall. When the hallway below quickly flooded, the waist-deep water began to empty down the second stairwell, which led into the engine room.

Even before the torrent of water had finished draining from the wheelhouse, Wallace Thomas raced up the stairs. The scene there horrified him. A giant rogue wave had smashed through the *St. Patrick's* "stormproof" windows, tearing most of the ship's navigational equipment from its mounts. Equipment hung from the dripping ceiling, swaying from the ends of strands of wiring, while much of the ship's electronics lay broken and scattered across the flooded floor. A bone chilling wind was gusting in through the holes where the windows had been.

The *St. Patrick* was listing about fifteen degrees to starboard at the time, making the wheelhouse floor slick and difficult for Thomas to cross. He spied his skipper lying amid the strewn equipment and broken window glass. Then he turned to Vanessa Sandin. She'd been only partially protected when the rogue wave shattered the windows and exploded into the room, and now she stood drenched and shaking.

Thomas had just finished helping Vanessa into her suit

when the fuel pressure alarm went off, clanging like an incessant fire bell. Then the main engines died and the lights aboard ship flickered, dimmed, and went dead. In the ghostly silence, a moaning wail became audible as winds approaching eighty knots howled through the steel cables of the mast rigging overhead and into the wheelhouse through the gaping window openings.

Jack Taylor found himself adrift at sea without steering or power. The only light aboard ship came from several battery powered lamps two flights below. Then a second huge breaker drove into the side of the ship, rocking her sharply, and two crewmen were thrown to the floor. Thomas heard Taylor yell. "Hey! We've got to get off this damned thing! Let's get into the life raft before she goes down!"

An icy spray drenched them as they fled from the wheelhouse. Moving out in single file, they crawled along through the wet, cold darkness, climbing over the twisted, wave-bent handrailings and through tangles of rope and gear.

When Thomas reached the stern, he groped for the raft. "It's gone! The raft's gone!" he screamed above the howl of the wind. A few disbelieving groans met the news and then the group slipped into stunned silence. Thomas heard the skipper yell again. "We've got to get off this thing before it sinks! It'll flip over and suck us all down with her!"

A half formed wave crashed against the far side of the St. Patrick and threw a wall of icy water over the crew. Those in survival suits paid scant attention. Clad only in his work clothes, Wallace Thomas was soaked and already ached with cold, however. He felt Vanessa grab him and heard her scream above the wind. "What are we going to do?" At that moment, Thomas spotted an amber beacon rising and falling off the stern. "It's the life raft!" he yelled. "It's got to be! Maybe we can swim for it!"

A crewman found a long length of rope and suggested

that they tie themselves together to prevent getting separated once they were adrift in the ocean. The skipper agreed. Someone had located a waterproof flashlight, and periodically a voice would call out "Could you give me some light over here? I can't see!"

Suddenly, the realization of what he was about to do struck Thomas. The time *twenty minutes* pounded in his head. From his instruction in wilderness survival, he knew that a man without a survival suit seldom lasted longer than twenty minutes in seas of this temperature. *If you go into that water without a survival suit,* he thought to himself, *you'll be dead in twenty minutes!*

The stem deck grew steeper as the unrelenting velocity of the storm rolled the *Saint Patrick* farther on its side. Like the rest of the crew, Thomas was sure the ship was sinking. For one long moment, he stood on the stern at the water's edge, and as the water licked up the sloping deck and over his feet, he grappled with the insanity of panic. He pictured himself alone in the darkness of the wheelhouse, stretching for air as the wintry Gulf of Alaska seas rose slowly over his head.

Soon, the crewmembers finished tying themselves together. They were about to abandon ship, and, irrespective of logic, Thomas felt drawn to follow. As his skipper and crew edged closer to the water and prepared to jump, Thomas bolted, however.

"Taylor!" he shouted to his skipper. "I can't go in with you! I've got to stay with the ship as long as I can! I'll die if I go in that water!"

The skipper seemed dazed. "What?" he shouted back.

"I don't have a survival suit and I'm not going in that water without one! I'll stay aboard until the ship goes down and call out more Maydays!"

"I think there's another suit in the captain's cabin!" the skipper yelled back.

Thomas shook with fear as he hurried back toward the wheelhouse. He was frantic, and his legs drove him forward faster than his numbed hands could interpret the shape of things. But the suit meant life to him and he scarcely noticed the skinned shins and bruises he acquired as he stumbled along. Entering by the rear wheelhouse door, he crawled along the wall through the rubble, feeling his way to the captain's cabin.

Thomas was on the verge of hysteria. It was the prospect of being abandoned alone on board the sinking ship that terrified him. He wanted to get back to the others waiting on the stern before they became too fearful and left without him. His hands slapped frantically against the walls as he crawled through the darkness. He realized he was in the bathroom and quickly backed out. His hands shook uncontrollably as they fumbled through scattered socks, shirts, boots, pillows, a suitcase, and supplies that lay shewn about the room.

"Where is it? Where is it?" he yelled aloud.

Then as he groped in the darkness, he felt the distinctive shape of a survival-suit bag. There was nothing in it! The suit had been taken! His mind raced. Was the skipper mistaken? Could there possibly be another suit in all this junk? Had there ever been an extra suit in the first place?

He plodded ahead blindly, bumping into one wall and then another. He tore through a jumble of bedding and clothes. Reaching some cabinet doors, he jerked them open. Inside, he felt the soft bulk of another long vinyl bag. There was a survival suit inside.

Thomas wiggled into the suit and felt his way back to the stern, where he raced to tie himself between Vanessa Sandin and John Blessing. John was one of three crewmen without a survival suit. He had slipped on every piece of clothing he could wear and yet still fit into a bulky life jacket. "We've got to get off this thing!" yelled the skipper again. "She could go down any minute!"

As they prepared to jump, Thomas looked around him and caught brief glimpses of the crew in the flickering flashlight beams. Their slick, wet figures looked ghostly.

Then Chief Engineer Curt Nelson yelled a warning. "When the water hits those batteries, they're going to explode!" Just then, a loud bang sounded from below in the engine room. A massive wave rolled by, passing as a black hulk just off the stern. Water swept up the slanting deck and over the crew's feet.

As the stern of the *St. Patrick* dipped and swayed, the youthful six-foot, four-inch frame of Art Simonton arrived. He had just returned from the bow. "Two guys just jumped overboard off the front deck!" he screamed, his eyes wide with terror. "We're going to capsize!"

"Okay," the skipper yelled. "Let's get off this thing!"

With the back deck constantly awash, Thomas could feel the ankle-deep water pulling at his legs. We're going down, he thought. We've got no choice but to abandon ship.

Bound together—around the waist and under the arms by loosely tied loops for easy movement, the crew shuffled down the steep deck. The railing before them had been torn away and now, timing their move with the downward roll of the ship, the crew stepped off the stern deck.

As they struck the water, the crew went under briefly. When Thomas's head bobbed clear, he gulped in the precious air. I'm all right! he thought, his mind racing. "I can breathe! I'm not dead!"

In the next moment, the massive steel hull of the *St. Patrick* flashed before his eyes as it plunged down beside him, narrowly missing crushing the entire crew. Thomas screamed, "Paddle! Paddle!" and the group stroked furiously to get clear of the ship's deadly stern.

They were afloat in the stormy darkness and except for the fragile beam of a lone flashlight, vision was impossible. Looking back, only a few yards into their journey, not a hint of the ship's outline remained. Yet distinctly visible in the battering night were two small portholes. Power still generating from the engine-room batteries filled the round windows with warm light, and now the circles soared and dived in the blackness. Moments later, the porthole lights disappeared. She finally sank, thought Thomas. We got off just in time.

No sooner had the nine drifting crewmen of the St. Patrick swum clear of her deadly stern than a wave began to lift them. Up and up it carried them. Thomas was certain they had neared the top of the steep, sloping wave when he heard a loud thundering roar coming from behind him and far overhead. He turned toward the booming rumble just as the first monstrous wave top collapsed down upon them.

The body of the wave carried whole fathoms of sea over them. It drove the struggling crew under and tossed them end over end. Like Thomas, some of the crewmembers had turned toward the wave when it overtook them and caught the full force of its fury directly at their faces.

No one could have imagined such a wave. Some in the party were washed out of their rope loops. They bobbed to the surface, gasping for air, and fought to remain upright as they groped blindly for the rope.

Hundreds of feet of floating excess line had become tangled around them. And seventy-knot winds whipped an icy spray across the water, blinding those who had forgotten to turn away and stinging any face not protected with a sheltering hand.

Wallace Thomas soon discovered that two people were hanging on to him. Vanessa clung to an arm and John Blessing was hugging him around a thigh. Blessing was already shaking violently from the effects of the cold.

Thomas shouted to him.

"You're going to be all right, buddy! Just hang on!"

"Count off! Count off!" someone screamed. Some of the crew seemed too disoriented to obey, while others were perhaps unable to hear the command.

Thomas felt another wave begin to lift him. It swept him up into the wind-torn blackness, ever higher and higher. Then he heard one end of the wave begin to roar as it folded over and collapsed through the darkness toward him.

"Look out! Look out!" he screamed. "It's another big one!"

The gigantic breaker rolled over the crew, submerging and tumbling them upside down as it passed. A few in the group had prepared for the approaching swell. Holding their breath, they had turned their backs to it. Though they still found themselves tossed and wrenched violently about, their recovery, once the wave had passed, was surprisingly rapid. Suffering repeated dunkings, others of the drifting crew soon adapted except, that is, for those without survival suits.

Thomas could feel John Blessing shivering violently as he clung to his leg. Less than twenty minutes had passed when his friend became delirious, moaning and speaking irrationally.

"It's cold! It's so cold!" he gasped in a painful, rasping voice.

Thomas tried to encourage him. "Hang on, John! You've got to ride it out!"

But the mountainous waves continued to sweep them high. And each time the wave crests folded over, they smashed down upon the ragged group of fishermen like concrete walls.

Then one of the crewmen cried out above the noise of the storm.

"So you guys think we should pray?"

Thomas was quick to respond.

"Now is the time if there ever was one!"

They recited the Lord's Prayer then, their voices dissipating quickly in the storm-lashed night.

"Our Father, who art in heaven, hallowed be Thy name; Thy kingdom come. Thy will be done, on earth ..."

They had completed less than half of the prayer when, without warning, another enormous wave broke directly over their heads, driving them deep beneath the surface.

The moment their heads again cleared the surface, there was heavy retching and gagging. Those tangled in the excess line fought frantically to free themselves before the next wave found them.

Wallace Thomas could see that John Blessing was in serious trouble. He wrapped his arm around the shaking man.

"Come on, John! Stay with us," he begged.

John stammered out his reply.

"My legs... arms... stiff... so cold."

John's moaning increased. Several times, Thomas felt his friend's quivering body go limp. When another large wave struck them, John was swept from Thomas's tiring grip and began to drift off. Stretching behind him in the wet darkness, Thomas managed to slap John with one hand. Then as he drew him near, he saw a small beacon attached to John's life jacket. He worked hard in the clumsy two fingered gloves of his survival suit to grip the beacon and yank it alive. His aching arm muscles told him he couldn't carry his friend much longer.

The tiny beacon had just begun flashing when John spasmodically flailed his arms and floundered out of control. Almost immediately, the wind and current swept him away. Thomas was horrified to realize he could no longer reach him. He watched helplessly as the tiny amber beacon light weaved off into the darkness and disappeared.

Someone yelled, "Was that John?"

"My God, yes!" Thomas answered. As he watched John disappear. Thomas felt Vanessa reattach herself to his arm. From the outset, Vanessa's suit had leaked steadily. It was becoming an ever-increasing struggle for her to keep her head above water. Together, they floated up and over the endless series of waves.

Vanessa Sandin prided herself in never getting seasick, even in the toughest weather. Several of her predecessors had lasted but a single trip. When Vanessa came on board, she was confronted by a galley that was dingy, dirty, and disorganized. She scrubbed the place from floor to ceiling. She emptied the cupboards and completely reorganized them. Then came the burned pots and pans, the oven interior, covered with burned grease and food, and finally the kitchen table, some twenty feet long.

She soon became known for having a good heart, and a mischievous sense of humor. When Wallace Thomas had his twenty-third birthday shortly before shoving off on their fateful final journey, Vanessa had prepared him a huge birthday cake. When he tried to cut into it, however, his knife chinked to a stop. Vanessa had taken a twelve-pack of beer, wrapped it in cardboard, and camouflaged it with a thick spread of canned frosting.

She could also cook. Each summer, she fished right along with her father on his gillnet boat in Bristol Bay. One day, when she had decided to prepare a dinner of sockeye salmon, her father, a long-time Alaskan fisherman, made the mistake of trying to tell her how to go about cooking it.

"You run the boat," she scolded him, "and I'll fly the fish. Now get out of here!"

The salmon proved to be the best he had ever eaten.

Vanessa, her father recalled, could not only cook but also tie knots, mend webbing, make a drift set, pick tangled salmon out of the gillnet, and navigate. One day, it came to him that she learned more quickly and with greater ease than he had as a young man. But now this adventurous young woman could only cling to Thomas through the night and pray to be rescued at first light.

As they passed over the top of another immense swell, Thomas felt something bump heavily into his back. Fearful that a log had drifted up on them out of the night, he shouted, "Get that light over here! Something just hit me!"

Thomas searched the darkness with the dim beam of light. Suddenly, he reeled in the water. There, adrift beside him, floated the body of Larry Saunders, another crewman who had abandoned ship without a survival suit. He was still tied to the crew's rope line. "Turn off the light and save it!" shouted Thomas. The light flicked off.

Close by, Thomas overheard the muffled conversation between Ben Pruitt and Jim Harvey. Harvey had been on his first voyage to sea in Alaska. He was the last of the original three without survival suits. Now he turned numbly to his crewmate and pleaded.

"Ben! Ben, I'm so cold! Could I borrow your suit for a little while?"

"Jim, I'm cold too! And the suit's leaking anyway! Just try to hang on!"

"Ben! What am I going to do? Help me! Please, help me, Ben!"

Thomas knew that there was nothing anyone could do. Hypothermia was the dangerous lowering of one's body temperature; more specifically, the temperature of one's core comprised of the heart, lungs, and brain. The moment the three frantic young men jumped from the stern of the St. Patrick without survival suits, they were doomed. Under such conditions, no man could live more than an hour.

A short time later, Jim Harvey began to moan and jabber incoherently. Eventually, he grew motionless and, still bound to the group by the rope line, his body drifted amongst them.

Eight hours after they had first abandoned ship, dawn slowly replaced the smothering black veil of darkness. In the dim gray light, Wallace Thomas could finally take in the unbelievable size of the massive seas. Raw winds whipped thin white streaks of foam across the moss green water. The waves moved under a bleak ceiling of sky, and he could make out blue-black rain squalls squatting low as they moved across the horizon.

Each time he passed over the crest of another wave, his eyes swept the desolate expanse of water. Then something caught his eye. "I can see somebody swimming over there!" he yelled. The six remaining crewmembers soon spotted him, too.

"Hey, it's the skipper!"

They yelled and waved and blew metal whistles that came attached to their suits, but Jack Taylor showed no sign of having heard them. He backstroked slowly away from them and was lost from sight.

Then Vanessa began to yell excitedly. "I can see land! I can see it! I'm sure of it!"

As he crested another twenty-five-foot wave, Thomas caught sight of it, too. Before long, he was able to make out two separate points of land. The spirits of the numb, pain racked crew soared.

"When I get back," promised Vanessa, "I'm going to eat the biggest pizza I can order!"

Hours later, when the low-lying clouds cleared adequately, a steep rock coastline loomed large before them. Its uppermost slopes were covered with rich shades of winter-browned grass and crowned with dark green stands of spruce trees.

The crewmembers decided to paddle for the nearest outcropping of land, but wave after wave struck them from the side, throwing them off course, and fog intermittently obliterated all sight of land.

"We're never going to make it this way!" Thomas called out. "We've got to swim more in line with the way the waves are moving! Then we can angle a little bit at a time in toward land!"

Swimming with the waves, they made steady progress, but soon Ben began to speak in fragmented phrases and suddenly collapsed facedown. The two crewmen on either side rolled him over.

"Come on, Ben! You've got to swim!" they screamed at him. "You've got to help us! We're not going to make it if you don't swim!"

Ben Pruitt tried. He flopped one weak arm and then the other out in front of him, but he was nearly unconscious. His two friends continued to encourage him as they pulled him along between them, kicking their numb legs and stroking with one hand while clutching Ben by the arm with the other.

Vanessa, too, was nearing the point of exhaustion. With her leaking survival suit now nearly full of icy seawater, her body ached with cold. If she was to survive, she would need constant help.

Then Wallace Thomas and Harold Avery devised a method. One of them would paddle on his back, carrying Vanessa on top of him, while the other trailed the pair, watching for land and verbally guiding them.

Paul Ferguson and Curt Nelson soon adopted this technique to carry Ben. Gradually, they grew weaker and their progress slowed appreciably. Their bodies were chilled from nearly fourteen hours in the near-freezing water. Hunger cramped their stomachs and they were becoming dehydrated.

The survivors had decided to save the bodies for decent burial. But then, under the sinking weight of the body of Larry Sanders, Thomas saw how Ferguson was struggling to remain afloat.

"We've got to untie him!" he yelled.

Thomas swam forward through a tangle of floating lines and loosened the rope line. The corpse quickly sank from sight. Without comment, the six remaining crewmembers regrouped and pushed on.

Ever since they had first spotted land that morning, the struggling crew had been swimming. Now, some eight hours later, the coastline seemed much closer. Thomas could see the black, flat faces of cliffs, perhaps a hundred feet high, lining the shore, but he could not see an accessible or calm stretch of beach. As they closed to within perhaps two miles, Thomas spotted the white explosions of waves bursting along the cliff bottoms.

The sight petrified him. He knew the deadly power of coastal breakers from years of surfing in Florida. Such seas were frightening enough, but to become entangled with one another in the rope lines in heavy breaking surf would be suicidal.

"Before we go in, we've got to untie!" he called out to the others. "It's too dangerous! We won't make it this way!" The exhausted, floundering members numbly agreed.

Now Ben Pruitt seemed on the edge of collapse. The two who had carried him no longer appeared to be able to do so. Thomas left Vanessa with Harold Avery and swam to Ben and held his blue face out of the frigid water. He was still breathing.

Then off to his right, Thomas caught a flash of something white on the water. As it rose over the crest of the next wave, he saw it clearly. "There's a ship!"

Those who were able began to wave wildly and blow their whistles. They swung their shivering arms back and forth until they no longer held them aloft. Thomas wore his tongue raw whistling and the taste of blood filled his mouth. The ship closed toward them for nearly a half hour. Wallace and the rest of the crewmembers were sure it was coming for them.

Then they watched in disbelief as their rescue ship began to turn away. As it changed course, Thomas could see the distinct lines of the ship's wooden hull.

"No! No!" he cried. "Why can't they see us? Please, please see us!"

But the vessel was soon lost from sight.

The collective disappointment was almost too much. Wallace Thomas was the first to break the silence.

"We've got to get swimming again, you guys. He didn't see us."

With disappointment showing in every stroke, the remnant crew once again began to plod ahead toward shore. They had hardly begun, however, when Ben Pruitt rolled facedown in the water. Paul Ferguson and Curt Nelson summoned all their remaining strength to roll him back over and give him mouth-to-mouth resuscitation, but there was no response.

"Come on, you two!" Thomas finally called, his voice breaking. "You've got to let him go now. You've got to save yourselves. We've done everything we could. We've got to take care of the living now!"

The remaining survivors of the *St. Patrick* were too exhausted to untie Ben's body, so they left it in tow and resumed swimming.

Less than an hour later, the five remaining survivors closed to within what they believed was a half mile of the shoreline. "I'll go on in," yelled Harold Avery, "and if it's all right. I'll wave for you to follow on in after me! I've got some waterproof matches and I'll get a warm fire going. So just watch for my signal and then follow me in!"

Thoughts of a crackling-hot fire lifted the spirits of the four remaining crewmen. Vanessa was shaking constantly from the cold water seeping into her suit. She was growing visibly weaker. With Vanessa lying across his lap, Thomas shuddered as he watched Harold swim away.

They were able to stop paddling then and, sighing with relief, settled back to await the signal from shore. As they drifted nearer to shore, they decided to untie themselves from each other in preparation for the swim in through the surf. Freed from the rope line, Vanessa and Thomas found themselves drifting away from Paul Ferguson and Curt Nelson. But the two couples were too fatigued to reunite.

Shortly, Thomas saw the two men drop into a hollow in the sea and disappear. That afternoon, he caught his last glimpse of them. They appeared to have stopped swimming.

Now, with Vanessa completely dependent upon him for her survival, Thomas drifted and waited in anticipation for a signal from Harold Avery. Each time, as he rose up and over another wave, he would search for his good friend and deckmate's wave from the distant banks. Drifting ever nearer, he studied the soaring rock precipices. He could see the ghastly black form of the cliffs, slickened with spray and rising abruptly from out of a pounding misty-gray surf, with fog rolling across its sheer granite face.

He contemplated that perhaps he had underestimated the size of the surf and cliffs along the shore.

Suddenly, he caught the flicker of something tiny and orange in the thundering surf. It looked toylike, about the size of a petite orange buoy as it was lifted up and tossed against the wet face of the rock cliffs. He watched it being swept out by the surf, only to be gathered by another massive wave and flung high against the stone walls.

Then as he drifted nearer, the true dimensions of the terrain ahead finally struck Thomas. The rock cliffs were not a mere one hundred feet high, as he had estimated, but in frightening reality towered more than a thousand feet overhead!

When he spotted the minute orange object again, it was suspended in a wave and being swept some thirty feet up the face to the cliffs, with spray exploding far above it. And at that moment, it dawned on him—the object he had been studying so intently as it surged back and forth against the cliffs was not a buoy. It was the lifeless body of Harold Avery.

The sight took his breath. His heart felt like lead. All seemed lost and utterly hopeless. The safety they had associated with the first sighting of land had been only another cruel illusion. Vanessa hadn't seen the body. Thomas decided not to tell her.

"We can't get in here!" he yelled to her.

But what if there isn't any accessible beach on this island's entire shoreline? he worried secretly.

As Vanessa lay across his lap, Thomas noticed that her condition was worsening. She could no longer move her legs, the feeling had gone out of her arms, and her lips had turned a dark blue. As he paddled on his back over the waves, he tried to parallel the coastline.

He, too, had begun to shake uncontrollably, and his legs felt stiff and weighted. Toward evening, Wallace Thomas's back and arms began to cramp badly. He felt he couldn't carry Vanessa much longer. As he lay back, he thought he'd close his eyes and doze for a moment. It seemed only seconds before Vanessa rattled him awake.

"Wally! Wally, are you all right? You're looking pretty bad!"

"I'm fine, Vanessa," he reassured her. "I was just trying to relax for a few minutes."

Then a loud thumping noise began to pound in their ears. As if out of nowhere, an orange and white helicopter roared past them, close by overhead. In an adrenaline-pumping rush of excitement, Thomas waved his arms wildly; Vanessa raised one quivering hand.

"It's the Coast Guard! My God, they've finally come for us! They know we're here! We've done it! We're going to be rescued! We're going to live!"

The helicopter sped out of sight, though. A few minutes later, they saw it making another pass in the distance.

Vanessa was too exhausted to wave.

"Did he spot us?" she asked in a weak voice.

"No. And he's too far away now."

He'd hardly finished speaking when another helicopter flew directly over them. As it passed, the side door slid open and Thomas could see a crewman standing in the doorway. He appeared to be looking right at them.

Thomas tried to rock forward, thereby rising slightly in the water, but Vanessa lay heavily across his lap. He screamed and waved frantically.

"Come on, Vanessa! We've got to signal to them! This might be the one time they see us!"

"I don't think I can anymore, Wally," she replied weakly.

The helicopter flew on out of sight.

"They didn't see us, did they?"

Thomas answered with silence.

"I don't think I'm going to make it, Wally," said Vanessa, her voice straining with pain and fatigue.

"Come on, Vanessa. We can still get out of this mess alive. We can float a good while longer if we have to."

"Oh, Wally," she replied in a disheartened voice, "I don't know. I'm awfully cold and there's a lot of water getting into my suit."

"Look over there," argued Thomas. "See that point of rock? Look past it. The waves aren't even breaking. There's a cove. We'll swim in around there somewhere."

Suddenly, Vanessa began to cough roughly. Then she jerked forward out of his arms and rolled facedown in the water. Thomas was horrified. He jerked her back upright and shook her violently.

"Vanessa! Wake up! Say something to me! Answer me!"

There was no response. Her face was chalk blue. Her eyes were glassy. She hacked deeply then and again wrenched free of Thomas's grip. Summoning what little strength he could, Thomas paddled to her side. He lifted her head and held her close. Her eyes were closed. Her body hung limply in his arms. She was no longer breathing. Vanessa was gone.

Thomas turned and slowly swam away. He was weary and heartbroken, and darkness was closing fast. His entire body ached with cold and now shook uncontrollably. He had been awake for more than thirty-six hours, twenty of them spent battling the stormy Alaskan seas. Now he wanted only to close his eyes and be done with it. His movements had grown sluggish to the point of immobility, but he fought to keep his tired mind on the task at hand. I'm dead! I'm going to die! he concluded.

Shortly after nightfall, Wallace Thomas spotted a ship's mast lights. He did not grow overly excited. The lights were miles off. Each time, as he rose over another wave top, he caught glimpses of them. They appeared to be headed in his direction.

As the ship drew closer, Thomas tried to gather his failing strength. He lifted his leaden arms and began waving, drawing an arm back down to rest now and again. Occasionally, he called out, hoping his voice would somehow carry to those on board the ship. Then the vessel pulled up even with Thomas, and he screamed, "My God, I'm here! I'm right here!"

He fumbled for his whistle and began blowing it frantically. Then he held his breath and listened for a reply. He could hear the sound of men's voices above the low rumble of the diesel engines. He could see the figures of crewmen working outside under the back deck lights. Yet the ship slowly lunged past him and disappeared into the night.

I'm dead, a goner. I'm going to die, he thought.

He struggled to come to terms with the finality of his predicament. He thought of his parents—how sad and wasteful losing their son this way would seem to them.

I'm sorry, Mom! I'm sorry, Dad! he thought, picturing them now in his mind. Such a lousy way to die, he pondered.

Thomas's shuddering body throbbed with cold. Then as he rode over the crest of a wave, he spotted tiny lights flickering in the distance. Only a few hours before, Thomas would have known that they represented another ship miles away, but his thinking had become disoriented. He was sure they were the lights of Kodiak. "I'll swim in there," he decided. But seconds later, he'd forgotten the idea and paddled numbly ahead.

Thomas knew he had to get out of the water. His body was just too cold to remain in it much longer. Several times, his legs grew so stiff that he was sure he no longer could use them. He knew he would soon pass out from the relentless cold. His wilderness training in hypothermia flashed through his mind. If you got cold, you didn't try to ignore it, he remembered. You act!

He crouched up into the fetal position then, and as he drifted in the darkness, he tucked his mouth down into his suit and for a time breathed heavily into it. His debilitating numbness and shivering seemed to diminish slightly.

Then, as he came off the peak of a big, sloping wave, Thomas saw something large in the moon-tinted darkness. It was floating beside him. It looked like a huge buoy, partially covered with dark green blotches of algae or seaweed, but its dimensions puzzled Thomas.

Maybe I can hang on to that and get some rest, he reasoned. I'll just float along for a little while.

He paddled toward the object, but oddly, he didn't seem to be getting any closer. A moment later, Thomas drew back, frightened of the thing. Now it looked like a whale, and, retreating, he splashed water at the massive creature in an attempt to frighten it away.

Eventually, Thomas came to realize that the whale he had feared was actually a point of land less than a half a mile away. Maybe it's not your time, he thought hopefully. You've got to at least try to swim for it! At least you can do that! He turned then and using the breaststroke headed in toward land.

"It's not your turn. It's not your time," he chanted to

himself. "Going to die if you stay out here any longer. May be the last thing you ever do. Might as well swim for it. Got to try."

Shortly, Thomas found his movement impeded. A swaying tangle of slimy fingers was bobbing about him, while others wrapped themselves around his arms and legs. Fear began to build. Oh, kelp, he realized suddenly. Must be getting closer. Must be.

He struggled on toward shore, and on either side of him, in the faint light, he spied tall pillars of blue-gray rock and moon-silvered breakers fanning out and bursting high against them. When he heard the roar of breakers exploding along the shore, he grew sick with fear. The vision of Harold Avery's body as it washed up against the cliff kept shooting through his groggy mind. Aim yourself in between those two pillars, he told himself. It's your only chance.

Wallace Thomas had no sooner decided upon his new course than he felt an immense wave pick him up and hurl him forward through the night. The wind blew sharply in his face and the water churned beneath him as it heaved him along toward shore. Then, without warning, the wave crest he was riding curled forward.

He felt suspended in air as he fell down its folding face. When he landed, the tremendous force of the pounding water shoved him under the surface and held him there. The boiling torrent of ocean surf pulled and pounded on him as if nothing short of his total destruction would satisfy it. It twisted him upside down, jerked him sideways, and rolled him about. The smothering black surf seemed to pull at his suit from all directions, and he could feel icy rivulets of water getting in around the facial opening of his hood.

Thomas fought to right himself and return to the surface. His lungs burned for air. He had already begun the involuntary inhalation of the salty water when his head finally cleared the surface. Thomas choked violently and gasped in a lungful of the damp sea air. Then another huge wave caught him and once again launched him swiftly forward through the night.

He threw his battered arms out in front of him and attempted to swim along with the thrusting power of the wave. Then he thought he felt a hand strike a rock and the foaming rush of water that had carried him there seemed to disappear from beneath him.

Thomas found himself lying facedown on the steep face of a solid rock bank. He clung to the steely cold surface in disbelief, his chest heaving for air. He felt too weak to move, but he knew if the next mammoth wave was to catch him still lying there, it might as well crush him with a single paralyzing blow.

In his mind, he stood to run, but his legs refused to move. It was as if they were no longer part of him! "Oh, God! Dear God, help me!" he cried, pawing wildly at the slick bare rock of the bank.

Thomas had managed to crawl only a single body length up the surf-slickened bank when the next wave exploded at his feet, drenching him.

A bitter cold wind was gusting along the shoreline and soon it chilled Thomas to his core. The short stretch of rock he had lucked upon was only a few yards wide. Too weak to stand, and shivering uncontrollably, he pulled himself along with his hands, and, lucking upon a shallow rock crevice, he instinctively rolled into it. There, out of the direct assault of the wind, Thomas closed his weighted eyes and almost instantly fell asleep.

Yet it was a fitful rest. The surf pounded loudly only a few yards away, and even in the naturally protected chasm, the razor-sharp wind found him.

Wallace Thomas awoke with a start, to see the figure of Art Simonton standing close by and staring at him. His former crewmate and friend wore street clothes and seemed unaffected by the arctic wind racing along the shore. Was it the visible apparition of a dead and departed friend, or had he survived?

"Art!" he called out. "What are you doing here?" When no answer came, Thomas took a moment to reposition himself and draw closer. But when he looked again, the figure had disappeared. He slumped back down and slipped into unconsciousness, lost in a merciful slumber.

The excruciating pain in his hands awakened him next. The arms of his suit were bloated with salt water forced in by the pummeling surf. He rolled onto his back, lifted his arms, drained the stinging water into the lower half of his suit, and fell back to sleep. When he awoke later, he found his hands had warmed to a point where he could at least open them.

The Coast Guard was finally able to verify that twelve crewmen had been aboard the fishing vessel *St. Patrick*. At first light, U.S. Coast Guard helicopter pilot Lt. Jimmy Ng lifted off from his base on Kodiak Island. Along with several other helicopters, C-130 SAR planes, and the Coast Guard cutter *Boutwell*, they began searching the area off Afognak Island for sign of survivors.

Lt. Ng worked his way around the steep rock shoreline of Marmot Island (positioned approximately four miles from the shores of Afognak Island). Some of the shoreline cliffs he encountered rose up in a sheer vertical climb more than twelve hundred feet above the water. A short time later, Lt. Ng located the first body. It was floating facedown in a small cliff-encircled cove. Oddly, the man wore neither rain gear nor a survival suit. The cliffs were too high and the cove too small to maneuver safely, so Lt. Ng hovered approximately fifty feet away and watched for signs of life. There were none, so he resumed his search around Marmot Island, and he soon came upon several more bodies.

"One body was off in the surf," he recalled. "He was

bouncing around in the rocks. And two others were lying up on the beach. All were dead."

With the discovering of the first body, the Coast Guard search for the missing crew of the *St. Patrick* intensified. Soon, USCG helicopters, planes, and cutters were scanning the waters and shoreline from Whale Island, just offshore from Kodiak, to Marmot Bay, to Iszuit Bay, and completely around the northern tip of Afognak Island, all in the hope of finding someone still alive.

~~~

Shortly after dawn, Wallace Thomas propped himself upright on a boulder. He sat shivering and studied the world around him. Overhead, rock walls rose as sheer and apparently inaccessible as those of a prison. More than one thousand feet above him, Thomas could see convoluted outcroppings of bare granite rock jutting into the sky, and beyond that, clinging to thin layers of soil, weather-stunted spruce trees bent in the wind. On either side of him, short stretches of narrow shoreline cut into the cliff rock and were strewn with boulders the size of dump trucks.

The cloud ceiling appeared to have lifted slightly but the freezing thirty-knot winds continued to blow without pause. The sea rushing up at him wore a blinding silver sheen. His pain-wracked legs still refused to support him, so he rubbed them furiously in an effort to restore circulation.

Thomas felt groggy and exhausted, miserably cold and hungry. But it was a maddening thirst that drove him finally to rise on wobbly legs and stagger stiff-legged along the cliff bottoms in search of fresh water. With water sloshing about inside, his survival suit hung heavily on him. He wanted to shed the suit but knew that to stand exposed to the Siberian-born winds in soaked clothing would mean death within hours.

Maybe I'll make it if I stay in the suit, he reasoned.

Thomas could find no fresh water close at hand. Walking

only a few steps exhausted him. If I'm going to survive, I've got to locate water, he told himself. But there appeared to be no escaping the cliffs lining the beach. The sharp-crested outcroppings of rock extended well out into the surf. They loomed impossibly steep and dangerous to climb.

The pounding surf before him, which had taken the lives of so many of his companions and nearly his own, now petrified him. He would remain trapped on the shore and take his chances with hunger and thirst and exposure before he would return to the ocean again.

Then as the surf receded to near-dead low tide, he saw an opportunity. The tide had receded enough to allow passage around the base of the jutting column on his left. Wallace did not hesitate. Leaning against the rock walls, he hurried around them as quickly as his buckling legs would carry him.

He discovered an even shorter stretch of enclosed shoreline. Large boulders covered most of it. He stumbled forward and fell on the bank, panting. Slowly, a faint dribbling sound stuck his consciousness. He spun and his eyes caught the movement of a tiny stream of water trickling off the face of a vertical rock bluff.

He rose, staggering and fell. He crawled the last few feet but found a small pond formed where the droplets had landed. He dipped his glove-covered hands anxiously into the clear pool and sipped the bounty. The water tasted salty and he spit it back out. His heart fell.

Damn! A tide pool! he thought angrily.

Then he sampled the pool again.

It *was* fresh water!

Thomas felt foolish. The salt he had tasted had come from the gloves of his survival suit. The water in the pool was fresh and cold. He drank down a few eager swallows and then stopped abruptly. He could feel the water cool him and he wanted to allow his body time to catch up.

Even with fresh water, Thomas doubted he could make it through another night in his wet clothes without food or fire. It had been nearly forty-five hours since his last meal and he was sick with hunger.

In an effort to hide from the painful and life-sapping cold of the December winds, Thomas hunched down between two huge boulders. From there, he could still command a view of a good portion of the ocean. As he waited, he shook so hard it felt as if all the bones in his body were rattling. Gradually, he thought he could make out the faint rumble of an engine. The noise dimmed, then grew stronger, only to fade once more. He debated whether to stand and look, exposing himself fully to the draining cold of the wind.

He had to try, he decided. His body was fast growing colder. He wavered as he stood, and his eyes squinted into the wind and swept quickly over the ocean before him. He was about to crouch back down when he spotted movement. It was the bow of a ship nosing its way through heavy seas off a point of land on his far right. Almost crippled with cold yet frantic with excitement, Thomas struggled up the side of a large boulder and began flailing his weary arms.

"They must be out looking for me! They've got to spot me! They've just got to see me now!" he cried out loud.

The one-hundred-foot ship drove nearly halfway across the open stretch of water in front of him before Thomas thought he saw it slow. Through watering eyes, he saw quick flashes of light coming from the wheelhouse.

Were those really signals? Have they actually spotted me? Or am I only imagining things again?

Every few seconds, the ship would crest the top of another swell and then slide into a deep trough, and then, except for the radar scanner spinning steadily atop the wheelhouse, it would disappear as if swallowed whole.

The waving seemed to take the last of Thomas's strength.

A sudden gust of wind staggered him, nearly toppling him from the rock. He dropped to his knees to maintain his balance. If they did see me, what will they do next? What could they do? his fuzzy mind puzzled.

On the horizon, Thomas caught sight of a small black dot moving directly toward him low over the water. Moments later, a four-engine C-130 U.S. Coast Guard plane roared overhead. Its deep, growling engines shook his insides like the blast from a cannon. Thomas was ecstatic. He blew kisses and screamed excitedly. "Yes! Yes, they've seen me! Thank God, at least they know where I am!"

Soon, he spied a U.S. Coast Guard helicopter moving toward him. "I'm here! I'm alive!" he called out.

The wind was blowing hard against the one-thousand foot cliffs behind him. The helicopter flew in twice over Thomas and hovered, only to clack noisily away.

Dear God, he can't get to me! he thought. I'm too cold! I've got to get out of here!

Then the bright orange, black, and white helicopter returned and hovered not fifty feet above him. The 110-knot wind churned up by the copter's blades whipped a mist off the water.

Thomas was thrilled when he saw the large steel body basket descend from out of the side door. But it landed well out in the breaking surf, and the pilot seemed reluctant to move in closer to the cliffs.

Gradually, the helicopter pilot maneuvered the craft closer, resting the basket in the surf on the edge of the shoreline. Though terrified of the water, Thomas shuffled down the embankment and fell into the basket. Fear that the next wave would catch him and batter him to death now that he was so near to being rescued raged in his mind. Yet almost instantly, the helicopter plucked Thomas up and out of the surf.

Thomas watched the shoreline grow minute in the

distance. A cutting wind whipped over him as the upward acceleration of the helicopter pressed his body hard against the wire-meshed basket's bottom. Then the helicopter leveled off and stood away from the shore, hovering noisily. Thomas could feel himself being lifted toward the door.

Far below, he could see the ship that had first spotted him and radioed his location. It was the *Nelle Belle*. She was throwing off heavy sheets of bow spray as she plowed through the waves.

The helicopter crew hoisted him in through the door and checked him for serious injuries. Next a radio headset was fitted over his head, and Thomas heard the voice of the chief pilot.

"Are you all right, young man?"

"Yes. I think so."

"How do you feel?"

"Well, you got me out of there! I feel so much better now."

"Look, you've got hypothermia! Do you understand that?"

"I kind of figured as much."

"Okay, so listen to what I'm telling you! Do not relax! Keep yourself charged up until we can get you into the hospital. You could go into shock right now and you could die before we could get you there! That has happened to us before."

The helicopter pilot was worried about a dangerous phenomenon called "after drop," the process in which a hypothermia victim's core temperature continues to plunge even after he has been rescued and wrapped in wool blankets. If not halted, this downward slide will continue until the victim suffers a heart attack from the cool blood circulating through his heart.

"Have you found anyone else besides me?" asked Thomas.

"No. You're the only one so far," answered the pilot.

The somber news shook Thomas. He had hoped that Paul Ferguson or Curt Nelson had somehow found a way safely ashore. He wondered about Bob Kidd and Arthur "Art" Simonton, whom he'd seen in his dreams the night before.

Bob Kidd had jumped overboard with Simonton from up near the bow minutes before Thomas and the rest of the crew had abandoned the *St. Patrick* off the stern.

When Wallace Thomas arrived at the hospital, his body temperature was ninety-three degrees Fahrenheit. Death can occur from heart failure at ninety degrees. The medical staff placed heated blankets and hot towels across his body and forced him to breathe heated oxygen. But it took little coaxing. The warm devices felt wonderful to Thomas's numb, sea ravaged body.

The next day, Thomas learned that one other crewmate had survived the ordeal. As he lay recovering in a Kodiak hospital bed, nurses wheeled in Bob Kidd for a visit. "I can't believe it," Thomas finally confided to his good friend. "I would never have believed that a ship built like the *St. Patrick* could have gone down as quickly as she did!"

Bob Kidd sat upright and turned and looked at Wally Thomas in astonishment. "Wally," said Kidd, "it didn't go down. It didn't sink. They found the *St. Patrick* floating the day after we abandoned ship. They're towing it in right now!"

The grim experience of Wallace Thomas contains important lessons for anyone who sets out to sea in Alaska, or anywhere else for that matter. Don't sail with a youthful untested captain or on a shabby vessel. Never sail without your own high-quality survival suit, one that is in good repair and of the latest design. And know where to find it, even in pitch black, stormy conditions. Be sure the suit has a strobe light attached to its arm. Better yet, take along a small waterproof survival bag containing various flares, an EPIRB, strobe light, waterproof matches, a knife, and emergency rations of food and water. But though these lifesaving lessons are simple and important, they pale beside the one overarching rule of survival at sea that was roundly ignored by all of the crew of the *F/V St. Patrick*: Never leave a floating vessel. Had they simply remained aboard, all would have lived. That is the most crucial of the many death-defeating lessons the crew of the *F/V St. Patrick* tragically and unwittingly taught us all.

Chapter Five

A man should know his limitations
- Clint Eastwood, Dirty Harry

BACK IN CORDOVA, I get some badly needed rest, have the VHF antenna repaired, and replace the lost anchor, then return a call from Lt. Randy Sundberg at the Coast Guard's Rescue Coordination Center in Juneau. From him I learn the Coast Guard deployed for a maximum search effort: two helicopters for close to shore, two C-130's for farther out to sea, and the cutter *Mustang* dispatched from Seward. They searched an enormous area from Cape Spencer near Glacier Bay up to Prince William Sound. With the help of my wife, they got my credit card numbers and traced all my credit transactions in Alaska, which means they got the names of some of the best bars in the state. They talked to the harbormaster at every stop along the way, checked my cell phone to see if I had even turned it on (somehow they can tell), and issued a press release resulting in TV and radio broadcasts asking for civilian assistance. In short, no stone was left unturned, for all of which I'm deeply grateful, though I was neither lost nor in immediate danger of premature death.

The dent in the U. S. Treasury for all this effort is enough to discourage an offer to contribute a share of the cost, though as I thought about it, I chip in every April 15. A Coast Guard officer later told me not to worry about the cost. In summer, they don't get many calls so they need the training time. Besides, he said, it gives the crews something to do other than shooting craps or scraping rust all day.

Had the VHF not malfunctioned, my calls could have easily been picked up by the Coast Guard's powerful receivers, and the whole exercise avoided. Had I known the VHF was defective, I could have used the backup handheld unit with the same result. I could have, and in hindsight should have, activated the EPIRB, but that would, I worried, sound an alarm and intensify the Coast Guard's efforts more than the situation called for. I could not know they would respond with the intensity they did. I expected a call on the VHF or, at most, that I'd be spotted by a low flying, single engine float plane searching along my route and the few protected anchorages. Instead, they sent out the cavalry.

A small crew from the cutter *Sedge* conducts a brief safety inspection, and I'm found to be in full compliance with all Coast Guard and other federal regulations—a long list indeed—except that I don't have two stickers displayed, one about dumping garbage in the water and the other about dumping oil (which, I couldn't know, would have a special significance farther along in the journey). The lieutenant in charge of the inspection says I have more safety equipment on board than any other recreational boat he's seen, but he'd like to see me get a single-side band radio that will allow me to communicate over long distances far beyond VHF range. I tell him I'll consider it, though it was my VHF's torn antenna wire, not its inadequate range, that caused the problem. Even a single-side band would be ineffective with a damaged antenna.

Ralph Bollis, the technician who replaced the defective antenna, discourages me from buying the bulky single-side band. Instead, he promises to call a remote lumber camp at Icy Bay and a tug boat based there, as well as a guy in Yakutat with a high VHF antenna, and others along the way, and alert them to my travel itinerary. Also, he says, in a few days, the fishing fleet will be operating in the Gulf, and they stand by, as do the logging companies, on VHF channel six. With these people available by radio at various points along the way and knowing the channels they monitor, I will have complete radio coverage to Yakutat, assuming my VHF works as it should. It's a patchwork arrangement, not unlike the jungle drums of Tarzan movies, but one commonly used in this harsh and remote area.

The lieutenant and I discuss survival suits. He says he'd like me to wear a suit while I'm under way, but I demur, because the bulky fingers would make it impossible to work the throttles or the small keypads of the boat's electronics, both of which require a deft touch. I decide, however, that it may be wise, if a bit overcautious, to don the lower half of the suit with the upper hanging at the waist, the Alaskan version of topless. He's right that putting one on while floating at sea, especially a stormy sea, would be impossible. I also plan to hook up to my clothing a lanyard that when pulled shuts off both motors. It's a standard feature on open boats, required by yet another law, so the boat won't run off if the operator is ejected by rough seas. Like every other boater. I've never seen a need to use it, since it makes moving around awkward.

At the opposite end of Kayak Island from Cape Saint Elias and near the mainland shore is a tricky channel, rock-strewn and violent with tidal surge and breakers. At dockside, the captain of a fifty-six foot fish tender tells me that at high slack tide I'll have no trouble getting through. This route means I can stay closer to shore rather than run the twenty miles out in the ocean required to pass Cape Saint Elias. It also means I'll burn less fuel.

I restock the boat with eighteen gallons of two-cycle oil. Since *Rascal's* motors burn six gallons of oil in every 200 gallons of gas. I'll have plenty. To the survival gear bag I add three marker flares, three parachute aerial flares, and a strobe light as additional safety gear. The survival gear bag and survival suit, will sit on the open deck next to me while under way. On the day of departure, I'll stock three days of food—sandwiches, fruit, and candy bars—all cold, as *Rascal* has no means of heating food, or me for that matter. After a few days of shore life in Cordova, I'm eager to get going again.

The same low pressure center that trapped me behind Cape St. Elias for three days is still in the area but slowly moving off to the north, and seas are still five to seven feet between here and Yakutat. But right behind this system is nautical bliss, a huge high pressure center moving onshore from out in the Pacific, which should bring blue skies, sunshine, and calm winds, or at least the Alaskan equivalent. It's about time.

An inadequate fuel supply was what got me into trouble behind Kayak Island, and it all traced back to the failed deck tanks. With them, I could have made Yakutat easily, after a rough ride through stormy seas. But with only two tanks still holding fuel, and those of seriously doubtful reliability, the margin for error simply got too tight. The storm and opposing current increased fuel consumption to the point that two tanks were not enough to make Yakutat with any level of assurance. If I'm to make it on the second try, some sort of reliable reserve fuel supply will be needed. Carrying extra fuel on board is not a satisfactory option. Jerry cans hold only five gallons each, and with so many required—ten at least—they couldn't be safely secured to the deck and in rough seas could break loose, creating havoc and a fire hazard. The only safe way to assure sufficient fuel is an en route resupply of some sort.

Ralph Bollis and his old friend Dan Farmer, a bush pilot, offer to help. At first we try to line up a tender boat. These are floating convenience stores that serve the gill net boats in the Cordova fleet. The tender operators buy the fishermen's catches and store them in their holds, allowing the gill netters to return to fishing without making the long run to the cannery and back out again. Of more importance, the tenders also carry extra fuel for sale, like seagoing tankers of a sort. The problem is that state regulators allow the gill netters only periodic time windows in which to fish, and the next window is not known until notice of it is posted the day before it begins. Thus my potential access to seaborne fuel depends on a window occurring at the same time as calm seas. Even then, the tender would need to be stationed far enough along my route to offer some advantage. Ralph and I visit all the canneries along the waterfront to gather information on tenders, but the situation doesn't look hopeful.

Finally, I decide I'll have an air taxi service fly ten five-gallon jerry cans of fuel into a remote airstrip (actually just a Gulf-front beach) on the east side of Icy Bay, drop them off where they can be reached easily, then fly the empties back on a later trip. We locate an air service that flies frequent supply trips to a logging camp along the route, and they agree to deliver the fuel for a modest fee. The pilot will land on a beach and taxi to a point nearest a small arm of Icy Bay. There he'll offload the fuel, leaving it at the end of the beach to be picked up whenever I can get there. With the extra fuel, I'll have enough range to explore Icy Bay a bit and a larger safety margin for the run to Yakutat. All I need to do is get to Icy Bay using *Rascal's* onboard fuel supply.

~~~

Ralph, Dan, and I drive thirty miles out of town on a graveled road across the vast delta of the Copper River to the Million Dollar Bridge. A railroad bridge completed in 1910, it was later converted for use by one-way vehicle traffic crossing the river. In the earthquake of 1964, one of its four spans collapsed, but a jury-rigged roadbed still allows the fearless driver to get across, though for no apparent reason since the road on the other side is grown over and impassable.

Off to the left of the bridge and across the river is the huge Childs Glacier, rising 200 feet above the far bank. With snowmelt in full force, the river is a boiling rage of silt-laden water and hurtling icebergs. Twelve hundred feet across the river from the glacier, the sounds of war reverberate: dropped bombs, lobbed artillery shells, hurled grenades. These are the sounds the glacier makes as it cracks open along its leading edge, sending great chunks of ice thundering into the river and splendid plumes of frigid spray erupting into the air. The Childs is an advancing glacier, growing two football fields in a year and, as it grows, the river's powerful current cuts at its base and bergs result. Every now and then, a monumental piece breaks off, creating a Holiday Inn-size berg and its consequent splash wave.

Just a few years ago such a piece broke off and created a wave that, even after traveling 1,200 feet across the river, was still over thirty feet high when it struck the far bank where I now stand. The result was localized devastation and two bystanders critically injured.

After our excursion, the three of us return to town in time for happy hour at the popular fishermen's bar on the ground floor of the slightly seedy Alaskan Hotel. Fishermen here, as everywhere, are a colorful lot, no less so their wives and girlfriends. As I walk through fight-scarred double front doors, a large, boozy woman seated familiarly at the bar and recognizing that I'm not a local, yells out in a gritty, tobacco-stained voice: "Hey, girls. At the front door. It's fresh meat!" It is revealing commentary on the state of romantic desperation among Alaskan women that a white-haired man in his mid-fifties should be thought of as fresh meat.

After the unexpected introduction, I survey my surroundings and right away begin to appreciate the place. It's dimly lit, but not in that halogen rheostat, soft light, romantic way. Most of the incandescent bulbs burned out a few years ago, and half the fluorescent bulbs over the pool table buzz and flicker. There's plenty of house dust, some of it gathered in corners in pale gray balls, the rest floating about in blizzards in the beer-dank air. Above the clack of acrylic balls from the off-level, drink-stained Brunswick pool table and the sliding twang of a steel guitar from a battered Wurlitzer, convivial giggles and belly laughs drift over the room, softened by a fog of cigarette smoke.

Off in a corner, two fishermen already a few sheets to the wind, just off their boats and still clad in orange foul weather gear, are loudly angry at what the government and fish-hugging environmentalists have done to their business. Another group of fishermen, half tanked and jovial, complain about their small catches. One, with a darkly satirical sense of humor, diagnoses the problem in yuppie-disease vernacular as FDS, Fish Deficit Syndrome. Most of the nonfishermen and women wear vests plump with quilted insulation, giving them the look of walking hand grenades. The furniture, carved upon, dented, bloodied no doubt, lends itself well to a good brawl. The solid oak bar, at least thirty feet long and stained a dark unidentifiable hue, has the regal pose of a battle monument, which on many nights it is.

My conclusion, after a careful examination of its features and based on years of solemn empirical study, is that this ranks among the best bars America has to offer. Thankfully, it isn't tidy or fern draped or filled with suits. Above the bar sits a TV set, but its technology is so badly out of date and the picture so fuzzed that it alone disqualifies the place from being labeled a sports bar, unless getting knee-crawling, toilet-hugging drunk can be considered a sport. Its menu—limited to popcorn, if you don't count the martini olives behind the bar—offers about all the nutrition you'd need in any proper bar. This is a place with a pleasing air of decadence and ambient sin, where sobriety is seen as a mild character flaw, and a place where I could easily waste a lot of time.

The loud woman who announced my entrance is Darlene, a half Asian, half white, bowling ball-shaped, fish net mender seated at the bar with a miniature Schnauzer in her lap (the salacious pun not intended). Standing next to her, slightly wobble-kneed, is her good friend Emily. Both are rough-hewn, salty babes. For me, the name Emily once conjured images of silk-fluttering, floral-scented femininity, but now I can see that picture was seriously flawed. Through a beer-brained cloud, Emily confides in me Oprah-like in the irksome, platonic way young women talk to white-headed men. I do my best to feign I-share-your-pain interest.

It seems she's recovering from a failed romance with a pony-tailed, heavily tattooed, Amana-size, sometime cannery worker and full-time Harley enthusiast, unimaginatively nicknamed Harley. From Darlene and Emily's description, I gather that he is a man of ornery disposition whose perpetually vacant expression betrays a mind untroubled by thought. He is frequently moved to imprudence, they say, and evinces a general disinclination to work of any kind. Agriculture is the career he professes, by which he means hiring others to harvest crops of marijuana grown secretively, not to say unlawfully, in nearby government-owned forests.

The love war between Emily and Harley started when on a recent night they got rip-roaring drunk, as they frequently did. Angry with him for some now forgotten reason, Emily rejected Harley's amorous advances—"cut him off" is I believe the way she phrased it—and locked him out of her house. Hurt by the rejection and homeless from the eviction, the ever-sensitive and romantic Harley became irritated, broke down the door, grabbed Emily by the arm, and threw her to the floor, thus making another of the foolish mistakes that, it could be said, had characterized his life thus far.

As Emily lay on the floor screaming obscenities, an alarming thought must have crept slowly to Harley's booze-addled mind: "Oh God, Emily has a pet dog!" It was at this unfortunate yet theatrical moment that Emily's lovable, fuzzy, but toothy and ferocious, 110-pound pit bull, ominously named Road Kill, arrived on the scene, an arrival that brought with it decidedly unpleasant consequences for her brutish paramour.

Several weeks later, when Harley emerged from the hospital with use of his left arm and shoulder regained in part, Emily and Harley agreed the encounter had had a dampening effect on their ardor, as well as a meat grinder effect on Harley's chrome studded, black leather, hog-jockey jacket. So now it's splitsville. In colorful language, she told him she never wanted to see him again, not at the moment reflecting how impossible that would be in tiny Cordova. She told him, "If the phone don't ring, it's me."

Smoke curling up from a long-ashed cigarette hanging limply from one corner of her mouth gives Emily a squint-eyed, pained expression and a troubled air. As the mournful strains of a Hank Williams tune drifts over the smoke-fogged room, Emily bemoans her chances of finding a new man to replace her Harley.

"Well, don't men outnumber women two to one in Alaska?" I ask, running low on pain-sharing interest in this conversation.

"Yeah," she says. "Alaska, where the odds are good, but the goods are odd. And to make matters worse," she prattles on, "the men don't stay married." A stunningly obvious revelation, and not exactly a problem novel to Alaska, I think.

"For a man in Alaska, marriage is like a ticket on the E-rides at Disney World. When the ride is over, they just go to the end of the line and wait until it's their turn again or move on to another ride"—this, an overly commercial assessment of Alaskan serial matrimony, but probably not far off the mark.

"And," she goes on somewhat randomly, "Alaskan men drink too much."

I can tell from her tone that she sees this last habit of local men as a flaw, though just why I'm not sure. The thought "too much, compared to what?" comes to mind. Being trapped all winter in a snowbound cabin with Emily might, after a time, make a down-in-front seat at a Twisted Sister concert seem appealing and expand greatly one's idea about how much drinking is too much. P. J. O'Rourke's two rules for traveling in third-world countries pops into my head: (1) never run out of whiskey; (2) never run out of whiskey.

Between gulps of beer and a few faintly audible belches, Emily, clearly despondent over her bleak prospects, says with a seductive gleam in her eye and a sultry grin that she is "available." It hasn't occurred to me until this moment that I might be the potential object of her affections, and the sudden realization that I am hits me like a ton of cold halibut. Alcohol has begun to cloud her judgment, as I'm sure it has often done in the past; but it hasn't clouded mine, not yet anyway.

The violence-prone Harley might still hold a possessory like interest in Emily, his encounter with Road Kill notwithstanding, and he surely wouldn't be amused if she shared her affections with me (nor would my wife). There isn't enough whiskey in this bar to anesthetize my judgment, compromise my virtue, and lead me to a libidinous night with the pining Emily, a thought too scary to dwell upon.

The Voice of Conscience, a little apparition that often perches on my right shoulder in time of need but seldom offers helpful or judicious counsel, now expresses a lukewarmness to spontaneous romance.

He whispers, "Hey, dumb ass! You're gonna get your neck broken and wind up mixed in with the fish puree down at the cannery. Time to get the hell outta here." My VOC, the keen-eyed reader will note, is interested only in self-preservation, a shallow and limited perspective but one that at this moment results in some pretty good advice. Now I have to put that advice into action.

Unprepared to respond coherently to Emily's suggestion that her affections are free for the taking, I resort instead to high dudgeon.

"That is so deeply hurtful, so insensitive. You make me feel cheap, like nothing but a sex object," I scold. "What kind of person do you think I am? Don't you know I have feelings? Don't you care how I feel?"

This outburst just about exhausts my rather meager supply of female bafflegab. I have not the slightest idea what I'm talking about. Still it's not a bad effort for having been called forth on the spur of the moment, and it has the effect of setting Emily back on her heels—perhaps a poor choice of anatomical metaphor under the circumstances. I feel almost self-righteous—like Jimmy Swaggart must feel when he's shedding sweat and tears onto the pages of his Bible, before, that is, he got caught with a hooker—though I know it is sanctimony.

Actually it is total b.s., though of a particularly high quality, and boldly delivered, if I may say so.

Just then, in my darkest hour of need, the doleful voice of Merle Haggard rolls across the bar from the juke box.

> "Could be holding you tonight,
> Could quit doin' wrong,
> Start doin' right,
> You don't care about what I think,
> I think I'll just stay here and drink."

That's a great idea, I think to myself, as I muster up a pretty decent angry-and-deeply-hurt expression, the kind guys learn from their wives after years of marriage (just kidding, darling), and storm off in a fit of faux pique to knock back yet another beer, virtue intact.

~~~

Plans now are to depart Cordova's docks at noon and arrive at the entry to the North Kayak Island channel just before peak flood tide. A recently announced thirty-six hour salmon fishing window, open to gill netters, means tender boats carrying extra fuel for sale will be operating in the area. Although the Pacific high pushing into the region is not yet fully in place, it is nearly so. Winds, though likely to be ten knots, increasing to fifteen later in the day, will be westerly and the seas following. If the sea gets too rough, I'll pull into Controller Bay and wait for the wind to slacken somewhat. Conditions aren't perfect, but they seldom are in the Gulf of Alaska.

At noon, I depart Cordova with oil and fuel tanks full and the tide just coming off the flood. After zigging and zagging out of the difficult Orca Inlet, weaving among lines of breaking swells, I make for the open sea, running five miles offshore of the Copper River Delta. Within thirty miles, I come upon a fleet of gill net boats working the near shore waters. Careful to avoid running over their nets, I continue along the coast in west winds at ten knots and seas a gentle two to three feet. Not an hour later, though, the wind freshens to fifteen, and the seas fester.

Astern of *Rascal's* present course, the earth-girding circle marked on nautical charts as sixty degrees of north latitude reaches west to Prince William Sound, the Kenai Peninsula, and Cook Inlet. Continuing west, it passes over the forbidding Alaska Range and miles of treeless tundra deeply iced over most of the year. Its last landfall in western North America is a windswept shore of the Bering Sea at a remote Eskimo village. West of there, the sixty degree parallel continues 1,240 miles across the desolate sea, where it encounters the north end of Russia's Kamchatka Peninsula, passes through Siberia, then Oslo, over the southern tip of Greenland, across the upper reaches of Canada's Hudson Bay, finally returning here to the Gulf of Alaska.

Off to starboard, the trackless reach of the North Pacific stretches to the horizon and beyond; the nearest land, the Hawaiian Islands, lies 3,300 miles away. To port, land is closer at five miles but no less forbidding than the vast seas. Along the shore stretch miles of marshlands, tidal flats, and bars of glacial silt washed by the Copper River. Behind these, the Chugach Range stands, a bafflement of low mountains interlaced with hundreds of miles of meandering glaciers, merely foreground for what lies beyond. Rising into the sky, towering over its grotesquely misshapen surroundings, are the dramatic peaks of the Wrangell and Saint Elias Ranges, arrayed along and defining the coast but distant from it. From *Rascal's* deck, the shore and the Chugach Range are overwhelmed by the faraway mountains painting luminous white the thin seam that joins earth to sky and adorning it with grandeur.

A sixty degree parallel of latitude also circles the globe in the Southern Hemisphere. Down there, below Cape Horn and Tierra del Fuego, the earth is belted by a line that is as distant from the South Pole as the northern line is from its pole. In 1914, just a few miles below that south line, the lives of twenty-eight men teetered on the navigation skills of one man and his sextant. That man, Frank Worsley, steered himself and five men in a twenty-two foot longboat from Elephant Island, a desolate, ice-bound rock off Antarctica, 800 miles across the South Atlantic to South Georgia Island, a tiny dot of a place. In doing so, Worsley saved the lives of all twenty-eight men of Sir Ernest Shackleton's ill-fated *Endurance*. That journey was one of history's greatest feats of celestial navigation.

Forty miles out of Orca Inlet, the fishing fleet is at work off the mainland coast; already I've burned thirty gallons of fuel. On VHF channel six, the fleet's working channel, I ask for a tender offshore of Grass Island. The *Lady Lee* responds and tells me I can find her in twelve fathoms, four and a half miles south of the west end of Grass Island.

After spotting her halogen mast light, brighter than the lights of any gas station, I pull alongside behind a gill netter unloading his catch. The fifty-foot tender is well fendered, but the seas are sloppy and the two boats bounce out of sync as a deckhand secures bow and stern lines and hands me the hose for *Rascal's* first refueling at sea.

The turbulent seas cause gas to belch from the filler neck and spew from the overflow vent. When she seems full, the meter reads thirty gallons, but I'm sure I've spilled at least two. [Note to Coast Guard: I was beyond the offshore legal limit when the spill occurred, and, anyway, I have a good lawyer, so back off!] After paying the deck-hand—fuel at sea runs double its shoreside cost—I cast off lines and head out. Just as I pull away, the deckhand yells that the weather fax on board the tender reports a storm coming and winds growing to twenty-five knots.

With that news I change plans. Instead of passing through the North Kayak channel on the peak flood and making for Icy Bay, I decide to pull into Controller Bay, just north of my old friend Kayak Island. There, under leaden sky, I drop the primary anchor, now with new chain, shackles tightly wired in place, and a trip line deployed, and sit until the next peak flood. Once the blow has passed, and if I have sufficient light, I'll continue on; otherwise, I'll wait for the next flood tide.

Kayak Island, one would guess, is named for the skin-covered watercraft used by the various Indian tribes of Alaska—but not so. Captain James Cook named it Kaye Island, after a man unflatteringly described as "a toadyish rector who had curried favor with Cook's family." Later the name was changed to Kayak, partly deferring to Cook and partly to the native boat. Just north across the channel from the island is Controller Bay. Fifteen miles across and five miles wide, the expanse is not so much a bay as it is a glacial mud flat at the seaward end of the broad delta formed by the Bering River and the meltwater coming down from the Bering Glacier. An island and a spit, both just accumulations of glacial silt on which trees have grown, are Controller Bay's only protection from the sea.

As I turn in for the night, salmon jump near the boat, birds squawk overhead, and wavelets slap the hull, none of which suggests the possibility of sound sleep. *Rascal's* small cabin, where I attempt to sleep, is vee-shaped with the pointed end of the vee at the bow. The legs of the vee are ninety-two inches long and twenty-four wide, and their bases are covered with thinly padded vinyl cushions. All my personal gear—a box of paper charts and cruising guides, a duffel bag of clothes for various weather, and assorted stuff—is stored on the starboard leg in comparatively dry conditions. On the port leg, there's just enough room for me to lie prone snuggled into a sleeping bag. The cabin's ceiling, two and a half feet above the cushions, makes the place less than appealing to claustrophobics.

Before trying to sleep, I check whether there is cell phone service—there is not—or anyone within VHF range—nobody responds to my calls over several working channels. Though remote, even from the fishing fleet I passed, I'm not completely shut off from the world, however, thanks to the generosity of Ralph Bollis, who loaned me a VHF designed for use on the sliver of radio band used by aircraft. With this handheld, battery-powered radio, I can contact planes flying anywhere near me, even commercial jets flying at 30,000 feet, and ask for help. One frequency is for emergencies only, while two others allow casual talk.

As I approach Controller Bay, *Rascal* flushes a small flock of tufted puffins as she has done many times since the voyage began. The puffin, partly I suppose because it is both endearingly cute and clumsy—like a Barbie doll after three martinis—has become a must-see item for the eco-tourist. If you were to set about designing a bird singularly ill-suited to flight, you would come up with something resembling the puffin. The size and general shape of a smaller-than-NFL regulation football with an absurdly oversized head attached, knobby orange legs, and a parrotlike bright orange beak, the puffin is a laughable accumulation of bird parts in a distinctly unbirdlike form. Its wings, far too short and stubby for the noble business of flight, beat at a blinding rate to generate lift. As if to demonstrate its physical handicaps, the puffin, when attempting flight from water, creates in the first sixty feet of its takeoff a long parallel series of embarrassing wingtip splashes before finally getting airborne. The term soar doesn't come to mind when watching puffins fly. Eagles soar, puffins, well, flutter.

To compensate for its ungainly flight, the puffin thankfully has an alternate escape technique that adults employ as a last resort and youngsters use for primary evasion. When its tranquility is threatened, such as by a roaring boat bearing down on it, the adult puffin first makes its comical attempt at flight, then, realizing the futility of its effort and sensing the loud monster closing in, simply abandons flight altogether, does what looks like a belly flop, and dives out of sight. The little ones, even more aeronautically challenged than their parents, don't even bother with attempted flight, perhaps a skill of sorts acquired only with years of practice, they just plop their heads in the water and dive. Both techniques, though humorous, are effective. *Rascal* never turned a puffin into nautical road kill.

~~~

At 3:00 a.m., the sky still lingering in twilight, I hoist anchor and fire up the motors, shattering Controller Bay's pastoral calm. Out beyond its shelter of the spruce forest, a line of ugly blue-black clouds comes into view, hanging over the horizon like hell-sent purple blisters. The entire landscape astern, the battlement of snow-draped mountains forming a backdrop to the bay, is fully enveloped in wool-thick fog, and the temperature has dropped to a damp mid-forties. The low light of early dawn and a misty fog sharply reduce visibility. These are not the conditions for someone foreign to these waters to be running the dangerous Kayak Passage, so I turn back, knowing the opportunity to leave must wait until just before the next peak flood. Again, I sit and wait, hoping the skies will clear in the meantime, and they do—slightly.

Before peak flood, I set out once more. Wending among water boils and suspicious currents betraying rocks below, eyes glued to the chart plotter and depth gauge, slowly, cautiously I pick my way through the passage. At last, clear without incident, I make for open sea and set a course directly for Icy Bay, sixty-eight miles distant. Just a few miles along the coast is the oddly named Cape Suckling. Captain James Cook, on his third voyage in 1778 and apparently in a dyspeptic mood, named it for another captain described as "weak" and "unimportant."

Congealed skies and thick fog still cover the coastal mountains above 500 feet, while winds are out of the west blowing fifteen knots at *Rascal's* starboard stem quarter. Seas are mostly following, running three to four feet. The ride is sloppy and uncomfortable but tolerable once I get the trim tabs lowered to dampen the boat's flight off wave tops and soften the crash when she lands. The price for this mild improvement in comfort is increased fuel consumption and reduced range due to the added drag. Good thing I bought fuel from the salmon tender.

Thirty miles out, the winds pick up to twenty knots and the seas, blown to sharp crests, are a field of frothing whitecaps. Now the ride gets rough, and I'm wrenched, twisted, and knocked around at the helm as *Rascal* pounds through the seas. Her motors strain and the hull shudders each time she climbs the back of a wave, grinding nearly to a stop, bow pointed to the sky. As the motors power her over a crest, the bow plummets, driven by horsepower and gravity, and slams against the sea with a loud crack, signaling the start of a head long rush down the steep face of the wave. Racing too fast down the face, nearly out of control, the bow burrows into the back of the next wave, penetrating its surface and sending a green plume of icy water crashing into the wind screen at twenty-five knots. The ride is wearing and no fun at all.

Three and a half hours later I enter the protected waters of Icy Bay, tense and beaten from the rough seas. In little Moraine Bay, a cove within the larger bay, I tie up against the *Cygnet*, a junk heap of a working tug used to tend log booms. Using two fallen trees with sheets of plywood nailed across them as a dock, I locate the essential fuel supply on the beach and pour it into the main tank, giving me plenty of fuel for the remainder of the leg to Yakutat Bay.

It's the Fourth of July, and the crews of the *Cygnet* and the nearby logging camp are off for the holiday, leaving *Rascal* and me in perfect solitude on an evening of exquisite beauty. Even for someone uneasy with religion, reverence comes easily here. Anchored in a blissful cove of Moraine Bay, I watch the sun set behind the enormous snow-shrouded Mount Saint Elias, festooned with glaciers of ancient ice reaching down into the bay like gaudy white ribbons. Glassy flat waters tinted burnt umber by the falling sun perfectly reflect the feral world around me. Fields of bergs drift silently by on the tide. With birds roosted for the night, not the faintest sound of nature is heard; only serene silence reigns, amid profound magnificence.

After a fitful night's sleep, I awake to a cloudless sky whose entire northern hemisphere is dominated by the colossal Mount Saint Elias. At this hour, clothed in a spangled blanket of pure white, the resplendent mountain seems so near I could reach out a hand and feel its cold skin, though I know it's thirty miles away. Reluctantly hoisting anchor, I leave Moraine Bay and attempt to enter the head of Icy Bay. There, the three large glaciers that flow into it are actively calving and, as a result, the head of the bay is hopelessly clogged by a broad field of bergs from golf bag-to SUV-size, clustered tightly by the incoming tide. Not wanting to play *Titanic*, I leave Icy Bay, making for Yakutat, seventy miles farther on.

Along the way, I pass pods of feeding humpback whales, their telltale spouts easily seen billowing white mist against the tree-lined shore. All along the coast, the majesty of Mount Saint Elias looms over me. For mile after mile, its great bulk fails to yield to the mathematical laws of perspective, never growing smaller, never fading into the distance. Adjoining Saint Elias, as ever so slightly smaller siblings, are Mounts Augusta, and Vancouver, and the larger Logan, decked out in matching shrouds of glimmering white. The four giants, along with countless neighbors densely arrayed around them, form the stunning backdrop for what must surely be the world's most majestic seashore.

At the dock in Yakutat, I'm greeted by Geoff Widdows, a long-time fishing guide who, to my good fortune, is without a customer for the day. We hit it off right away, and he takes me a mile up the road in his truck to the first hot meal I've had in a few days. Over a last cup of coffee, Geoff volunteers to be my guide on a sight-seeing trip, an offer I eagerly accept. Back at the harbor, we board *Rascal*, crank up the motors, and set out to visit the great Hubbard Glacier in Disenchantment Bay, at the head of the much larger Yakutat Bay.

At eighty miles end to end, the Hubbard is one of the longest glaciers in North America, beginning in Canada and finishing here. To get to it, we make our way among spruce-covered islands, along the sheer mountainous east shore of the bay, through kelp beds and broad swaths of icebergs, some house-size, drifting on the tide. As we near Hubbard, a cruise ship is just leaving, so we have the place to ourselves. Four or five ships visit this easily accessible glacier each day in the peak summer months, so we're fortunate to have solitude. Geoff cautions me not to get too close to the Hubbard's six-mile long, 300-foot high face. The calving ice can create enormous waves with devastating consequences, as I learned at the Childs Glacier back in Cordova.

The Hubbard is particularly active, advancing and retreating, con-stantly moving. In the mid-eighties, it advanced so far that it closed off a narrow passage into the Russell Fjord, bottling up all the sea life caught there and causing the water to rise over a hundred feet inside the fjord. It also caused animal lovers to suffer acute public angst over the fate of the trapped creatures. But soon enough the Hubbard retreated once again, releasing an enormous volume of water along with the captives. Recently, the gap closed again and reopened a short time later. When open, it can be easily passed through in a small boat—but at the risk of having an iceberg drop on your head, a risk we decide not to take. After a pleasant day, we return to the dock, and then drive to Geoff's home for a treat of moose burgers with his wife Kris and friends.

Geoff and Kris once worked their own boat, fishing for salmon. Starting as gillnetters, they soon moved to a seiner, but as the years went by the allure of commercial fishing began to fade. The work was hard, and it was dangerous; the financial rewards for the work and risk started to diminish. Prices for their catch began a downward trend they rightly perceived would not reverse. Finally, one day they made the prescient decision to get out of the business. Abandoning the only livelihood they knew wasn't easy, yet they also understood they had little choice. After selling the boat and all their gear, Geoff set out on the painfully slow process of developing a new business as a sportfishing guide in summer and pursuing what odd jobs he could find in winter. Kris helped out with whatever jobs she could find. They lived frugally but comfortably and raised a daughter, now off to college. By all appearances, life has treated them kindly.

Next day, Geoff has a fishing charter and graciously lends me his truck for a self-guided tour of the area. Kris suggests I might enjoy the "beach," a freighted word that for me evokes images of bikini-clad volleyball players and coolers of iced down beer. In Alaska, a beach is something else entirely.

I head for a coastal rain forest just behind the sand flats and dunes of the Gulf beach, where a gravel trail barely wider than the truck twists its way through miles of eerie woods. Here, under a dark canopy of Sitka spruce and red cedar is a tortured ground, not so much as a yard of it level. Littered with deadfalls lying helter-skelter in gnarled heaps and twisted shapes, every surface painted over with mosses and lichens and funguses in all the shades of green, sprays of tropical ferns reaching out of the mire, it seems as if the Amazon River should be nearby, not the Gulf of Alaska. This is surely like the place where the first amoeba crawled from the primordial soup and began its long journey that so far has ended with the human, one of whom now stands gawking at a modern replica of his species' place of origin. There are no bikinis or beer coolers in sight.

After saying goodbye to Geoff and Kris early the next morning, I fire up the motors and make my way out of Yakutat Bay, headed for Cape Spencer and the Inside Passage. It's a rare day in coastal Alaska that brings cloudless skies and radiant sunshine, but this is such a day. Though the skies are clear, stiff winds out of the southeast drive head seas up to six feet. When I set the trim tabs to their maximum extension in an attempt to slice through the waves and smooth the ride, the fuel consumption rate increases sharply, making it a dicey matter whether I can make the next refueling stop. The winds continue to blow and pick up speed as I get farther out into the Gulf. Small white caps grow larger and the seas steepen.

Chastened by the experience of my adventure behind Kayak Island, I decide to wait for a calmer day and return to Yakutat. After tending to neglected details and scrubbing her clean, I sit down on *Rascal's* stern and admire Mounts Logan, Vancouver, Augusta, and Saint Elias dominating the sky just across the bay. Rising above forests of spruce and hemlock and cedar lining the foreground, the mountains paint a set piece of operatic flamboyance.

~~~

In true Alaskan fashion, the weather today is sharply different from that of yesterday. A gray blanket of tenebrous clouds has replaced blue skies, warm has turned to cold, and a a light breeze of southeast winds has freshened to twenty knots from the southwest. Seas are an uncomfortable five to six feet, but today attack from abaft the starboard beam. So at 4:00 a.m. in the dull light of clouded dawn and with an unshakable anxiety somewhat short of fear, I leave the calm of Yakutat Bay—foolishly, I later conclude.

Closely spaced ocean swells greet me, the result of ebbing tide running headlong into wind-driven sea. Each wave stands *Rascal's* bow in the air at a precarious angle and, as I pass over it, slams the bow into the trough. Even setting the trim tabs at their maximum is not enough to soften the blow from the badly wrinkled seas. When I emerge from the mouth of the bay, past the tide's effects and into open water, I ease the tabs and the bow moves freely, starboard leading the way, causing the boat both to plunge into the trough at a cockeyed angle and to roll, jerking me about simultaneously on two axes. Up the face of one wave, down its backside, then up the face of the next, I head for Cape Spencer, 120 miles away, where, at the entrance to the Inside Passage, I will find welcome relief from the badly churned Gulf of Alaska.

Navigation along this route is simple enough: Keep the mountains to port and the ocean to starboard and don't hit anything. The charts reveal no obstacles offshore of the breakers along the beach, though the bars at Dry Bay and Lituya Bay break up to two miles offshore in a strong ebb. A wide, fanlike delta of the Alsek River, itself fed by the meltwater from a glacier of the same name, Dry Bay is laced with shallow, shifting, unmarked channels. These course through fields of alluvial sand accumulated over thousands of years, seen at low tide as sand flats. Dry Bay is said to be the only place in Alaska where dust storms are a threat to human life, as though Alaska needed another.

The mighty Alsek is one of the wildest and least explored rivers of North America. As yet, no Butterfield and Robinson ten-speed and chardonnay picnic trips are available there. With a water volume twice that of the Colorado, the Alsek drains a vast area of Alaska and British Columbia. It is the only river that has slashed and eroded its way through the Coastal Range and its complex of ice fields and glaciers to disgorge itself into the Gulf of Alaska. In a pinch, Dry Bay might serve as a haven from storms, provided the seas are calm and the tide isn't ebbing—a highly unlikely set of conditions along this coast. Lituya Bay is another possible refuge, but it too can't be safely entered on the ebb.

~~~

The coast of the Gulf of Alaska between Yakutat Bay and Cape Spencer, the northernmost entrance into the Inside Passage, is one of the world's most exuberant monuments to the surpassing might of Mother Nature. Along this route is an overpowering parade of gleaming white mountains, sitting fat and gaudy, coruscating against the sky. A stretch of this coast, from the absurdly misnamed Cape Fairweather (by Capt. James Cook in 1778) to Cape Spencer, is the grandest of all, a coastline dominated by the Fairweather Mountain Range. Starting at the north end of the coast and overwhelming the world around it is the 15,300-foot Mount Fairweather, followed in succession moving southeast by one after another of icy monoliths painting across the sky a panoramic wall of serrated grandeur. Along the foreshore are seaward slopes and alluvial plains, scabbed with forests of weather-stunted Sitka spruce, western red cedar, and hemlock.

In the midst of this melodramatic coast, undetectable from the sea, is the extraordinary and mystical Lituya Bay. Technically a fjord of some 500 feet in maximum depth, the bay is tiny by Alaska's scale, just two miles across and eight miles long. At its head, two covelike inlets form the crosstree of a tee, each home to a large glacier calving ice. A third glacier calves into the tee's peak.

Called "the Yosemite of the North" and "perhaps the most extraordinary place in the world," Lituya Bay is among the earth's most spectacular and serenely beautiful and at once latently sinister places. Its eastern shore is a nearly vertical 7,000-foot high wall of gray rock, sheathed yearlong in ice and snow, its northern and southern shores slightly lower versions of the same. Thus surrounded on three sides, the bay becomes a deep pond set in a walled basin of rock, snow, and ice, softened on its lower reaches by carpets of forest.

A low spit tightly constricts the bay's only entry from the sea. Its name, the La Chaussee Spit—French for "the chopper"—is appropriate for the place where in recorded history more than 200 men have lost their lives. Much of the death and hundreds more wrecked boats were the predictable result of an attempt to enter or leave the bay during an ebbing tide. Because the enormous volume of water trapped inside the bay's basin escapes only through the narrow opening at La Chaussee Spit, the tidal flow surges through at up to six knots, among the fastest flowing tidal waters anywhere in the world (think of a thumb placed over the end of a flowing garden hose). And if the tide is ebbing when ocean swells and wind are from the northwest, thus colliding with the onrushing tide, tumultuous waves of cold green sea result, waves through which no vessel could hope to pass, though many have tried. The Coast Pilot says simply that "entrance [into the bay] is dangerous and should never be attempted except at slack water ..."

~~~

The perils of La Chaussee Spit are predictable. Tides, ebbing twice every twenty-four hours at precisely known times, are easily avoided and are not in themselves catastrophic. Not so predictable was an event that struck Lituya Bay on the evening of July 9, 1958. For a few weeks before that date, a large fleet of salmon trollers was working the fishing grounds offshore. As the Fourth of July holiday approached, most of the boats headed for the tiny village of Pelican, where a rowdy annual party took place every year (and still does) at Rose's Bar and Grill. After the party, the boats went off in different directions, some returning to Lituya Bay.

By late that afternoon, eight mountaineers from Canada arrived on Lituya's shore following a successful climb of Mount Fairweather. After stowing their gear in an abandoned cabin on tiny Cenotaph Island in the middle of the bay, the climbers had settled in for the night when a Royal Canadian Air Force amphibious plane landed, pulled up to the beach, and ordered the party to pack its gear and board the plane at once. A nasty storm was coming, and they had to be evacuated quickly. When the loaded plane took off, its pilot had unknowingly saved the climbers from a disaster far worse than any approaching storm. Another climbing party, this one of ten men, was scheduled to reach Lituya on this same day but was delayed. They too were saved by sheer chance.

As the day ended, Howard Ulrich and Sonny, his six-year old son, anchored their small fishing boat, the *Edrie*, in the southeast corner of the bay. Also at anchor in the bay but out of sight of the *Edrie*, were Bill and Vivian Swanson aboard the *Badger*, and Orville and Micky Wagner on their new forty-seven-foot *Sunmore*. As the arctic-long day waned, Howard Ulrich and Sonny finished eating their dinner, then looked out across the placid, mirror-finished surface of the bay. Off in the distance, gulls and terns, which should have been bedded down in their nests, were oddly restless, circling noisily. The Ulrichs didn't know it at the time, but the birds' unrest was an ominous warning that Lituya Bay's serenity was about to end.

Just after the Ulrichs bedded down for the night in the *Edrie's* forecastle, they heard an engine. Sonny went to the wheelhouse and saw the *Badger* approach Cenotaph Island then turn and make for the entrance. At 10:17 p.m., the *Edrie* began to pitch and roll violently, this in the same water that moments before had been flat. Thinking his boat had dragged anchor and struck the shore, Howard Ulrich ran to the wheelhouse and in his own words this is what he saw:

"The *Edrie* was still tugging at her anchor chain as she rolled and heaved, but the scene at the head of the bay drove all thought of her from my mind. I called Sonny and together we watched the peaks which rise steeply from the water's edge to heights of six and seven thousand feet, with the lofty giants of the Fairweather Range behind.

"These great snow-capped giants shook and twisted and heaved. They seemed to be suffering unbearable internal tortures. Have you ever seen a 15,000-foot mountain twist and shake and dance? At last, as if to rid themselves of their torment, the mountains spewed heavy clouds of snow and rocks into the air and threw huge avalanches down their groaning sides.

"During all this I was literally petrified, rooted to the deck. It was not fright, but a kind of stunned amazement. I do not believe I thought of it as something that was going to affect me. This frozen immobility must have lasted for two minutes or longer. Then it came to a dramatic end. It so happened that I was looking over the shoulder of Cenotaph Island toward the head of the bay when a mighty seismic disturbance exploded and there was a deafening crash.

"I saw a gigantic wall of water, 1,800 feet high, erupt against the west mountain. I saw it lash against the island, which rises to a height of 320 feet above sea level, and cut a fifty-foot-wide swath through the trees of its center. Then I saw it backlash against the eastern shore, sweeping away the timber to a height of more than 500 feet. Finally, I saw a fifty-foot wave come out of this churning turmoil and move along the eastern shore directly toward me."

As the fast-approaching disaster finally registered in Howard Ulrich's stunned mind, as he realized that he and his son were about to be crushed under tons of icy water, he sprang into action.

"First, I got a life jacket on Sonny. Then I started the engine and tried to pull the anchor. To my horror, it wouldn't budge. The wave was almost upon us and we were fastened to the bottom with a heavy chain. I let the chain run, then, all of it, to where the end was made solidly fast. Perhaps, I thought, we can ride up and over the wave while the anchor holds us from being swept away. It proved to be a vain hope. Using the engine and rudder, I headed the *Edrie* into the oncoming mountain of water and waited for the impact. Then the wave reached us. Heroically, the *Edrie* met the challenge. She lifted, rising up and up the face of the wave ... the chain snapped and a short end whipped back and wrapped around the pilothouse.

"As we were swept along by the wave, over what had recently been dry land and a timber-covered shore, I was sure that the end of the world had come for Sonny and me and our boat. I wanted my wife, back in Pelican, to know where and how her husband and her firstborn son had been lost, and I grabbed the handset of my radiophone and yelled into it: 'Mayday! Mayday! This is the *Edrie* in Lituya Bay. All hell has broken loose in here.' I faltered a bit then before I added, 'I think we've had it. Good-bye.' After what seemed an eternity but must have been only seconds the great wave, still carrying us with it, changed course again. It bounced off the eastern shore and started westward across the bay. The water was filled with icebergs of all sizes, tree trunks, and other debris, and even [though] the long twilight of an Alaska summer evening was fast fading, I managed, however, by using all the power of the *Edrie's* engine, to avoid the worst of the debris, get her under control, and pull her out of the wave before she could be swept to the west shore."

What had struck Lituya Bay was an earthquake of epic proportions, registering eight on the Richter scale, its epicenter just south, a few miles out in the Gulf off Cape Spencer. The quake hit all along the Fairweather Fault that runs through the high mountains and glaciers at the head of the bay. Boats at sea were struck by violent tsunami waves that shook them down to their keel timbers, shook them as if they were flimsy detritus, not stout fishing vessels. The VHF radio sets aboard all the boats came wildly to life as frantic pandemonium, voices tense with fear, filled the airwaves. Finally, a semblance of order was restored, and the boats began to call out their names and positions. Soon all were accounted for—all but two, the *Badger* and the *Sunmore*.

Bill Swanson on the *Badger* saw an entire glacier rise several hundred feet in the air, spewing great chunks of house-size ice as it shook in spasms of geologic rage. After what seemed an interminable period, the violence stopped as abruptly as it had begun. The glacier, risen from its resting place of thousands of years, plummeted back to earth, its splash spewing forth a fifty-foot wave that quickly inundated a point of land six miles away then aimed straight for the anchored *Badger*. The Swansons, helpless and dressed in their nightclothes, could do nothing but hold on. The giant wave lifted the little boat to its crest and swept it across the bay, over the top of standing spruce trees, up and over La Chaussee Spit, and into the Gulf of Alaska. There she landed and sank stern first, battered by trees swept along in the wave. The Swansons somehow managed to climb into a tiny skiff in time to watch their beloved boat with all their possessions sink into the black sea.

Bill Swanson reported that just before the wave hit he turned and saw the *Sunmore* making for the entrance under full power and dragging her anchor. The boat and her owners, Orville and Micky Wagner, were never seen again. Up the coast at Yakutat Bay, three more people died when the south end of the island they had been picnicking on suddenly rose into the air, dropped back into the ocean, and sank amid deadly waves.

Aboard the *Edrie*, Howard Ulrich and Sonny were astounded they were still alive and afloat. In the dark of night, they were in a wide field of crushing icebergs, some larger than the boat, and rafts of wave-mown timber shorn of bark. Howard knew they had to get out of the bay if they were to survive, but this meant running an entrance that would be clogged with icebergs and debris, that might be filled with its own seabed disjointed by the earthquake and risen from the deep. Worse, the tide was ebbing. His choice was to leave the bay through the ebb tide or be crushed among the icebergs; he chose to run the chopper. The *Edrie* forged ahead into a line of seething breakers surrounded by the night, and almost immediately her bow buried completely. Water crashing over the wheelhouse, the little boat shuddered to a halt, her motor groaning against the strain of trying to plow through the seas that would engulf them. As smothering water cascaded off her decks, she broke free, fought through two more breakers, and at last reached open ocean, which this night was, ironically for Howard and Sonny Ulrich, a place of safety.

The earthquake at Lituya Bay ranks up there with the truly big ones, but that day will forever be remembered as the day that saw the greatest tsunami in recorded history. The wave stripped timber and earth and every living thing from the faces of its enclosing mountains and polished the rock clean to a height of 1,720 feet! Later, geologic studies concluded that when the Fairweather Fault shifted, it sparked not just the otherworldly uplift and displacement of mountains and glaciers that Howard Ulrich saw but a gargantuan rockslide to a depth of 300 feet, 2,300 feet wide, and 3,000 feet long, starting from an elevation several thousand feet above the bay. The slide dropped into the head of the bay forty million cubic yards weighing ninety million tons and sent the terrible wave racing across the water at 100 miles an hour, the wave that terrorized the Ulrichs and Swansons and killed the Wagners. Geologists say the same fault line *will*, not may, shift again and the results will be the same. It could all happen again at any time.

According to the *Coast Pilot*, "... giant waves are a recurring phenomenon in the bay, and other catastrophic waves were observed in 1853, 1874, 1936, and 1958. Steep shattered cliffs at the head of the bay [the work of the Fairweather Fault] present a continuing hazard of avalanches; destructive waves caused by rockfalls, can occur at any time."

~~~

A curious flaw of human nature compels some otherwise sensible people to accept with complete indifference the mortal yet avoidable risks they well know surround them. I have flaws, to be sure, but this is not one of them. I take seriously the *Coast Pilot's* warnings and avoid spending too much time in Lituya Bay.

After entering the bay on a flooding tide and exploring its shores for a few hours, I leave in a froth of beerfoamlike white spindrift blown shoreward from offshore breakers still visible in the fading light. Pressing onward toward Cape Spencer, I pass along yet another shore of breathtaking beauty. Just behind the foreshore are more snow sheathed mountains of the Fairweather Range standing side by side like a picket fence guarding the land and separating the Gulf from Glacier Bay just to their east. After Mount Fairweather, the fourth highest peak in North America at 15,300 feet, come Mounts Quincy Adams (13,560 feet), Salisbury (12,170 feet), Lituya (11,924 feet), Wilbur (10,820 feet), Orville (10,495 feet), Crillion (12,700 feet), Dagelet (9,550 feet), and at last nearing the end of the chain, lying just east of Icy Point, La Perouse (10,756 feet).

Just in front of Mount La Perouse, right on the beach, is a glacier of the same name, an enormous wall of solid ice 300-feet high and four miles across its face, one of the world's largest coastal glaciers. In tiny *Rascal*, I motor warily not more than fifty yards from its seaward face towered over by this massive wall of ice. Ragged and pockmarked from the shards it has calved these summer months, it reflects opalescent colors in the pale light of approaching night.

At last I arrive at the 1,800-foot high headland of Cape Spencer after four grim hours of being battered by wind-tossed sea only to discover that I've timed the arrival badly. The tide is ebbing hard out of the mouth of Cross Sound, around the rocky point of Cape Spencer, and into the face of the southwest seas. In my eagerness to escape the Gulf, I've followed a course too close to shore, rather than swinging wide four or five miles off the cape, and now find myself caught in a maelstrom of cresting waves, the rinse and spin cycle of nature's washing machine.

For the moment, the wind-driven ocean swells from the sea overpower the ebbing tide, and the waves, though towering, crest toward the sound, trapping me in a following sea. It's too dangerous to turn back, a tricky maneuver among steep waves, so I press ahead, easing the trim tabs to let the bow rise and keeping the boat square so it isn't flipped by cross waves or slewed off course to a broach. The unexpected thrill ride is over in twenty minutes as *Rascal* emerges from the turmoil onto a slick sheet of tide-boiling water. The Dangerous Coast is at last behind.

Rascal tied up to the Cygnet in Icy Bay, Alaska.
Million Dollar Bridge over the Copper River near Cordova, Alaska.

Childs Glacier, Cordova, Alaska.

The author in Controller Bay off the Gulf of Alaska.
Chugach Range, Prince William Sound, Alaska.

Yakutat Bay at twilight.
Yakutat Bay, Alaska.

Yakutat Bay, Alaska.
Yakutat Bay harbor.

The author at Hubbard Glacier.
Geoff Widdows at Hubbard Glacier.

Hubbard Glacier, Yakutat Bay, Alaska.

Disenchantment Bay, Alaska.

Lituya Bay, Alaska.
Cape Spencer, Gulf of Alaska.

Cape Spencer, Gulf of Alaska.

La Perouse Glacier, Gulf of Alaska.
Astrolabe Rock, Gulf of Alaska near Cape Spencer.

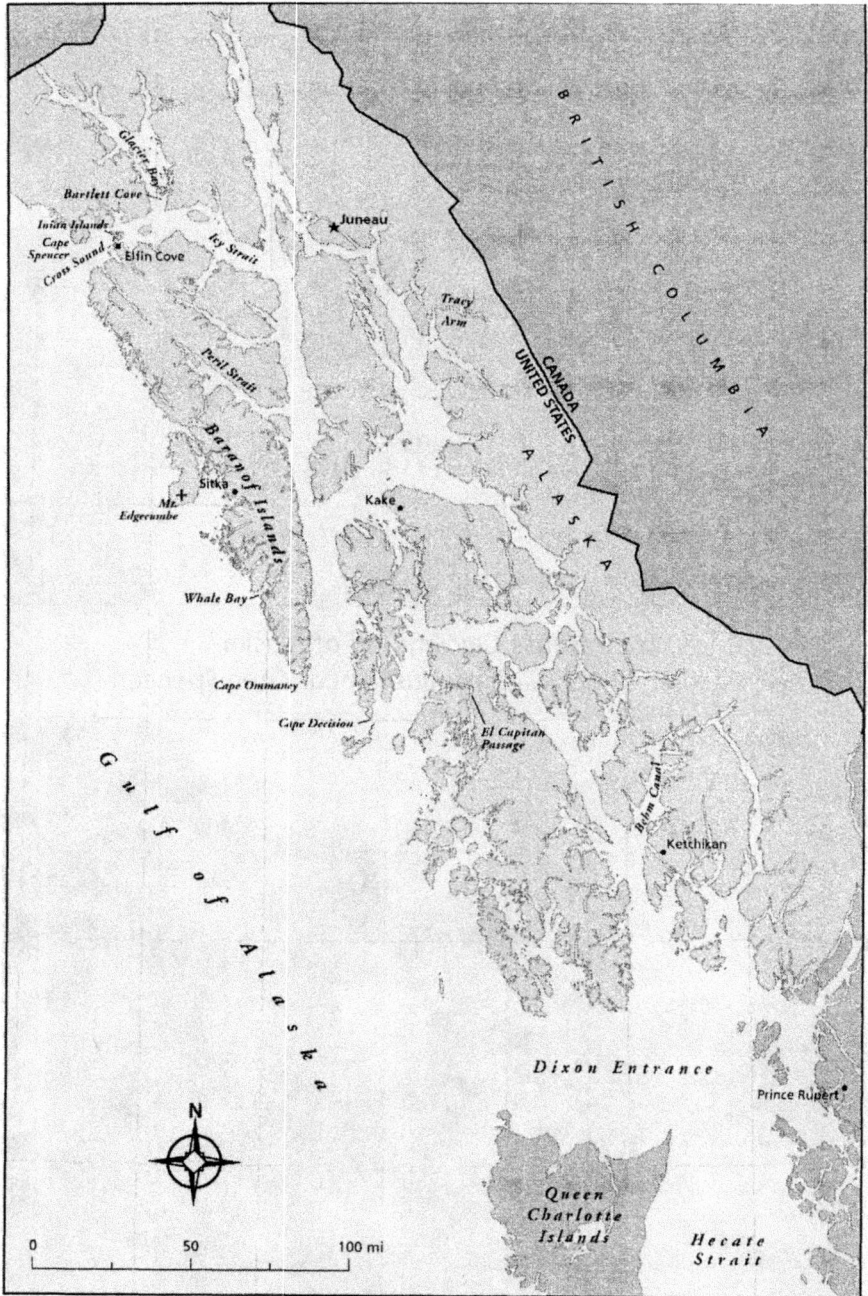

Chapter Six

The more contact people actually
have with nature, the less likely they are
to "appreciate" it in a big, mushy
ecumenical way. And the more likely
they are to get chiggers.
                                   - P. J. O'Rourke

ITS NORTHERNMOST POINT lies on the shore of the small Alaskan town of Skagway or perhaps at the end of the Tarr Inlet in Glacier Bay at about the same latitude. From either place, the Inside Passage proceeds in a generally southeasterly direction through Southeast Alaska and coastal British Columbia to its southern terminus in Washington state's Puget Sound. A thousand miles long, the Inside Passage is a labyrinth of tidal bays, inlets, canals, rivers, fjords, sounds, and straits that, depicted on nautical charts, resembles the wild profusion of splotches and splashes on a house painter's drop cloth. One stretch, four hundred miles long and a hundred wide, is crowded with nearly a thousand islands, ranging from backyard-size chunks of land to several larger than Delaware. The islands are a chaotic jumble of mountainous granite, some fully clothed in dense forest, others thinly clad in patches of verdure, while a few are solitary slabs of rock that rise from the sea bare as the day they were formed.

Mostly protected from the tempestuous Gulf of Alaska, the Inside Passage offers the world's most extensive waterway with channels so deep that giant cruise ships, and on occasion U.S. and Canadian warships, ply its tortuous waters. Cape Spencer, the Gulf-front promontory I now pass, marks the entrance into Cross Sound and is the northernmost of the few entries from the Gulf into the Inside Passage's quieter waters.

Elfin Cove, a miniature clapboard village hidden among the rocks in a tiny cove—thus the name—lies just east of Cape Spencer. The community's quaint doll house buildings, spread along narrow boardwalks, attach precariously to the mountainous faces of the shores that enclose the cove. It's the first place I've encountered in Alaska that could be called, without too much exaggeration, reasonably attractive. Its excellent harbor is bounded by sheer cliffs covered in dark, drooping spruce trees that when not catching rain from above are dripping it to the ground below. The village caters mostly to sport fishermen staying at one or another of its lodges and to cruising boaters as well as passengers on the few small tour boats that stop here.

After refueling under a glorious sky, I travel a few miles to North Inian Pass and there visit briefly a fetid colony of Steller's sea lions. Its resident stud muffin, who closely resembles Jabba the Hutt, roars at me ferociously, seeming certain that I plan to make off with one of his harem. Fifteen miles away is the opening in the shoreline that is the entrance into Glacier Bay National Park. When Captain George Vancouver passed by here in 1792, what is now the bay was then a massive field of ice, a confluence of many glaciers cascading down from the Fairweather Mountain Range. Just eighty-seven years later, the glaciers had retreated to reveal the magnificent bays and fjords that John Muir discovered for the Euro-American world.

After checking in with the U.S. Park Service office, I cruise up the bay's east arm, past feeding humpback whales and more colonies of sea lions. The shimmering water is surrounded by massive snow-dabbed cliffs and magnificent contortions of granite, and peppered with spruce-covered islets. I travel in search of the sailboat Surprise, whose owner, a friend of a friend, I'm scheduled to meet by prior arrangement. Locating Surprise coming out of one of the fjords off the east arm, I agree with its captain to meet at Sandy Cove, where we'll anchor for the night. Rascal gets there in half an hour. Surprise in three, just at twilight, as a humpback feeds noisily along the shore a stone's throw away. I raft up and join the captain and his wife and guests for a fine meal and a genial evening.

~~~

Early the next morning I'm off again, after watching a pair of moose and two bear cubs search for their breakfast along the shore of the quiet cove shimmering in early light. Arriving at park headquarters in Bartlett Cove at mid-morning, I refuel, but not without an incident that requires elaboration.

In the not too distant past, when state laws, or court opinions interpreting those laws, wrote of the "abominable and detestable crime against nature," it was universally understood to be a sanitized reference to a particular sexual practice then thought to be a perversion. Today, the locution seems merely quaint, since most of what were once thought to be perversions are now just "lifestyle" choices.

In another context, however, the words are accurately descriptive of the currently fashionable righteous indignation, with overtones of religious fanaticism, surrounding the new perversion: pollution. This would be just a minor irritant to more rational people—one easily dismissed with a chuckle—were it not for the unfortunate fact that some pollution is now a crime—a crime, as in *felony*, time in the slammer, the same charge made against serial killers, rapists, and child molesters. It's no less a crime when the act of pollution—the "crime against nature"—is inadvertent. Human error, which all of us encounter every day of our lives—Murphy's Laws come to mind, along with acronyms like snafu and fubar—is not a defense to an act of pollution in waters of a national park. It may lessen the penalty, but the act remains criminal. In keeping with the quasi-religious fanaticism on which the laws are founded, *any* pollution, no matter how slight, constitutes an illegal act. Thus a thimbleful of motor oil is as morally contemptible—not to mention criminal—as a tankerful; less messy for sure, but no less felonious. Birds, bears, moose, whales, fish, seals, sea lions, all are free to foul the water, and the more of them that show up to do so, the better. It is cause for celebration. But let one human pee in the water or, God forbid, accidentally spill a drop of

motor oil, and jail time and a fine may be the result. It is into this sur-
real legal world that I inadvertently gain admission during the stop at
park headquarters in Bartlett Cove.

The refueling of an outboard powered boat offers two opportunities for criminal mischief. First is the process of filling the gas tank.
As gas displaces air in the tank and its filler neck, the air escapes
through a tiny vent on the boat's exterior surface. All such boats have
these vents; they're required by law (what else?). When the gas level
reaches nearly full, the escaping air becomes mixed with gas and
sprays out the vent in modest quantities, usually not more than a few
ounces. When this overspray, which simply runs down the side of the
boat or is washed off with fresh water, hits the sea in a national park,
a crime occurs. It's of no consequence that the quantity is miniscule
or that it's mixed with sea water flushed twice daily by the tides or,
as I have noted, that it is the result of inadvertence. It's still a crime
with all the potential consequences of that label. All along the west
coast, I encountered people whom the Coast Guard had threatened
with severe legal consequences, like the closure of their marina or the
confiscation of their boat or jail time, because they were claimed to
have fouled the sea from this or a similar source.

The second opportunity for criminality occurs when the oil tanks
are filled. On *Rascal*, this is done from filler necks located on top of
the transom. Oil is poured into the necks slowly. Pour too fast and
displaced air will prevent the oil from settling in the tank, and the oil
will back up in the neck and bubble over the transom. It was down
this avenue that I traveled toward a life of crime.

While tied up to the fuel dock in Bartlett Cove near the Glacier Bay
Park Ranger Station, I am filling the oil tanks when, briefly distracted, I
allow a small quantity of oil to overflow onto the transom, some even
seeping into the splash well where the motors are mounted. Without
giving much thought to criminal consequences, as say a bank robber
might, I grab a small bucket, scoop up a few gallons of sea water,
and splash it against the oil stains. The resulting runoff, containing
all of a half teaspoon of oil, runs down the transom into the splash

well and, in a fateful moment, out a drain hole into, of all places, the pristine waters of the sacrosanct Glacier Bay. If there is a mortal sin in the catechism of environmentalism, this is surely it. I have peed in the Holy Font.

From the mouth of the fuel dock attendant, an overly earnest and of course environmentally hypersensitive young college student on a summer job, comes a horrified gasp, the same gasp one might expect from a witness to a grisly chainsaw murder, so heinous is my offense. I have spilled a pollutant, not just into any old water but—gasp!—into the waters of Glacier Bay. It's as though I had robbed not just a bank but the entire Federal Reserve System and had done so in plain view of the cops, or at least one of their functionaries. I think to myself that this would be a fun time to announce, in jocular tone of course, that I've come to evaluate the area as a site for glittering condo towers, a spiffy Wal-Mart, and a really swell Disneyesque amusement park, but as I can't detect a sense of humor in the attendant, I think the better of it and keep quiet.

Promptly following the man's audible gasp, as if on cue, the offending pollutant bursts forth across the surface of Bartlett Cove in a flamboyant sheen, a kaleidoscope of hydrocarbon rainbow colors broadcasting to the world the true scope of my crime against nature. The attendant's face turns back to me, contorted into a grimace of moral repugnance mixed with the haughty disdain with which the self-righteous regard the sinner, a modern Torquemada glowering at a heretic. Thankfully, he doesn't have the authority to lock me up or I might be writing this from the Glacier Bay jail.

After paying the man, a commercial ceremony noticeably lacking the usual "have a nice day" or "thanks, come again" pleasantries, I head out of the now sullied bay bound for Juneau. At once, the VHF comes to life with a raspy, crackling chatter that I can't make out likely due to more of the antenna problems I had earlier experienced. All I can make out of the static jumble are the words "Ranger" and "*Rascal*," nothing more, so I reply that I can't understand the transmission, but will call tomorrow by phone. Something tells me this may have to do with my crime against nature, but frankly I'm in no mood to deal with tiresome petulance, so I continue on my way, thus becoming a fleeing desperado.

At this moment, my Voice of Conscience appears and says, fully in the spirit of the moment, "Let's get the hell outta here, like rapido, dude. Pedal to the metal, baby! Those crypto-Nazis back there catch you it's firing squad time and you'll be on the wrong end of the bullets."

"But it was a harmless accident involving a thimbleful of oil. That can't be a crime. It was unintentional," I protest naively.

"Don't matter to the Greenies. You are to the eco-whackos what Al Capone was to the Christian Temperance Union, and you know how fun-loving and forgiving those sober-obsessed pests were. Time to haul ass."

After a brief visit to Juneau for minor supplies, unknowingly just one step ahead of the law, I travel in fine weather and calm winds to the magnificent Tracy Arm Fjord with its sheer cliffs rising from a narrow canyon carved by an ancient glacier. Then it's south, down Stephens Passage over waters grown increasingly choppy from the afternoon winds. As the day fades to twilight, I pull into the harbor of the Tlinkit Indian village of Kake for the night.

First thing in the morning, I call the Park Ranger's office at Glacier Bay to ask what the jumbled VHF call was about, and I'm told, not to my surprise, that I was being summoned back to the fuel dock concerning the "oil spill." When I failed to return, the man said charmlessly, he went to Juneau by official launch in search of me, the scofflaw.

Promptly a visual image leapt to mind. A posse of armed and crisply uniformed Environmental Enforcers aboard a government gunboat speeds across the water toward Juneau. Their mission: Find, arrest, and bring to justice a notorious member of the Dark Side thought to have committed a heinous crime against nature. Images come to mind, too, of moonshiners fleeing the revenuers, Bonnie and Clyde evading the FBI, and Butch Cassidy and the Sundance Kid chased by Pinkerton men, not to mention Al Capone dogged by Elliot Ness.

My pursuer seems certain I had intentionally evaded his search, but he is thankful, for my sake, that I have called just as I said I would. This fact would allow him to be more lenient, he says. My temper begins warming to the occasion.

Exercising some discretion, I tell the man calmly what I think of a law that designates a person as criminal, with all the potential consequences of that label, when he has done nothing more than accidentally spill a half teaspoon of oil in the water. I also tell him that unburned hydrocarbons spewing legally from the exhausts of *Rascal's* motors soil both the air and water far greater than my peccadillo. "The law is the law," he responds.

I don't tell him—because at the time I have not yet learned it—that near Santa Barbara, California, a submarine fault in the earth's crust oozes daily hundreds of gallons of raw crude oil into the Pacific, where many square miles of it sit on the surface as fetid sludge. "To whom would you issue a citation?" I would have asked, "God?" Nor do I ask why birds, bears, whales, fish, seals, and sea lions can freely defecate and urinate and thus pollute the water, while humans are forbidden to do so. Are we second class citizens in the animal world and, to use a currently popular whine, the victims of discrimination?

When the sensible goal of improving the quality of the world around us becomes not rational policy but quasi-religious fanaticism marked by rigid intolerance, an offense against the policy takes on the trappings of a sin against the new god. Zealotry, whether religious or environmental, knows no limits.

[Author's note: The result of all this was that I was issued a federal summons to appear in U.S. District Court in Juneau on charges of polluting the waters of Glacier Bay and violating Alaskan pollution laws for which I would need costly legal representation. I would also have to make a 10,000 mile round trip to Juneau. In lieu of contesting the charge, I could pay a fine of $200 and thus avoid potentially more severe penalties, including up to six months in stir. As I wrote the check, a paraphrase of a maxim from Benjamin Franklin leapt to mind: Those who would give up some of their freedom to obtain security are destined to have neither. I am not at all proud of paying the fine, ashamed even at my capitulation, but I paid because under the law I had no defense.]

~~~

While waiting for the tribal-owned fuel dock to open, I walk to a nearby restaurant for breakfast, open its door, and step inside. A loud, friendly voice calls out, "Hi, what are you doing in Kake? Sit down." This is how I come to meet the gregarious and instantly like-able Paul Martin, owner of the restaurant and a lifelong resident of Kake, though not an Indian.

Along the shore of Kake's harbor, when the tide ebbs, a long, wide swath of beach is exposed. At one place just down the road from Paul Martin's restaurant, a particularly broad stretch of beach reveals itself, strewn with kelp, clams, rocks, and assorted debris. If you look carefully at the beach, you'll see in the distance a piece of steel rebar protruding ten feet into the air with a triangular red flag attached at its top. Exactly twenty-five yards to its left is another ten-foot high rebar, and exactly sixty-five yards to its left is a third. To the casual observer, these would seem to be just crude, randomly spaced channel markers, but not so. Each day when the beach is exposed and Paul Martin can escape from his duties, he can be found exactly 150 yards to the right of the flag-topped rebar, posted astride a sheet of plywood to which is affixed a sheet of green artificial turf. He's stand-ing there hitting golf balls at the 150-, 175- and 240-yard rebar yardage markers on his ersatz driving range. His yellow and red golf balls are easy to find among the kelp and rocks and clams.

The people of Kake like the easily likable Paul Martin, and most regard his unusual hobby with bemused indifference. Some think he's moderately eccentric, and a few are sure he's quite mad. If a court hearing were held to determine Paul Martin's sanity, the evidence would show that for years Paul has vowed never to spend another winter in Alaska and that each fall he and his family move to Palm Springs, California, for warmth, and of course lots of golf. Paul's makeshift driving range is just the place where he prepares for the winter. Case dismissed. Paul isn't nuts, he's smart.

~~~

I leave Kake in the early afternoon and once again face windblown chop on the way to Sitka under now black, rain-blurred skies. Fifteen miles out, gas spews over the stern deck from a torn seam in one of the two remaining bladders and runs into the bilge. In these bumpy waters, I can do nothing about it except slow the leak by taping the hole. In the calmer waters of a protected cove, I transfer gas from the bladder into the main fuel tank, using a three-gallon plastic bucket, add water to the bladder to dilute the residue, thoroughly wash down the deck, flood the bilge, then pump it out to remove the fire hazard. That makes three of the four new fuel bladders that have proved defective so, in hindsight, I was prudent not to rely on these in running the Cordova-to-Yakutat leg, and I'll certainly not rely on the one remaining.

By now the weather has degenerated into thick, cold mist hanging low over the water, making it difficult to locate the channel markers through the treacherous waterways leading to Sitka. Luckily, I overtake a sixty-foot power catamaran, the St. Eugene, making thirty knots and winding through the channel as if the man at the helm has done it all before. After calling him on the radio to be sure he's headed for Sitka, I tag along in his wake until he leads me an hour later into the harbor.

~~~

Since rounding Cape Spencer and entering the Inside Passage, the coastal towns have become remarkably different from those in other parts of Alaska I've visited. Homer and Seward, and certainly Whittier and Cordova, and the little village of Yakutat, are organized around their principal industry, fishing, mostly commercial but some sport too. Tourism exists here, but it's not a major part of the economy. Fishing in some years is good, but most years, like this one, it's not. Strict regulations severely limit the time periods, or openers, when fish may be caught and thus the quantity taken. Meanwhile, the costly boat and gear, not to mention the fishermen, sit idle, a terribly inefficient use of capital and labor, the result almost entirely of government policy. The locals are faced with, of course, severe competition from other salmon fisheries, including the productive Bristol Bay region of the Bering Sea, Kodiak Island, and elsewhere. Thousands of gill net, seine net, and trailer boats ply Alaska's coastal waters in search of a day's catch.

To make matters worse, farm-raised salmon, mostly from foreign countries, are taking an increasing share of the world market and are cheap to produce. They are a predictable, reliable source of supply year-round, not subject to severe seasonal variation or regulatory restrictions on the catch. Prices, as a result, are under constant downward pressure, and the fishing towns and villages show it. They are functional, unadorned working towns, slapdash places, not dilapidated yet but not handsome either.

By contrast, some of the towns of the Inside Passage, including the village of Elfin Cove, the towns of Juneau, Sitka, and Ketchikan, though still essentially devoted to fishing and logging, get a substantial tourist trade. Since they can't be reached by vehicle, the visitors arrive by sea on enormous cruise ships, state run ferries, or on yachts, and by air. Tourists spend their money in shops, restaurants, and bars, and on hotel rooms and rental cars. Some rent cottages for a time in the summer, and a few buy second homes here. They use flight-seeing and local tour services, rent kayaks, and hire outfitters for fishing and hunting expeditions. Competition ensues among providers of these goods and services with the result that the consumer gets a wide range of choices of price and quality. The towns, in short, become better places to live, and their residents earn more money and enjoy a higher standard of living than places without so much tourism. It shows, even to the casual observer like me.

~~~

Brown bears are numerous throughout most of Alaska; indeed, the state has the world's highest concentration of bears of all types. But the critters are especially populous on the Alaskan islands of the Inside

Passage. Those found along Alaska's coasts are the world's largest car-nivorous mammals, growing up to 1,400 pounds and eleven feet tall. Brown bears living in an inland habitat are commonly called grizzlies, while those in coastal areas are called, simply enough, brown bears. The enormous browns found on Kodiak Island have been genetically isolated for so long they are now classified as a distinct subspecies. With so many bears wandering around Alaska, it's no wonder, but still disturbing, that attacks on humans occur with some frequency. Most involve a hapless soul who stumbles upon a cub with a mother nearby who perceives a threat to her offspring. Potential disaster lurks in such chance encounters, as Mark Matheny and Fred Bahnson discovered the hard way.

It was a brisk September morning when Matheny and his companion, Bahnson, set out on the trail bowhunting for deer. Conditions were near perfect and so was their luck. Right off, they downed a four-point deer, field dressed it, and hung the carcass from a tree with the intention of returning the next day to claim it. They pressed on down a wooded trail single file with Matheny twenty yards in the lead. As he walked over a low rise, Matheny spotted something moving in the trees to his left. That something was the bizarre sight of two brown furry balls the size of large dogs flying through the air thir-ty-five yards away—and that's when it hit him. They were bear cubs that had been nursing at their mother while she lay on her back. When she sensed his presence, the sow jumped to her feet, tossing the cubs in the air. Matheny knew right away he was in serious trouble.

Without a moment's hesitation, the huge grizzly charged, racing straight for Matheny at lightning speed. "I remember seeing those little black, beady eyes," Matheny said. "And the anger—like an aura around her." He spun around, searching desperately for a tree to climb, then ran toward Bahnson yell-ing, "It's a bear, get your spray." Weeks before this hunting trip, Bahnson had bought a canister of Karate in a Can, a pepper spray for use against human muggers that he thought might prove useful against bears. Matheny had planned to buy some himself but, as he later said, "I just never got around to it."

If a waving red flag incites a bull to charge, a fleeing human positively enrages an already angry bear to do the same. "A total mistake," he later admitted. "It doesn't work. You can't outrun them. They're like missiles homing in on their targets." Bahnson saw the toothy freight train charging at them and dove off the trail. Matheny got behind a nearby log, turned around, and there she was just a few feet away. "I couldn't help thinking what a beautiful, magnificent animal—silvertip, healthy, maybe 400 pounds. But that thought was quickly replaced by fear."

In a vain attempt to discourage the bear, Matheny stabbed at her with his bow. "She whacked the bow out of my hands with one paw and leapt over the log. It all happened so fast. Next thing I know, I'm just seeing teeth and trying to jump out of the way." It didn't work though. The bear sprang at him with jaws agape and bit him on the face and neck." I could feel my face ripping," he said. She then flattened him, her full weight pressing him into the fresh snow and moist earth, teeth gnawing into his skull.

"She's got my head, she's killing me!" The sound of Matheny screaming in terror only caused the sow to attack even more aggressively. And that's when he realized, 'I've got to play dead or I'm gonna be dead.' It was at this terrible moment, the worst of his life, that Matheny had an epiphany. "When she put the head bite on me, I felt the power she had to kill me. Time just stopped then. I remember thinking, 'My time on earth is done. I'm going to miss my wife and kids. Now I'm going to meet my creator.'"

Not just yet. With pepper spray in hand, Bahnson charged

at the bear, screaming like the mad man he had become at that moment, trying to save his friend. Not frightened in the least, only distracted, the bear let go of Matheny and charged this new threat to her and her cubs, knocking Bahnson to the ground as he shot her in the face with a blast from the pepper spray. As Bahnson fell, Matheny "started squirming away like a mouse, as fast as I could. That got the bear off Fred. She turned back to me. I saw her coming, so I covered my head with my arms. Then, whoom! She pounced on me like a cat on a mouse. I remember the weight of her, the incredible pressure against the ground. She started ripping at my arm, shaking it violently. I thought she was going to rip it off. I didn't feel any pain. It all happened too fast."

The bear, who had earlier been feeding on the fetid carcass of an elk, stank of offal and death. "Like rotting, decaying flesh," as Matheny described it. He made himself lie still, feigning a carcass himself as the bear smacked him. Returning now to Bahnson, the great beast charged headlong, aiming to destroy the last threat to her children's safety. Bahnson hit the bear full in the face with the last puff of aerosol irritant, and that was the end of the attack. The sow and her cubs ran off into the dark woods, she coughing and snorting as they fled, leaving a badly maimed and profusely bleeding Mark Matheny lying on the ground.

Bahnson, a physician, assessed the wounds and assured Matheny he would not die. The bear had ripped open the entire left side of Matheny's face, his cheek dangled from the little skin that still secured it to his head, the jaw muscle was torn from the jawbone, and the salivary gland and larynx were sliced through. The bone at the eyebrow was punctured between the brow and the eyeball, as was the top of the skull. Another bite, the one that nearly killed him, got to within a hair of his jugular vein. When they finally made it to the hospital, repair required more than fifteen inches of stitches. Matheny's arm, though severely bruised and sore for weeks, was not broken. The constant headaches would last two years. Bahnson's wounds were less severe in part because of the heavy coat he had worn. He was bruised and his skin abraded, and he had some separated ribs.

For Mark Matheny, the encounter proved to be a life-altering experience. At first, "All I could think about was bears and bear stuff. I needed to make my peace with it." He returned to the outdoors he had always loved so much and began to heal. Then, by way of a call from a pepper spray manufacturer, Matheny became "obsessed with the subject of pepper spray as a bear deterrent." In the very best tradition of American entrepreneurs, he ultimately developed his own improvements for the product and launched a new company to make and sell the spray, a company with the ungainly name of Universal Defense Alternative Products that today successfully sells its Pepper Power brand of bear deterrent. Matheny now happily travels the country educating people about the potential for bear attacks and how to ward them off.

~~~

We may be at first uncomprehending of the sow's vicious attack on Matheny and Bahnson. Were the cubs really threatened? Was it necessary to gnaw away at a man's face while he was pinned helplessly? Might a scare have been enough? As humans, we are quick to ask such questions and to judge harshly. But Roger A. Caras, in *Monarch of Deadman Bay: The Life and Death of a Kodiak Bear,* reminds us that we should be reluctant to judge cruelty in nature. Here, in an excerpt, he tells us about a sow Kodiak and her two cubs confronting another sow and her four cubs.

One afternoon as the family was edging down through a clearing between two rings of stunted alders that girded a hill, the sow stopped short and rose to her hind legs. The movement was smooth and effortless. Straining against the inadequacy of her vision she moved her head from side to side. The cubs came tumbling up against her legs and began to frolic. She issued three rapid, harsh commands and in a comic imitation of their mother they attempted to rise up to see what had caught mom's attention. The longer she held the position, the more nervous the cubs became. They sank to all fours and moved in close against her legs. The female cub began to whine, and again the sow grunted peremptorily. She was listening to the winds and sampling their chemistry. She sensed another bear in the vicinity—and it was close by.

On the lower portion of the slope, another sow stood among the alders and stared myopically up to where the bronze female towered. Victim of a natural anomaly, this bear had *four* cubs huddled by her legs. This extremely rare occurrence does happen from time to time and the sows involved are generally all but overwhelmed by the responsibility. With so much more to do, with so much more to worry about, their whole attitude is one of profound bewilderment.

A small current of moving air that had begun at sea and picked its way across seaweed-covered rocks, through patches of brush and trees, was working up the slope to the worried mother of four. The energy behind the breeze was reinforced by other currents from over the surface of the water and the wind flowed and rippled across the clearing. It passed the sow in the alders, snatched away her secret and eddied past the female on the slope peering down, alert but uninformed. Instantly, the bronze sow located the intruder in the valley. Her sudden head movement and grunt caused the stranger to move and to shift her position ever so slightly. The bronze sow was able to detect the movement and determine her visitor's shadowy outline. She gave a sharp bark and lumbered two steps forward on her hind legs before dropping to all fours, facing downhill. Her cubs were already on their way up to the ridge. They bawled in terror as they ran.

With front legs stiff, each step jarring her great frame, the sow hurried down the slope.

In the alder growth, the other female, too, had gone to all fours and, determining that her cubs were well concealed, started out into the open.

The two sows faced each other over a distance of a couple of dozen yards and circled slowly until they were on the same level. In a kind of displacement activity, as if to relieve the unbearable tension that had been mounting, the intruder stopped and pulled free a mouthful of grass. Jerking her head up she quartered away and stood with her head turned to the side, looking in the direction of her opponent with the grass drooping comically from the corner of her mouth. In an imitative movement the bronze sow did the same.

Then, without warning, after having given it all the thought of which she was capable, the bronze sow charged. She hurtled across the intervening yards and caught the intruder in the shoulder as she turned and half rose to bring her great forepaws into play. They slapped ineffectually as she was rolled over twice by the weight of the impact. Her reflexes had been a beat too slow and the blood flowed from an open wound where the sow had sunk her teeth.

The momentum of her charge carried the bronze sow well beyond her target and when she pulled up and whirled about to charge again she was struck by the intruder barreling down on top of her. She felt a terrible, stunning shock as a paw as large as a platter, with powerful claws spread wide and angry, descended with the full force of half a ton behind it. One of the bronze sow's cheeks was opened and her teeth showed through the wound. Again she charged, snapping furiously, but the intruder had already begun to retreat. She caught up with the darker female and managed to sink her teeth into her rump before she vanished into the brush. Her great body crashed through the growth with all the intensity and result-ing noise of a two-ton truck.

The sow patrolled the edge of the trees, coughing and grunting. She didn't dare enter the thicket with an opponent so aroused and one that had the benefit of cover. The air cur-rents between the trees could not be trusted and her eyesight would be all but useless.

The bronze sow's two cubs and the intruder's four had witnessed the battle huddled in two groups a hundred yards apart. They would have played together had they been allowed, for they were still endowed with a social sense that enabled them to tolerate their littermates. In time, they would lose this trusting innocence, though, and were learning a les-son for now that would stay with them as long as they lived.

Both females bedded down almost immediately after returning to their cubs. They were no more than a hundred and fifty yards apart in the two groups of alders that bounded the small clearing. Throughout the night they both remained awake, sniffing, listening for the sound of any movement. On several occasions each moved to the edge of the trees and stood facing the other, although neither could know for sure the opponent was there.

On the following morning the sows again each spotted her rival. They did not clash, although some short charges were made by both as gestures of threat. They drifted apart after a few minutes and did not see each other again for several hours, when once more they came within sensing distance of each other. Several defiant movements resulted, but, again, no direct conflict occurred.

On the morning of the third day, shortly after feeding her cubs their first meal of the morning, the bronze sow moved down to the edge of the trees. There, not more than a dozen feet away, the intruder grazed with her four cubs strung out behind her. The wind was blowing again from the sea and the scent and sound of the intruder carried clearly and unmistakably. The sow sank back on her haunches and sorted out the messages. With a wild roar, almost a scream, she burst from her cover. The four cubs scattered but one was too slow. Snatching it up with her great jaws she ended its life with a single snapping action, dropped its small body, and spun again to re-enter the woods where her own cubs were wailing.

Whether or not it was immediately clear to the intruder that she had lost her smallest cub we cannot know. Her remaining three were running and tumbling down the slope in abject terror. The charge of the great bronze sow out of the brush so close at hand has produced a stunning impact. Only their training enabled them to break away from the paralyzing effect of the attack and get away at all.

The intruder spun around, perhaps seeing the body of her cub lying limp and oozing blood, and crashed into the brush after her opponent. Roaring, wailing, grunting, and chopping her jaws, she smashed down brush, and, with a gesture of wild defiance clubbed a sapling an inch and a half thick to the ground with one sweep of her forepaw. Rising to her full height, her jaws still chopping in anger, the great sow circled slowly, worrying everything in her way. In her passage she destroyed the nests of three ground-nesting birds. The yellow yokes from a dozen shattered shells seeped out and the parent birds circled overhead, bemoaning their loss. Diminutive mammals of several species fled before the onslaught, and a mouse nest toppled, spilling its pink inhabitants to the ground. When the sow had passed, a weasel emerged and took the little bodies for a snack before the mother mouse could find them.

The furious charge of the intruder into the brush was to no avail. While the intruder beat her way through the bushes and between the trees, the bronze sow and her cubs vanished over the ridge above. They were close to a mile away by the time the intruder emerged grunting and coughing on the downslope side to sit wailing beside her dead cub. She left the valley that day and never returned.

As if her cruelly violent deed had reminded her of the danger that surrounded her own two cubs, the sow was unusually alert in the days that followed. She was even short-tempered with her charges and their obedience had to be ever more unquestioning to satisfy her. She cuffed them often and bit one on the flank hard enough to make it whimper for several minutes. Thoroughly cowed, it returned to her to be fed and found her forgiving.

The intruder that had come to the valley to lose her cub remained confused and miserable for days. She never quite realized that he was gone and grunted angrily several times when her commands brought only three cubs to her side. She would look for him and stand bawling when he did not appear.

The savage cruelty of this encounter cannot be overstated. Food was plentiful enough in the area for both families, and the females need not have fought. The killing of the cub was senseless and, indeed, an unthinking man might despise a species whose behavior is seemingly so cruel. Such a man should reflect on his own behavior, though, and think of cities bombed and the young of his own kind dead in their smashed beds and broken gardens to understand and forgive that which is savage in nature. Although such wanton killing is bewildering in any species, man and animal alike, at least among bears it can be accounted for. Bears are not equipped to feel pity and cannot reflect on agony they cause another. Bears know only how to survive. They instinctively destroy that which seems threatening to them and are extremely intolerant of any annoyance, however slight. They have no capacity for guilt. Man, who has that capacity, seems unable to act upon it. The most imaginative of living creatures, he is also the crudest, and he is in no position to judge another species harshly.

~~~

Inconveniently sited, Sitka is located, as befits an Alaskan coastal town, on a narrow apron of land at the base of a mountain on the west shore of Baranof Island, where it is shielded from the ever-threatening Gulf of Alaska by a maze of tiny offshore islands. To reach Sitka from the main waterways of the Inside Passage requires winding through a long series of straits, including the aptly named Peril Strait.

In most towns, the countryside can't be seen. It's out there beyond the last traffic light and shopping center, out where cows graze, corn grows, and snuff is dipped. Sitka is semi-encircled by neck-craning walls of countryside that blot out large parts of the sky and loom over daily life like a permanent thunder cloud. Its countryside is impossible not to see, making the town, by contrast, seem obscure and temporary.

Off to the northwest, just across the harbor, is the magnificent Mount Edgecumbe, a 3,201-foot volcano, the apparent twin of Japan's Mount Fuji. Edgecumbe doesn't seem sinister, but the knowledge that it has erupted in the recent past and is likely to do so again has a disquieting effect. Its innate malevolence is clothed in distracting beauty.

From Sitka on to Ketchikan, my next port of call, I must choose between two routes. One lies back through Peril Strait, traveling in reverse the same route that brought me here, and going miles out of the way but in calmer protected water. The other way to my destination is to run out in the Gulf along the western shore of Baranof Island. I've chosen the latter because it's new for me, is not commonly used by pleasure boats, and offers the prospect of adventure. So after a few days of lolling about town collecting mildew on my wardrobe, rum-dwelling toxins in my brain, and Pioneer Bar logo caps on my head, it's time to move on.

The National Weather Service issues constant daily updates from its Sitka office over VHF channel two. Its marine forecast for today says what's hand-slammed-in-the-car-door obvious when I arrive at the docks at 5:30 a.m., eager to get underway. A weak low pressure system has moved into the Gulf of Alaska just offshore from Sitka, bringing scattered rain—meaning it's unlikely to rain indoors—heavy clouds, and cold. Winds are southwest moving to southeast at fifteen to twenty knots and seas are five to six feet. Another day of awful weather is in store.

As I idle out of the harbor past a Coast Guard cutter, rows of seine net fishing boats, and a few yachts, the sky is a low rankle of dense cloud, the landscape a murky scouring pad gray. The entire natural world around me—air and land—drips, saturated beyond its capacity to hold water. Light misting rain forms droplets on the windscreen, blurring my vision. If I stand to one side, I get both a stiff breeze and rain full in the face. Though the temperature is in the mid-forties, the sodden air feels much colder. In fleece-lined storm hat with ear flaps secured, insulated rubber gloves, long johns, wool socks, rubber boots, wool sweater, wool pants, heavy jacket, and foul weather pants, I'm still cold, and I haven't even come up to speed yet. The harbor water is black, its surface flat and languid, rippled only by *Rascal's* small wake and the bigger wake of the *Sally Ann*, a sixty-foot seine netter headed to sea.

As I make my way with the help of the chart plotter, the channel turns to the southwest where seiners are working, and I encounter the first ocean swells, gentle undulations six feet from crest to trough with a period of six seconds between them. When I bring *Rascal* up to speed, the swells force the bow up then let it down abruptly, so I lower the trim tabs to smooth the ride. Exiting the seaward end of the buoyed channel, I change course to the southeast, running with the swells, and begin to weave among a maze of mist-shrouded offshore islands and rocky, spruce-covered crags. These, and the larger Kruzof Island nearby, shield me from the swells, and the sea becomes a laminar sheet. White mist and diaphanous clouds surround the coastal mountains, enveloping their upper half but leaving the lower half visible, weirdly truncated. Shorn of their higher reaches, the mountains look as if they're a ridge of mesas rising from black sea. Loose kelp and floating logs dot the ocean's surface.

Soon I'm out of the lee of the small islands, running several miles out in the open Gulf of Alaska. Swells, still gentle, quarter the stern on the starboard side. Wind that to now has been calm in the rain-drenched quiet of the early morning freshens to the forecasted fifteen to twenty knots and begins to shift direction. No longer blowing in concert with the swells, the gusts now oppose them, though at an oblique angle, and generate their own waves that collide with the ceaselessly billowing sea. A tempestuous brew is the result, following only a few minutes after I have been lulled by somnolent seas. This route is beginning to look like a poor choice.

~~~

A ship's motion while underway in a sea is described by marine engineers as the six degrees of freedom: pitch, roll, sway, heave, surge, and yaw. Two of these, sway and surge, are of little significance. A third, yaw, is controlled by rudder or, in the case of outboards, by the turning of the motors themselves. The remaining three, pitch, roll and heave, are of the most concern to the captain of a vessel. How a boat handles in a sea will depend on its hull design and the power driving it, the characteristics of the surrounding waves, the attitude of the hull with respect to wave direction, and its velocity over the water. Trim, influenced by speed, tilt of the motors, and trim tabs, also plays an important though lesser role.

Unlike steel ships or large motor yachts designed to plow through the water. *Rascal* is a small, cork-light boat designed to run at speed, skimming across the surface. At idle, she is fiberglass flotsam. While she runs at her usual thirty-five knots, the hull moves about in the critical three degrees of freedom, rolling beam to beam, pitching bow to stem, and heaving up and down on the waves. In any but the calmest waters, she'll exhibit at least one, and often two of these motions simultaneously. In turbulent seas she'll move on all three axes at the same time, constantly. When she reaches the limits of a move in one direction on one axis, always with a jarring halt, she snaps back in another direction on the same or a different axis, while simultaneously duplicating the series of motions on the other two.

This for the captain is something like wrestling Hulk Hogan on a trampoline. To tolerate it, the captain has to hold on to the welded aluminum grab bar conveniently located next to the helm for just that purpose and stay loose, letting his knees, midsection, shoulders, and neck move fluidly as the deck pitches wildly beneath him. If he fights it, he will tire quickly, grow even more tense, and be sore next morning.

If all the seas of the world were always flat, tooling around in a small boat would be much like driving a car down an interstate high-way. Smooth, quiet, uneventful—and painfully dull. Waves give the sea its character, its personality, its allure, and its fearful challenge. As the waves change—and they do so constantly, hour by hour—the sea's effect on a boat changes and so too the demands on her captain.

Waves are creatures of the wind. They grow from a sea that is—at an imaginary beginning—a gleaming, flat membrane stretched over a vast expanse. With the first gentle breaths, the surface is ruffled ever so slightly. These little imperfections begin to perturb the flow of air as it continues to waft over the water. Now a pressure differential develops between the low pressure on the wavelet's steep leading or leeward face and the higher pressure on its more gently sloped wind-ward side. This differential causes the wave to lift from the surface and climb above it, much as a wing provides lift on an airplane. As the wave grows, the wind has a still greater surface to blow against, so the wave grows still more. Its air pressure differential increases, and it grows yet again. This continuous symbiosis between air and water changes calm seas to a light chop, then to white caps, to rough seas, and finally, in severe storm conditions, to terrifying towers of energy known to reach one hundred feet high.

The effect of wind blowing over water is magnified when the water itself is moving in opposition, as in the case of tide ebbing from an inlet. When these two implacable forces collide, waves get higher as well as much steeper. Wave height is also affected by the distance of open water over which the wind blows, called fetch. The greater the fetch, the longer time the wind has to disturb the water and the higher and steeper are the waves. Shallow depth also affects waves by compressing and driving them up. Waves rolling into shore from far out at sea pile up on coastal shoals, crest, and break.

Along the Pacific Coast, swells are common. These long, usually harmless, slow moving blobs of water have nearly the same slope on their leading and trailing surfaces. Generated by storms as far away as Japan, they roll unobstructed across the Pacific depths, gradually losing height and power, the dying remnants of once great waves. It is the swells whose period is reported in marine weather forecasts. Waves, in these same forecasts, mean wind-driven waves kicked up by local weather systems. A weather report, broadcast over one of the VHF channels dedicated to such matters, may say "Swells are ten feet with a period of twenty seconds. Waves are three to four feet." Though it sounds pernicious, a ten-foot swell spaced twenty seconds apart is just a big rolling teddy bear of a wave. In a fast boat like *Rascal*, swells are fun, like marine roller coasters. Wind-driven waves, though, are angular and closely spaced and are the bumps and wrinkles that disrupt a small boat and jangle its captain's nerves.

Sometimes, but rarely, swells and waves are both going in the same direction, a state of relative harmony at sea. The confluence of the two at least unifies and coordinates nature's attacks on a hull. And when these two forces are directly opposed, a rare condition, they will tend to cancel each other out. The wind will reduce the swell, and the swell will diminish the waves, so that life aboard a boat will be nautical delight, or at least tolerable. It's when the forces come at each other on the oblique that things begin to go awry. Formless, unpredictable, and unmanageable, the resulting roiled mess is rightly called "a confused sea," though the term "whip-ass sea" is both more apt and more colorful.

The sea at any moment is a wide spectrum of waves, both height and period, and a confused sea adds to this a variety of directions that the waves take. Nothing, short of cresting breakers in a violent storm with wind speeds exceeding forty knots, is so punishing to a small boat as a confused sea. This was the condition that I encountered between Cordova and Kayak Island, when a shoreward swell, a perpendicular tide set, off-angled winds, and a 1.5 knot current collided to turn the surface of the Gulf of Alaska into wicked turmoil.

~~~

Soon I spot and round Cape Ommaney at the southern end of Baronof Island, where a pod of orcas is feeding near the chiseled cliffs of the shore, their dorsal fins cutting easily through the stormy surf. At low ebb and now out of the Gulf, I pass over calm waters to Cape Decision, where harbor seals and humpbacks are on the hunt, then I maneuver through El Capitan Passage. Finally at 7:00 p.m., after thirteen hours of weaving among rocks and islands, picking through narrow channels, and flying along wind-buffeted boulevards of water, always in cold, misting drizzle, I arrive in Ketchikan utterly exhausted.

~~~

Ketchikan is a prosperous, busy little place spread along a harbor front. Just a twenty-minute walk end to end and three streets deep from the waterfront, the village has the chocka block, disheveled aspect of a turn-of-the-century mining town, which, as it turns out, it once was. Back then the place was a ramshackle collection of flimsy, unpainted wood shacks. Now, still flimsy and made of wood, the shacks have been tarted up for the carriage trade. The once graying wood siding has been slathered over in colors of seafoam green, robin's egg blue, and Georgia peach. More historically evocative colors would be flesh-tone pancake, hooker rouge, and red-light lipstick. The same places that today are too-cute-for-words boutiques were not all that long ago whorehouses, where women of sporting morality plied their trade among the sourdough miners, fishermen, and loggers. One such cute shop, Dolly's House, is a museum of sorts, commemorating one of the more popular of these bordellos.

As I recover from the day's travails in a fine bar that night, just down the hill from my hotel and a few blocks from Dolly's House, I learn from the bartender that the cathouse business in Ketchikan has not faded with the Gold Rush, it just has relocated down the street. In summer, the town is choked with fishermen away from home for the season, loggers in bunkhouses, transient tourists, and cannery work-ers, most of them men. "And, well, you know how it goes," he says with a knowing grin. A lesson from some long ago class in elementary economics comes to mind: Where there is demand, supply will soon follow.

When I arrived here last night, no cruise ships were in port; this morning there are three, each with nearly 2,000 passengers. Tourism is vital to the local economy and, as we have seen, is the single fac-tor that distinguishes the vibrant towns of the Inside Passage from their duller sister towns farther north. Still, a place that has 4,000 to 8,000 new tourists descend upon it in a sudden flood every few days instinctively develops a protective barrier, keeping the invaders iso-lated where they and the alien cultures they bring with them can less easily infect the locals.

Since cruise ship tourists seem not to be fond of walking long dis-tances as a rule, geographic isolation, confining the locusts to an area a few blocks from the ship's docks, works just fine. Enter the zone and you're confronted by a plethora of gift shops, tee shirt shops, "art galleries," and the like, some owned by the cruise ship companies, and all aswarm with tourists. It's a waterfront shopping mall where aging ladies patrol the shops alert for bargains, vacuous expressions hiding their glee at the prospect of another purchase. Trailing behind them, always behind, are the senescent husbands, vividly clad, trying, with skills honed from years of practice, not to appear as bored with the whole thing as they surely are.

Step back a block or so and the picture changes. Just a few steps too far for the tourists are the fishermen's supply store, the outboard motor repair shop, and the dingy bar with felt-worn pool table and the aroma of stale beer and cigarette smoke. These are the places where the locals go about their daily routines as oblivious as they can get to that other world just around the corner. The arrangement seems to accommodate both groups nicely.

Early in the morning, I board *Rascal* preparing to leave Ketchikan after a few days' visit, turn on the VHF radio, and tune it to one of the weather channels. The National Weather Service offers a faint glimmer of hope for relief from the miserable conditions I have endured now for several days. "The weak low pressure system in the Gulf of Alaska just offshore of Sitka will be moving out of the area today. Visions leap to mind of radiant sunshine, cloudless skies, and even warm breezes. I'll change to a short sleeve shirt, maybe shorts. This momentary flight of fantasy is sadly crash landed by reality. "It will be followed by another weak low pressure system ...." The words "low pressure system," I have learned through soaked experience, are weatherspeak meaning some god-awful mix of wind, rain, fog, and cold, and that's what I encounter, again, motoring slowly, damply out of Ketchikan.

Wind, rain, fog, and cold are one thing if you're sitting in a home by a blazing fire or even perched on a captain's chair in the dry, heated confines of the pilothouse atop a fishing boat or motor yacht. Such unfortunate weather conditions are quite another experience when standing under a narrow canvas tee-top behind a three-foot wide windscreen, ripping along at a brisk thirty-five knots over icy Alaskan waters in an open boat designed for sport fishing in the subtropics. In my original planning for this trip, I reasoned that shelter from the elements, though commonly provided by hard-surfaced facilities like houses and pilothouses, could nearly as well be provided by clothing. Dress properly and all would be warm and cozy. That one ranks near the top of the long list of bad ideas I've ever had, right up there with the momentary adolescent brain warp that maybe I should become a Democrat. Despite layers of high-tech fabrics, old-fashioned wool, and foul weather gear, my hands, feet, and face are cold, and they stay cold all day, and damp too. John Ruskin once said, "There is really no such thing as bad weather, only different kinds of good weather." Wherever John may have been when he made this laughable statement, he was nowhere near southeast Alaska, or nowhere near sober.

Leaving Ketchikan's harbor, I cruise along the western edge of the Misty Fjords National Monument, apparently named by the Weather Service to commemorate the ever-present low pressure system. It's a park of 2.2 million acres, where annual rain and snowfall of 150 to 200 inches nourishes a darkly beautiful—and darkly wet—coastal rain forest, a giant petri dish perfect for growing shower curtain mold. Despite the grim weather, the water surface is eerily calm. Only raindrops, falling intermittently when the cold air can no longer hold all the moisture it collects, mar the slate-gray surface. The world around me is an enveloping miasma of cold gloom; there is no sky. Out there where the horizon should be, cold gray water meets cold gray water-filled air. Along the shore, as if to tease, the opaque shroud lifts its skirt a few hundred feet and a brooding landscape appears. Low mountains, scabrous with colorless patches of trees and fields of ancient granite outcrops, are truncated below their peaks by the menacing veil. Pressing ahead, I'm desperate to leave this bleak world behind.

~~~

A year after completing the voyage that is the primary subject of this book, I returned to Alaska for yet another adventure. I had become enthralled with the raw majesty of coastal Alaska, and I couldn't shake the place from my thoughts. This second trip was different from the first, however, in three important respects. First, because of the experience with a short fuel supply that resulted in a Coast Guard search, I bought a new boat with a 350-gallon fuel capacity, rather than the 200 gallons of the first boat and, with more economical motors, double the range. Other than cosmetic details, this was the same type boat as the one used on the first trip, and it too I named *Rascal*. Secondly, this subsequent trip began, as did the first, in Homer, Alaska, but it ended in Vancouver, British Columbia, and so covered what was for me the most alluring and primitive region of the first trip. The third, and by a long measure the most important difference, was that I took along my twelve-year-old son, our only child, as first mate.

The trip was for both Grant and me an important milestone, a watershed event that brought us together as never before. He was, he told me, deeply honored to be asked to go, and he proved throughout the voyage, whether on land or at sea, to be a stalwart companion and friend. His unfailing good humor, infectious laughter, and barely contained excitement never failed to amaze me. And through it all—rain, cold, fog, pounding seas, danger—he never complained.

We followed the same route as the first trip, with some minor variation in Prince William Sound and the Inside Passage, and slept many nights in the tiny cuddy cabin that, as with the first *Rascal*, had no head, running water, galley, or heat. Grant was designated chief cook, which meant that most nights he heated cans of chili and made hot chocolate on our one-burner camp stove. As first mate, he deployed and recovered the anchor, kept lines neatly stowed, and generally kept the boat clean and orderly. When in ice fields, Grant manned the boat hook to fend off bergs that might damage the hull. Together we saw a bear cub, adult bears, orcas, humpbacks, sea lions, and seals. Grant flew out of Homer with Jose de Creeft into the Katmai Range over pretty much the same route I had flown with Jose a year earlier.

Geoff Widdows in Yakutat took him fishing—Geoff had room only for one more in his charter party that day—and Grant thrilled at catching door-size halibut and golf bag-size king salmon. We drove to the Childs Glacier and the Million Dollar Bridge out of Cordova, talked with fishermen, and observed up close as a long-liner unloaded at a cannery its holds of halibut, salmon, and ling cod, watched as the fish were weighed, beheaded, and iced down. Together we walked the streets of Alaskan and British Columbian towns. Decked out in bright yellow foul weather gear and fishermen's rubber boots, my brash and personable son easily adopted a manly swagger and told everybody we encountered all about our adventures to that point. As he told the stories, he gushed with animated excitement and his blue eyes sparkled, each word spoken through a broad smile.

We had some serious talks about girls, life, and adventure, about what it means to become a man, about honor and integrity and character, about working to attain goals, respecting himself and others. I told him that all I really expected of him was that he make me proud of him. I said I was sure he would screw up along the way, stumble and fall and pick himself up, but in the end I knew he'd make me proud. I also yelled at him more often than either of us liked, but he always took it in stride and, within minutes, we were best friends again. We agreed that despite our age difference and our familial relationship, we are each the best friend of the other. I told him what he already knew too well, that his father was some twenty years older than the fathers of his peers and that one day, at an awkward time in his life, I would die. And when that happens, I said, he would be on his own, and from then on is when I'd especially want him to make me proud.

In the 1,800-mile, one-month voyage we took together, one of our many shared experiences stands out above the rest. Its setting was the Queen Charlotte Islands off the coast of British Columbia, and Grant's role in the events gave me good reason to swell with pride. What follows is a recounting of those events.

================================

Grant and I are bound for the Queen Charlotte Islands, our first stop in Canada. To get there, we'll have to cross one of the two broad expanses of open water where the Gulf of Alaska cuts deeply into the protective barrier of the Inside Passage. Dixon Entrance, where we are presently, and Queen Charlotte Sound, have fearsome reputations for the terrible seas they can produce. Crossing winds, colliding tides, and currents make both at times worse even than the Gulf. But this morning, Dixon Entrance is slick, black, and pavement smooth. Concerned that conditions may soon change for the worse, I push the throttles up and cross the sixty miles to Rose Spit on the northeast end of the islands, then run a final sixty miles along the east shore into Queen Charlotte City with fuel running low.

Crossing the border into Canada by boat is notably different from crossing it by car. Here, out in the wilderness of the Inside Passage, nothing suggests a transition from one country to another, except for the charted tick marks of an international boundary barely discernible on the GPS screen. There are no patrol boats, no uniformed function-aries, no gated border crossing and, of course, no chain link fence. In short, the government apparatus of customs and immigration that greets us on land is absent here. A person not devoted to scrupulous compliance with red tape might easily and simply not bother with border formalities. He could stop in Canadian towns, stay overnight in hotels, and be on his way again, all without the slightest hindrance, though compliance is just a phone call away. I suspect that many travelers on the Inside Passage, perhaps most, ignore the border and its rituals.

To call a place with a population of 1,200 a city is to engage in hyperbole that would make even an infomercial flack blush. Queen Charlotte City is at best a village spread helter-skelter along a two-mile waterfront, and with just a single traffic light, it devoted to the ferry loading ramp. The community's population, a large number of whom are members of the Haida Nation of Indians, engages in commercial fishing or logging, shopkeeping, and the like.

For the outsider, the principal attraction of Q. C. City is that it's home to the Information Center for the Gwaii Haanas Tribal and National Park Reserve. This modest frame building—whose clapboard, neo-rustic, modern-Canada, whatever, design shouts government building—is the place to which visitors must report to get a permit, and of course pay a fee. Though the Haidas who manage it seem determined to make access to the reserve as troublesome as possible. Reservations are required, often months in advance, and upon arrival visitors have to endure a *one and a half hour-long* orientation session.

In the information center, a videotape is played on an ordinary TV set in a tiny room accommodating me, Grant, and a dozen other tourists. On the tape, a voice-over spoken by a Haida chief in the desultory cadence of the Noble Savage describes how the Indians (he calls them Native Americans, perhaps forgetting their ancestors came over the Bering land bridge from Mongolia) have always been as-one-with-the-raven (by which he means closely attuned to nature) and lived according to a clock set by nature. His paean goes on to paint the Indian in green eco-glow tones as the environmental version of Jesus of Nazareth. In contrast, he says, as the camera pans across a commercial logging operation, the capitalist white man only brought greed and destruction of the wilderness. He fails to mention five-star golf resorts, 200-mile an hour sports cars, and a one-pill cure for erectile dysfunction. He says the white man tells you to climb the ladder of success but does not tell you where the ladder leads, thus making a compelling case for a new OSHA ladder sticker saying "Up", with an appropriately aimed arrow.

In a peroration of self-pity, a statistic is flashed on the screen: Before the white man arrived, umpteen thousand Indians lived along the Inside Passage; years later a lot fewer remained. The locution has the intended purpose of causing the viewer to make the logical leap that the grim attrition was caused entirely by the white man. The statistic does not say this, of course, because it's not true, and the truth would be off message, would diminish the guilt white viewers are supposed to feel. So effective is the illogic that a very large woman seated next to me becomes lachrymose, amazingly, over events alleged to have taken place more than 300 years ago. It's as if I should become maudlin over what those Yankees did to my whoever-they-were, dirt-road ancestors in antebellum South Carolina. Her tears are misplaced, not to mention quite a bit tardy.

What happened, mainstream scientists now agree, was that the internecine and intertribal wars that always plagued the Indians swelled in bloody intensity, fueled by advances in war skills and a periodic decline in the salmon population. Raids by one village on another increased in frequency and ferocity to produce thousands of captured slaves taken as human sacrifices, worked to death, or often just killed for sport. The cruelty of the tribes knew no limits. Chiefs commonly ordered slaves, and even lower members of their own tribe, to be trussed and laid prone where they served as human rollers for dispatching massive war canoes, less costly that the modern float-off trailer that launched *Rascal* in Homer but a sight messier.

Live slaves were jammed into post holes and huge timbers dropped on them to bring good luck to the hut the timbers supported—harder on the population than the harmless but equally silly feng shui. Ample evidence exists of widespread cannibalism. Certainly the arrival of the white man contributed to the carnage by providing an expanded market for slaves, introducing advanced weapons and alcohol, and even spreading disease, but his arrival was not, as the film's statistical half-truth is meant to imply, the sole cause of a decimated population.

Of course nothing in the film suggests the white man may have benefited the red man, for example by introducing iron fish hooks, nails, cutlery, firearms, and other innovations passed along from an advanced culture to one barely removed from the Stone Age. Or that freedom, democracy, and capitalism, Western civilization's greatest contributions to modernity, might somehow have had a more serious and beneficial impact on the red man than did a mystical affinity for the raven. And not a word hints at the embarrassing fact that those white men who climbed the ladder of success—without directions from OSHA—now too generously support those Noble Savages who have become unproductive citizens and shameless whiners.

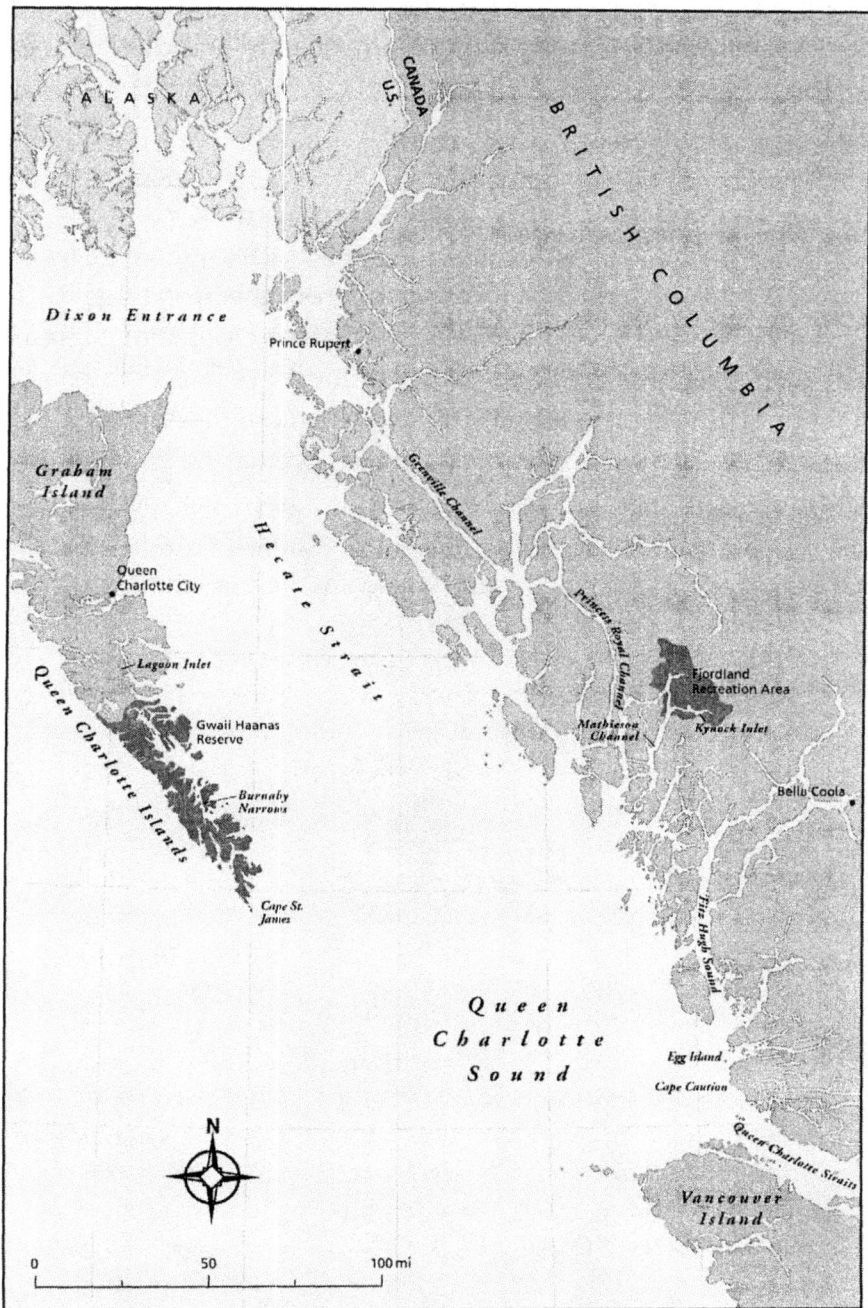

ALASKA

CANADA
U.S.

BRITISH COLUMBIA

Dixon Entrance

Prince Rupert

*Graham
Island*

Greenville Channel

Queen
Charlotte City

Hecate Strait

Lagoon Inlet

Queen Charlotte Islands

Gwaii Haanas
Reserve

*Burnaby
Narrows*

Princess Royal Channel

Fjordland
Recreation Area

*Mathieson
Channel*

Kynoch Inlet

Bella Coola

*Cape St.
James*

Fitz Hugh Sound

*Queen
Charlotte
Sound*

Egg Island

Cape Caution

Queen Charlotte Straits

N

*Vancouver
Island*

0   50   100 mi

My tolerance for eco-blather exhausted, Grant and I head out of the city, setting course for the reserve. Shallow and rock strewn, the nearshore is a field of whitecaps the color and froth of a perfect beer head, but in just fifteen miles we enter the sanctuary of the reserve's protected waters. The Queen Charlottes, known to the Haida as Haida Gwaii, or Place of Wonder, are called, with some reason, the Canadian Galapagos. Lying variously sixty to 120 miles off the British Columbia coastal archipelago, they stand so far out to sea that, quite unlike all the other islands along the Inside Passage, they are untouched by the power of glaciation. So remote are they that the islands evolved a separate ecosystem, claiming thirty-nine endemic subspecies, including mammals and birds. Nowhere are the natural wonders of these islands more apparent than among the 138 islands, the tidal inlets, and lagoons of the Gwaii Haanas.

Its differentness is obvious from one glance at the charts. In the many diverse fjords I have visited, from Kenai to Prince William Sound, from Sitka to Grenville Channel, the depth contours are all the same. Steep rock walls plummet from high peaks straight into the depths, up to 1,000 feet below the surface, and do so uniformly on both sides. The bottoms of these starkly defined chasms are smooth and free of variant conditions, because once upon a long lost time they were scoured clean by the glaciers. But here in Gwaii Haanas, wildly erratic contours describe a corruption of the seabed and betray the absence of glaciation. Pinnacles, shelves, clusters, peaks, shoulders, and valleys, all sculpted from granite, litter the bottom in chaotic assortment. This is not a place ever shaped by the razored shave of glaciers.

Navigation through the Gwaii Haanas is fraught with peril. Where rocks are near the surface, acres of sinewy kelp gardens grow, marking the danger. If they can be seen in time in the dull light, the kelp is easily avoided. Miss spotting them and *Rascal* becomes entangled in a brown-leafed thicket, like Tar Baby caught in the briar patch. Roots and leaves wrap around the feet of the motors, shut off the flow of cooling water, and cause the heat alarms to sound. Without glaciers to grade smooth its bottomland, the waterways of the reserve are

littered here and there with rocks jutting to the surface for no apparent reason. Without logical connection to nearby depths or shore,
they are aberrant and so dangerous. I can't simply fly along blithely
over what appears to be unobstructed water. A constant eye on the
GPS is required along every mile.

The reserve's landscape is marked by the low hills of the San
Cristoval Range, a lateral ridge of mountains 3,300-feet high at its
peak and layered over with forests of cedar, spruce, and hemlock.
Under the overstory lies a temperate rain forest, where clusters of
fern, bogs of sedge and alder, and patches of dark, moss-covered
deadwood give the place the feel of Yoda's homeland. The mountain
ridge, a result of plate tectonics, rises into the sky but not nearly so
far as a nearby valley drops into the deep. Just a mile out in the Gulf,
the ocean depth reaches 6,000 feet.

Marine life here is so well fed from the nutrient rich tidal waters
that one place, Burnaby Narrows, is said to contain the highest concentration of marine biomass in the world, outside of a sushi bar.
Passing over the shallow narrows, I can see in the clear water a collection of bat stars, a flimsy-armed starfish that comes in a wider variety of colors than Saturday night lip gloss: magenta, tangerine, and
lavender are just a few. And these are only a hint of the menagerie of
creatures found here.

As daylight wanes, I gingerly coax *Rascal* out of the main channel,
through the inrushing tide stream of a ten-yard wide keyhole in the
rocks, and pass over a kelp bed into the solitude of Lagoon Inlet. Its
black water, polished by the stillness to a flat-light sheen, perfectly
reflects the tousled carpet of forests that rise from the shore and the
faded-gray hues of the sky at subarctic dusk. A lone brown bear, just
at the tree line, forages without the slightest hint of fear in our presence. Just offshore of a grassy meadow at the head of the lagoon,
Grant wrankles the surface with dropped anchor, and we sit together
in perfect solitude, savoring wild, unblemished beauty.

Early next morning, as the first rays of sunlight bathe the lagoon,
Grant hoists anchor, and we make our way out through the keyhole.

Plowing easily across waves of inrushing tide, we pass through the narrow slot and onward over more splendid miles of the Gwaii Haanas, until the weather turns colder and gray drizzle falls. Turning about, we return to the city in a nasty chop kicked up by twenty knot winds on the stern.

The Canadian weather service announces over the VHF that a high pressure center has affixed itself to the north end of Vancouver Island, just 120 miles south of the southern tip of the Queen Charlottes. That tip, Cape St. James, has the dubious distinction of having the highest and most frequent winds in all of Canada—that's all of Canada, not just British Columbia. North of this high, where we are at the moment, sits another of the ever-present weak low pressure centers. Between the two, out there in the notorious waters of Hecate Straits, is a trough—more descriptively, a wind tunnel—where wind speeds are thirty to forty knots with gusts to fifty. It's a roughly accurate rule of thumb that wave height in feet is half of sustained wind speed in knots. That means waves out in Hecate Strait are running fifteen to twenty feet.

Thus confined to port by high winds and rough seas, Grant and I search out, and over four days exhaust, every possible form of diversion and entertainment (that I can write about in a published book) the place has to offer. Among these are a drive around Graham Island, including fifty miles of gravel forest road, the annual Q. C. City Hospital Day dance, beer sampling at all four of the local pubs (Grant not included), and many racks of nine ball against the best of the Haida pool hustlers (again without Grant).

The Haida, rare among Native American Indians, are a warm and gregarious people, my experience at the Gwaii Haanas Information Center notwithstanding. To their credit, my opponents took not the slightest offense, and even laughed heartily, when I described a string of my pool table triumphs, using a feeble association, as Custer's Revenge! Some of the humorless, overly earnest American ethnic groups could learn from the Haida that they need not take themselves, and certainly not their ancestors, too seriously.

Growing restless as the winds continue to blow, Grant and I begin searching for any way to get off the Queen Charlottes, across Hecate Straits, and back to our travels. Desperate, I finally concoct an escape plan borne of plain boredom, and it comes to me the very moment I first see the Prince Rupert-to-Queen Charlotte ferry. The *Queen of Prince Rupert*, at well over 300 feet long, is a ship. Displacing nearly 6,000 gross tons and four decks high, it carries loads of up to eighty cars and trucks, high stacks of pallets bearing equipment and supplies, and up to 500 passengers, across Hecate Straits between Queen Charlotte City and the Canadian town of Prince Rupert.

Though it can travel in most weather, the ferry is in port here in Queen Charlotte City some six hours behind schedule due to the fearsome seas out in the straits. The idea that comes to me is to use the mass of the ferry for lee protection from the wind and sea, much as I used Kayak Island "but as a mobile barrier." Behind this floating shield, we'll travel across the straits in nearly flat water. A stroke of pure genius! Or so it seems.

After refueling, the ferry casts off its lines and pulls away from the loading dock. It executes a slow, graceful turn in the harbor and begins making its way out of the marked channel into the straits with *Rascal* dead astern. When the ferry turns northeast across the straits, we'll pull alongside and cozy up to our blocker. At the end of the long ship channel, following the shore of Graham Island, the seas already are getting rough even though we're not yet fully exposed. When the ferry at last makes its turn and takes up a northeasterly course at its cruising speed, reduced in these conditions to fourteen knots, an enormous flaw in my brilliant plan appears. The ship's bow and stern wakes, fifteen-foot high, steep faced waves, trail away from its hull at forty-five degree angles. I try to place *Rascal* between these parallel wakes, but they are too close together, and the sea in the lee of the ship is not as calm as I had predicted. Now Grant and I must face not just wind-driven waves shattered by the ship into a hull-wrenching jumble, but also the stern wake, a wall of water on our tail, chasing us down should I slow too much, and the bow wake, a cliff lurking ahead should I go too fast.

This is clearly no place for us to be, so I devise an alternative plan on the spur of the moment, which is easy to do since it's the only plan available: I drop back dead astern of the ferry and follow in its prop wash. Now fully exposed to the wind-blown and now also prop-churned seas, I become tense and anxious. Grant, seated beside me, has not uttered a word of complaint, but I can see from the expression on his expressive face that he's concerned. His childlike laughter stopped when we made the turn and had to drop behind the ship.

I tell him to crawl on hands and knees up to the forward locker where the life jackets are stowed, keeping his body below the gunwales for protection should we take a breaker over the beam, get a child-size and an adult-size jacket, and come back to me at the helm. "Yes, sir," he replies, and promptly carries out his orders. When he returns, I fasten his life jacket securely, then don my own. Next, I tell him to remain low to the deck again and recover our two survival suits from their aft locker. Once again he says, "Yes, sir," and completes his assignment. But this time when he returns he looks at me earnestly, alarm approaching panic spread all over his face, and says, "Dad, I'm scared."

I reply in a voice as reassuring as I can muster, "Grant, I know you are. That's a perfectly normal reaction to these conditions. I just ask you to remain calm as you have so far on this trip, do what I tell you to do, and look on the positive side. We have a big ship as our escort, we're in a fine, well-equipped boat, and I have a lot of experience in conditions like this and worse. We'll be okay."

He nods in agreement. "Okay, Dad."

From the wave troughs, high walls of black, spume-laced water loom overhead, blocking the sky. From the crests, a vast, wind-torn sea spreads out before us, reaching to the horizon. Though attacking the beam, the waves don't break into the boat but cause it to ride up and down their face, heaving, yawing, pitching, and rolling. *Rascal* is tossed around by prop wash and ship-broken waves and waves that missed crashing into the ship and come at us untamed.

As my anxiety grows to just a notch below fear, I reach up to the overhead electronics box and, despite the wildly dancing deck, manage to grasp the VHF microphone. Using channel and volume controls on the mike, I call on channel sixteen, the international emergency and hailing channel: "*Queen of Prince Rupert*, this is the pleasure boat *Rascal* on your stern on channel one-six."

After a brief pause, just long enough to bring to mind the memory of a failed antenna off Kayak Island, I hear: "*Rascal*, this is the *Queen of Prince Rupert*."

With the sounds of crashing waves and straining motors, the voice is barely audible, even with the volume turned to maximum. I reply: "*Queen of Prince Rupert*, switch and answer channel one-one." This will get us off the emergency and hailing channel and onto another public channel suitable for extended conversation. Anybody within range can turn to channel eleven and hear us; there is no privacy on the VHF. We both change channels, and the ferry captain replies. In a voice tense with the drama of the moment, I tell him that Grant and I are aboard the small boat on his stern, that we'll follow in his prop wash to Prince Rupert, and that the rough seas, now running twelve to fifteen feet on the beam, are giving us a hard time. I ask him simply to keep an eye on us, and he says he will do so. A short while later a ferry crewman appears, standing behind the bulwarks on the ship's fantail, and there he'll remain until ferry and *Rascal* reach calm water. Now I at least know that if we broach or pitchpole we'll have both a watchman to report it and an expert rescue team at hand. The sight of this man standing there with his eyes fixed on us is deeply comforting.

Rascal travels on plane as fast as forty-five knots or as slow as twenty-two knots, or off plane as fast as twelve. At the ferry's speed of fourteen, I am obliged to accelerate ahead on plane, getting as close to the ship's stern as I dare, then reduce throttle, drift back off plane as the ferry pulls away, then accelerate again. Off plane, the boat's hull does not handle the seas well. Without power, she is squir-relly, wanting to yaw excessively. Twice, while off plane, a sea slams into the starboard beam, pushing the boat over the watery cliff of the ferry's portside stern wake. Racing down the steep wake out of con-trol and at a bad angle, I apply more power and port helm, square the boat to the wave to regain control then, past its trough, work back up the wake into the prop wash now become our lifeline.

Halfway across, in the full grasp of blowing seas with wind gusts reaching fifty knots, I am startled by the riveting wail of the overheat alarms on both motors. Rising sharply from the ambient sounds of howling wind, tormented seas, and straining motors I have heard now for three hours, the sound of the alarms sends a tremor of fear coursing through my body. I'm sure Grant feels the same, but he sits bravely and impassively, relying on me to get us out of this fix. To ignore the alarms risks damaging both motors permanently, and this is no place or time to be without power. There is no choice but to shut down the motors and attempt a repair. When I shut them off, an eerie silence follows. Without the shrill alarms or the groaning thrum of the motors, there are only the sounds of wind keening through *Rascal's* tee-top and tumultuous seas, one wave train followed closely by another. For the first time, I smell the pungent diesel fumes from the ferry's 7,700 horsepower engine, an engine slowly driving our guardian farther and farther away.

Once again in fear-taught voice, I call the ferry on channel eleven, which we had agreed we both would monitor. "*Queen of Prince Rupert*, this is *Rascal*."

The answer comes in a cool, professional tone that helps calm my jangled nerves. "This is *Queen of Prince Rupert*. Go ahead *Rascal*."

"The overheat alarms on both motors went off and I had to shut them down. I'll raise the motors and try to find the problem and will let you know what I find. Please standby."

"Roger, standing by," was the reply, brief but reassuring.

I'm almost certain that sea-driven kelp leaves have wrapped around the lower units and blocked the cooling water intakes. With a press of the electric tilt switch, the lower units of the outboard motors rotate up and out of the sea revealing, sure enough, glistening sheets of kelp attached to the motors like leaches. As the deck tosses wildly without the stabilizing effects of power, the hull turned beam to the waves, I begin to fear a broach. At first I think that as the stronger and more experienced I should be the one to crawl aft and remove the kelp leaves, but then I realize if I get swept overboard Grant can't operate the boat well enough to rescue me. He's also more agile, a quality more important for the task than strength. It's better he remove the leaves. Remaining at the helm, I instruct Grant to stay low to the deck and, on his belly, crawl aft to the transom and over it to the splash well where the motors attach to the hull. He must then grab the slimy leaves and tear them away from the motors. He follows my instructions perfectly and without the slightest hesitation or complaint, and I'm deeply proud of him. As he crawls back to the helm, I get the motors lowered and restarted without alarms and notify the ferry that all is well.

Onward through mountains of black seas, the ferry plows ahead, mother duck leading her duckling. Twice the ferry changes course, to avoid shallows I assume, and twice in lockstep so do I. My eyes fixed on her stern, I will not wander from the narrow avenue of white prop wash that connects us to her. The seas are so harsh that even at 6,000 tons the ferry slews badly, especially on a downwind leg. I can imagine the helmsman high on the bridge turning this way to correct. then back to correct again, as the ferry absorbs energy from the punishing waves and wallows in reaction. Even mother duck is having her problems in these seas.

At long last, after seven gut-wrenching hours of fighting the helm, managing the throttles, getting slammed around, tense, anxious, combating fear, Grant and I arrive at the calmer waters of the Inside Passage. Making our way up the ship channel behind the ferry, we wend our way among the mountains of the British Columbia coastal archipelago over flat waters undisturbed by the gale winds out in the straits.

Then, just as we start to relax and our nerves begin to calm, we're struck on the starboard beam by a hurricane force blast of clear, frigid air. *Rascal* rocks on her keel and is blown off course, until I regain control. The powerful wind blows up closely spaced, choppy waves and knocks the crests off these. White froth, the atomized remains of the crests, skitters across the surface like beer foam in the wind. Grant and I have just been hit by a williwaw, roaring over the top of a mountain off to starboard, down its lee slope, and across our path. In fifteen minutes, we pass through it, going from forty knot winds out in the straits, to calm in the ship channel, to perhaps eighty knot winds in the williwaw, to dead calm again, and all in the space of just a few miles. Alaska's weather gets, and keeps, your attention.

On a flat sea, the seven-hour crossing of Hecate Straits would have taken two and a half hours, and we would've arrived fresh and ready for more. Now we're both thoroughly spent, depleted of every ounce of energy, and I'm badly in need of a stiff drink, or two, or three. At a fine dinner treat that night, I honor Grant for his courage under stress, and he beams with the glow of his achievement.

~~~

At Prince Rupert, a tidy fishing and logging center for coastal British Columbia and a major railhead and port at the mouth of the important Skeena River, *Rascal* is docked at the Prince Rupert Yacht and Rowing Club. The name evokes images of the Henley Regatta with proper gentlemen in morning coats and silk top hats escorting dowdy ladies hung with pearl strands parading imperiously under enormous sunbonnets. Here the image fizzles. I see no morning coats, top hats, or sunbonnets, though dowdy ladies abound, even if without pearls.

Canadian fishermen are in the midst of an opener. Their boats, nets, and bright orange floats clog the entrance channel as we weave among them. These are gill netters, but unlike the fleet in Cordova the boats are mostly stern pickers, with their wheelhouse forward and the working deck aft. The drum of the hydraulic winch over which the net is wound is set in the stern, and the net is deployed and recovered from there. One man operates the boat with remote controls and handles the net and its catch, all on the stern deck.

Boats of the more modern Cordova fleet are nearly all bow pickers. The wheelhouse is set aft, while the hydraulic winch and remote controls are in the bow where the net is deployed and recovered. Cordova boats have an extremely shallow draft, nearly flat bottomed, and are driven by hydraulic jet drives instead of conventional props, which allow the boat to run over the net without fouling. These innovations allow the boats to operate in shallow waters, like those of the Copper River Delta.

A gill net, which by Canadian law can't exceed sixteen feet in depth, hangs in the water from a surface line kept afloat by a series of small white buoys. The line, up to 1,200 feet long, is anchored at each end by an orange ball float that lets others know where the net is set so they can avoid it. Holes in the net are a size, established by government regulation, that will entrap only fish of a legal size. Too small fish can pass through the net unharmed and those too large can't become entrapped, or so the theory goes. Fishermen set their nets in a straight line across an area where the salmon are expected to run, wait a short while, an hour or two, then step on a button mounted on the deck. This activates the winch drum, which rotates, dragging the net up and over the stern and with it wriggling salmon. Fish are removed from the snare by hand, one at a time, and tossed into an ice-packed hold. Once emptied, the net is reset, and the process begins anew.

In the world of commercial fishing in Alaska and British Columbia, the gill netter is the smallest of the small businessmen trying to earn a living from the sea. He is the sole owner and operator, though his wife may keep the books and a son or daughter may lend a hand. Both the technical skills and the amount of capital needed are modest but then so is the potential profit. The low level of skills and capital mean that when prices are high and fish are plentiful, a rare combination, a lot of new entrants come into the business seeking what for the moment seems like easy money. Then prices plummet, or the catch falls off, or both, or the already stringent government regulations become even more so, and the ruthless calculus of seeking a profit from gathering a regulated natural resource asserts itself. To bad economics is added the high risk to life and limb and the often grueling hours and working conditions.

We're left to wonder why anyone would want to be a commercial fisherman, especially a gill netter. The answer, so far as I can determine, seems to focus on what the fisherman describes vaguely as lifestyle. He works outdoors in some of the most dramatic scenery on the globe, is his own boss answering to no other person (unmentioned here are his creditors, especially the canneries that extend generous trade credit, and government regulators), and works and lives among his friends, the other fishermen. He will not say it, though it is a fact, but he enjoys a lot of time off. He'll work very hard during the short salmon season, but only in the brief periods when fishing openers are allowed; otherwise he's mostly idle. A person who places a high value on leisure may find fishing for a living appealing, but it remains only a marginally profitable and dangerous business.

Inside Passage.

Inside Passage.

Inside Passage.

Cross Sound, Alaska.
Phil, Grant, and Kitty Phillips.

Elfin Cove, Alaska.
Grant Phillips at Elfin Cove, Alaska.

Grant Phillips, age twelve, at Thunder Bay in the Kenai Fjords.
Geoff Widdows and Grant Phillips at Yakutat dock.

Grant Phillips on Rascall II, berg bit in hand. Columbia Glacier. Columbia Fjord, Prince William Sound.

Glacier Bay, Alaska.

Near Sitka, Alaska.
Bartlett Cove, Alaska.

El Capitan Passage, Alaska.
Burnaby Narrows, British Columbia.

Humpback whale.
Sea lion colony.

Salmon boat, Cordova harbor, Alaska.
Prince Rupert, British Columbia.

Chapter Seven

Theirs not to reason why,
Theirs but to do and die.
- Alfred Lord Tennyson,
Charge of the Light Brigade

H & P BROTHERS SHIPYARD on Oak Street in Biloxi, Mississippi, sits along the shore of a quiet bayou, a tidal backwater of the Gulf of Mexico. Owned by Mr. John Nguyen, one of the many Vietnamese who came to the Gulf Coast in the aftermath of the Vietnam War, the yard built shrimp boats. When the price of shrimp was high and hauling in trawl nets filled with them was profitable, it built and sold a lot of shrimp boats.

Eager buyers sought inexpensive boats, so inexpensive boats were built, using various shortcuts to hold down costs. Instead of hiring a marine architect, the yard copied the plans of other boats, modifying them to suit their buyers' needs, often without any thought of how the changes might affect stability or even basic seaworthiness. Welding rods, the steel glue that holds a boat together at its seams, were another source of savings. The heavy rods used by reputable boat builders to weld sturdy hulls and decks and superstructures were costly, so the yard often used lighter rods, which was like building the structural frame of a house with fine-stemmed finishing nails instead of heavy ten-penny nails.

In 1988, H & P Brothers Shipyard completed the steel-hulled shrimp boat, *Sea Power*. Built without benefit of a marine architect or formal detailed plans, the *Sea Power* was a stretched-out version of a tested sixty-foot design. It had a narrow beam, perhaps befitting a sixty-foot boat but skinny for a ninety-two footer; a rounded bottom, fine for the shallow drafts of near shore shrimping in the Gulf of Mexico; and a jaunty upswept stern.

When its bare hull was completed, *Sea Power* was launched and set afloat. Into it were set various double-bottom fuel tanks in the bow, wing tanks to port and starboard; hydraulic oil-, lube oil-, and sewer-holding tanks; fresh-water tanks; freezers for storing the catch; and a diesel engine. On deck, stanchions, hydraulic winches, and roller gear to handle a trawl net were set in place. Next came steering gear and the pipes, conduit, cable, waterlines, hydraulic lines, and drain lines needed to make the boat a working vessel. Finally, its interior was fitted with crew quarters and lockers for food stores and ground tackle, while the pilot house was equipped with navigation electronics and control systems.

Had it been properly engineered and constructed, displacement— its actual weight in the water—would have been measured. This is done by taking various dimensions at points along the waterline to the deck, yielding, after further calculations, the mass of a hull below the waterline and thus its displacement. These and other dimensions were not measured, yet they would be critical to the vessel's inherent stability. They would be needed to tell her captain which fuel tanks to fill and drain and in what sequence, which fish freezers to fill first, and how to balance its load of chain, nets, lines, bait, fish catch, and stores.

After displacement was determined, in the proper order of things, the *Sea Power's* builder would have run stability tests to determine the material strength of the hull and its equilibrium. The stability of a vessel is measured using a crude but time-proven technique. A simple plumb bob is hung on deck while thousands of pounds of concrete weights are loaded aboard and shifted about. With the movement of each load, the floating vessel rolls this way or that, then returns to level trim. The angle of the roll measured from the pendulum swing of the plumb bob and the time the hull takes to return from the roll are measured. These determine the vessel's center of gravity, its ability to right itself from a roll, and how far it can roll and still right itself. The process of making these calculations is called inclining.

The maximum angle at which a vessel can roll and still right itself is the righting arm, and in well-designed boats it is commonly in the range of thirty to thirty-five degrees; the minimum standard is twenty-five degrees. Some Coast Guard cutters and modem yachts are known to sustain rolls of as much as ninety degrees and still right themselves. Beyond the righting arm, a vessel, especially one with a high superstructure or with a stacked load on its decks or, common in the Bering Sea, one that accumulates layers of ice above its decks, is susceptible to capsizing.

With the stability tests complete, the boat's designer should have used the data gathered during the testing to prepare a stability letter. This set of guidelines assists the captain in operating and loading the vessel and balancing its load to minimize roll. Using the stability letter and a handheld calculator, a captain can figure the consequences of various loading variables, including factors for weather and icing. Balancing loads to achieve stability, called trimming, is far from the exact science the stability letter suggests. A captain's experience plays an important role, as does the vessel's feel underfoot. A badly trimmed boat is a floating potential disaster awaiting only the right circumstances to become fatal. The Coast Guard has determined that material failure, or the lack of stability, accounts for eighty-five percent of vessels lost at sea and half of all seaborne fatalities.

Among the many vessels that have sunk as a result of poor trim were the modern, state-of-the-art crab boats *Americus* and *Altair*, or the A-boats, as they became known. Both boats were somewhat unstable to begin with, as the result of the addition of extensive heavy deck gear, a modification done without a follow-up amendment to their stability letters. And when they were loaded at dockside, their stability was compromised further after their decks were stacked too high with heavy crab pots, their crab storage tanks were flooded with seawater adding topside weight, and fuel was improperly allocated among the various tanks. It was a wonder both boats didn't turn turtle sitting right there at the docks. Just twenty-five miles out of the harbor, both boats, traveling together in calm seas, capsized, and fourteen men, the entire crews of both, died as the direct result of instability and poor trim.

Although inclining a vessel and loading it with the aid of a stability letter is good practice for a boat owner and an important element of a vessel's seaworthiness, it was not required by law when the *Sea Power* was built. Though the law did not require it, however, insurance companies usually did, and for the boat owner, meeting the conditions required to obtain marine insurance was essential. So, as a matter of practice, most large fishing vessels had stability letters bound into booklet form and stowed in the wheelhouse or the captain's cabin. The *Sea Power* did not.

John Nguyen lost the *Sea Power* in bankruptcy in 1991. Renamed *Tenacity*, the boat was converted to a head-and-gut trawler working out of Seattle. As part of a twenty-five boat fleet, the *Tenacity* targeted bottom fish in the Bering Sea and Gulf of Alaska. Flatfish, Atka mackerel, rockfish, Pacific cod, and sole were caught using trawl nets dragged along the bottom. When the nets were hauled in, the catch was sorted, the rejects discarded overboard, and the keepers beheaded and eviscerated—thus head and gut—and sent below to a freezer hold where they were held until the boat returned to port.

Todd Wheeler, who served for a time as manager of its fish processing crew, said that when a net full of fish was hauled aboard, "if the seas were bad, we'd really rock and roll. With the added weight on top, we would really feel that." He said that once in rough seas the weight of a large catch forced the stem under the surface. Kevin Ward, who captained the boat on a trip to India to investigate the fishing potential there, found it to be tender, difficult to keep evenly balanced. He thought it had an unnatural roll. One day, in comparatively calm seas, the boat heeled over so hard as a result of a problem net that it threw Ward out of his chair.

After its then owner went broke and a bank foreclosed, the boat languished for a while at the docks in Seattle with a *"For Sale"* sign posted in its wheelhouse window. It was finally bought by Dave Olney, owner of Seattle-based Arctic Sole Seafoods, who promptly renamed it the *Arctic Rose*. Olney had started fishing in the waters of Puget Sound and Alaska when he was seventeen years old and by the time he was eighteen had bought his first boat. When he bought *Tenacity*, he had been fishing for thirty years and was in the midst of dealing with a potentially ruinous event in the little niche of the fishing industry he worked in.

The federal government, through authority granted by Congress to the National Marine Fisheries Service, had regulated marine fishing for many decades. Over the years, regulations had piled up one on top of the other to form a regime that would make George Orwell say, were he around today, "See, I told you so." Everything not expressly permitted is prohibited. The rules had the laudable goal of reducing the total catch of each of the fished species to a level approximately equal to its reproduction, called sustainability, though the term implies far greater scientific knowledge than actually exists.

But, as each regulation took effect, the iron law of unintended consequences intervened, and the regulations' desired effect was gutted just as surely as the fish on Dave Olney's boats. Government regulates as if the world is a static place easily managed by fiat, never comprehending that its edicts cause behavior to change. People, especially including the fiercely independent fishermen, respond to increased regulation in ways that protect their own self-interest. They will not simply sit by and see their livelihoods eroded without employing their intellect to adjust to the new environment.

One new rule, labeled "Amendment Forty-nine," threatened to drive all the head-and-gut boats out of business. The rule was meant to address the problem of unwanted fish caught up in the trawl nets, sorted out from the targeted species, and tossed overboard. By the time they were sorted and discarded, the fish were dead. So each year more than 650 million pounds of unwanted catch, or catch that might have been valuable but not in compliance with other rules, the so-called bycatch, was lost.

For the massive factory trawlers, the bycatch is of little or no concern. They convert nearly all of a catch into marketable fish products. These boats, ships really, from 150-to 350-feet long, employ enormous trawl nets that sweep up anything in their path. After just a few hours of trawling, the nets contain up to 150 tons of fish. When a trawl is complete, the nets are hauled by powerful hydraulic winches up onto the trawl deck (the aft part of the main deck), where they are dumped through a hatch to the processing factory below. Here, the catch is sorted, processed, and frozen while the empty net is returned to the sea.

The size, sophistication, and technology of the processing factory distinguishes the large factory trawler from the more primitive head-and-gut boats. These factories are highly efficient, employing their capital to make profitable use of nearly all of a catch, with end products that range from valuable filets, to processed fish sold in Asian markets for use as faux crab (called surimi), to lowly fish meal. That same capital also employs lobbyists and lawyers and makes political contributions. It buys power and influence that result in favorable regulations that result in bigger catches at the expense of other fishermen.

The NMFS decided that the problem of trawl netting was excess waste—that 650 million pounds that gets tossed overboard every year. So, it must be obvious, the solution is a rule that prohibits waste, at least of certain species. Thus was born Amendment Forty-nine. It provides that all pollock and cod caught as bycatch, regardless of gender or size or whether they are marketable or were wanted in the first place, must be processed and kept. It is not just coincidence that large factory trawlers primarily target pollock and cod and that head-and-gut-boats are responsible for a large part of the discarded bycatch.

With limited processing area and freezer space, the head-and-gut boats could not make profitable use of these low-value fish. These boats are actually small factory trawlers that intend to catch higher-value groundfish, like flathead sole. For these boats, the cost to catch and process pollock and cod is higher than the market value of the fish, so a rule requiring they keep and process low-value fish was a rule pushing them toward the abyss of bankruptcy. Only marginally profitable to begin with, head-and-gut boats could not long survive if they were required to process some fish at a loss. We can only assume the large factory trawlers would not miss the head-and-gut boats on the Bering Sea.

Facing this potentially ruinous government regulation, and without access to the capital required to get into the large factory trawler business, Dave Olney looked for a way to continue operating profitably in the only business he had ever known, a business now very different thanks to Amendment Forty-nine. His answer was to buy an existing boat as cheaply as he could and retrofit it to meet the requirements of the amendment. He bought *Tenacity* (nee *Sea Power*) for a song, but he knew it could operate profitably and safely in the Bering Sea only after extensive modifications. So he invested a lot of money, some his own, some that of investors, and some borrowed, to bring the boat up to seaworthy standards, including the addition of a new motor and improved electronics.

But the most important and innovative improvement Olney made was to weld onto the main deck, aft of the wheelhouse, a new processing factory. Made from sheets of heavy steel, it was beefy enough to take the punishment it would encounter in the Bering Sea. By moving the tiny, inefficient existing factory area from below decks to the new larger factory on the main deck, Olney had, in one bold stroke, increased the size and efficiency of the factory and freed up space below to enlarge the size of the freezer hold. Now he had a better shot at surviving the brutal competition made worse by Amendment Forty-nine.

When stability tests became a requirement of federal law in 1999, the *Arctic Rose* was tested and determined to be stable, but only upon compliance with a set of highly restrictive loading requirements, necessary even after more than seven tons of lead had been added to the keel for ballast. To make it as profitable as possible, Olney wanted the boat to be able to handle a deck load of 40,000 pounds, more than enough to handle the average catch of 24,000 as well as the maximum catch of 30,000 pounds. But even with all its modifications, the *Arctic Rose*, under the best conditions, was limited by stability restrictions to a maximum load of only 21,000 pounds.

To achieve even this modest level, the boat was required to keep the number one fuel tank in the bow, containing fully thirty percent of its fuel, fully loaded for ballast. The other seventy percent was held in four tanks along the port and starboard beams, which had to be drained in a specific sequence to keep the boat stable. The fish processing factory that had been added to the main deck was required to be kept free of excessive water that, sloshing on deck, would compromise stability. Still, the stability report said, the boat could not handle the maximum deck load without further ballast low in its hold, and that could only come from storing caught fish in the freezer. Load the deck without a hefty freezer load, and the *Arctic Rose* would become dangerously unstable.

Though it might not have been the most profitable boat in its fleet, the *Arctic Rose* never had any trouble recruiting a crew from the plentiful supply of novice deckhands hanging around Seattle's waterfront looking for work. Called "Discovery Boys" by the old salts, these men were attracted to high adventure on the Bering Sea by the documentary stories they had seen on the Discovery Channel. But the big money they could earn was the real attraction. All around the country young men in search of high adventure or easy money or both had heard the buzz. You could make $1,000 a day, $60,000 for just a few months' work—big bucks for a young guy, the kind of money that changed lives and opened doors to the American Dream.

The rumors started a minor gold rush of sorts. Vagrants, fraternity boys, fugitives, construction laborers, and farm hands showed up on the docks in Seattle or Bellingham or Anacortes or any of the other places where Northwest fishing fleets ported. They wandered the

docks in spring, 15,000 of them every year, pestering any boat captain they could find, begging to be taken on for a share of the profits.
Some came from the Midwest and had up until now been no closer
to the sea than a canoe ride on a lake, yet they daydreamed wistfully
of high adventure and big payoffs. A handful of the seekers actually
landed jobs, but the money they earned rarely got within spitting distance of what they had hoped for.

Still, they made more than they might have back home, and when
they returned inland after a season, they exaggerated the sums
and embellished their tales. The rumors grew and spread, and more
bedazzled soldiers of fortune flocked to the docks. Most went away
disappointed, their dream of life-altering riches shattered in the reality of too many men seeking too few jobs.

Problem was, the best jobs went to family and friends of the captain and his boat owner. The formula that applies in most of competitive life applies in fishing as well: Ten percent of the boats catch eighty
percent of the fish. With each crewman getting a percentage share of
a boat's profit, the captains of those ten percent boats weren't about
to hand out jobs, even as lowly deck hands, to greenhorn dreamers.
Those jobs were fat plums handed out to experienced fishermen who
the captain knew personally, men he knew he could depend on, often
from the captain's or owner's hometown, places like Bellingham or
Anacortes or Port Angeles

The small gill net and trailer boats didn't need extra hands. They
were run by their owners with help from wife, son, or daughter.
Long-lining for halibut could be profitable, and deckhands were often
needed, but the season was so short and the job applicants so many
that captains could pick and choose, taking only the most experienced
men. Crabbers sometimes hired raw hands, but most of these were
among the ninety percent of boats that caught twenty percent of the
crabs. The vessels were rusting hulks, poorly equipped, manned by
indifferent crew, and run by lethargic captains. With small catches,
the hired hands got small shares of small profits.

The purse-seiners seem to offer the best shot at a job. Though small—the legal maximum length is fifty-eight feet—they need three to four hands to run the mother boat and another couple to run the skiff that hauls the net around, encircling the catch. A green kid from Iowa or Montana or Alabama might make $10,000 to $12,000 for two months of hard labor. Might, if the fish are caught in sufficient quantity, if the price of the catch holds, if the weather cooperates, and if.... Not bad for a fresh kid, but a long way from the far-fetched rumors, and not enough to open the door to the American Dream.

Those Discovery Boys knew the risks of fishing in Alaska. It was a common topic of conversation in the dingy waterfront bars where they hung out. They listened to tales of this boat or that boat that had sunk, of friends, or friends of friends, lost in the frozen wastes of the Bering Sea. They heard about wind-driven mountains of icy water collapsing on a boat, blowing out the specially designed stormproof windows in the wheelhouse or ripping off hatch covers or punching effortlessly through carelessly dogged doors and flooding the engine room. Powerless, the boat would turn crosswise to the heavy seas, roll, and sink. They passed around stories of a boat whose steering gear had been torqued by the stresses of raging seas and, without steering, crested over a wave just a little awry, plummeted down its face out of control, veered off wildly, broached, and sank.

In the manner of young men everywhere, the storytellers embellished the tales, and both told and heard through an alcohol fog, the stories grew in their intensity and sheer drama. If they did anything at all, the tall accounts magnified the risks of fishing in Alaska. Their purpose was, after all, not to entertain the listener, but to enhance the perception of the storyteller's manliness. Anybody willing to put to sea on a fishing boat bound for Alaskan waters was a real man, and after the stories puffed up the risks, the teller became a brave man, a swashbuckling mariner on the high seas. Lurking between the lines of all these tales of bravado, but unsaid and not comprehended, was that thin, imperceptible line separating courageous from foolhardy. That line, often crossed with deadly consequence, never stopped the annual flood of young men walking the docks in search of a job fishing in Alaska. They came, they signed up, and they died.

Most Northwestern fishing ports have memorials near the docks commemorating the deaths of local fishermen. You couldn't miss seeing them. In Anacortes, a small port north of Seattle, there stands at the docks an obelisk twelve feet tall, and on it is inscribed the names of all the town's fishermen lost over the past fifty years. The most recent total was 112. That's more than two a year from a small town of 10,000 people with just a fraction of its population engaged in fishing. Other memorials have been erected in Anacortes, dedicated to those who died in World War II, the Korean War, and Vietnam, but the fishermen's memorial contains more than three times as many names as those on the three war memorials combined.

Nathan Miller, a restless man, twenty-five years old, was a typical Discovery Boy, and one of the few who landed a job. Assigned to work in the factory area of the *Arctic Rose*, he recalled that the main deck often took on seawater that came up higher than his boot tops; the pumps frequently clogged; watertight doors, instead of being properly dogged shut were left standing open; overboard scuppers and drains plugged so the boat often took on more water than it shed; and, worse yet, the *Arctic Rose* carried much of the additional water high on its main deck. High water alarms sounded most nights in rough seas, and with the burden of high water added to the weight of the new fish factory welded to its aft deck, the boat seemed top-heavy to Miller. He noticed that the engine room, which had to be kept free of invading water at all cost, had a hollow wood door not a steel watertight hatch. After just over a month on board, often working sixteen hour days beheading and gutting fish, Nathan Miller had had enough. He quit.

On January 13, the *Arctic Rose*, with a crew not including Nathan Miller, set out from Seattle, getting a late start on the fishing season in a boat small and slow by Bering Sea standards. Its captain, thirty-four year old Dave Rundall, led a crew of fourteen men, including nine Discovery Boys, who had never before been at sea on a fishing vessel, and one man for whom this was a second voyage.

As the *Arctic Rose* left port, the boat seemed to be in disarray. Routine maintenance had not been performed, rust splotched its hull, dirty oil covered the main engine, the propeller shaft was corrosion-pitted and leaking water, and tools and oily rags lay about below deck. The boat's engineer, Mike Olney, the forty-seven year old brother of Dave Olney, and his assistant, twenty-five year old G. W. Kandris, began attending to some of these deficiencies and to the many other mechanical problems fishing boats always have. The boat made its way out of the Straits of Juan de Fuca, rounded the southern tip of Vancouver Island, and turned northwest across the Pacific Ocean.

Traveling at eight knots, the *Arctic Rose* took ten uneventful days to cover the 1,700 miles to what would be its temporary home port at Dutch Harbor in the Aleutian chain, the main supply depot for one of the world's most productive fishing grounds. Under the supervision of first mate Kerry Egan, thirty-five, the crew worked along the way to repair the boat and prepare themselves for the hard days of fishing that lay ahead.

Sitting on barren, windswept Unalaska Island, its shores washed by the icy water of the Bering Sea, Dutch Harbor is a crude, ramshackle fishing settlement. With its unpaved streets and dilapidated storefronts, it has the forlorn look of an Alaskan gold mining camp or a Wild West movie set. It's the last American frontier town, one filled with every temptation a young Discovery Boy could dream of. Its leading cultural institution, the Elbow Room, located in an incongruously purple clapboard A-frame, is called by *Playboy* magazine "the raunchiest bar in America."

With all the essentials of a fine bar—juke box, bandstand, popcorn machine, dart board, painting of a reclined nude, and busted-up, dinged and dented furnishings—the place is second home to the fishermen working out of the scruffy port. Here, they brag about their catch or lament it, down tequila shots and, in the old days, snorted coke, complain about their captain or the weather, swap tips on crew vacancies, and sing the fleshly virtues of the hottest babes in the local whorehouses. Ring the ship's bell at the bar and you announce you're buying drinks for everybody. When the fishing is good, the bell rings a lot, and the babes are busy.

In Dutch Harbor's harbor sit fleets of trawlers, seiners, crab boats, scallop boats, long-liners, and floating processors the size of modern freighters. Cargo ships and freight boats, ocean-going tugs, and tramp steamers come and go regularly. Along its shore are lined one cannery after another, enough to produce two million pounds of fish products daily, giving the place an unforgettable aroma of rotting fish guts mixed with diesel fumes.

During the fishing season, as many as 5,000 new visitors descend on Dutch Harbor each day. These are not like the kids who swoop down on Daytona Beach at spring break, nor the holiday crowds that clog the streets of Nantucket in summer, nor even like the throngs of tourists that disembark from cruise ships onto the towns of the Inside Passage during the summer and fall. Its visitors are a rough and rowdy crowd of randy young men who have been at sea too long, so it comes as no surprise that the businesses of Dutch Harbor are there to accommodate them. Since none of the visitors has a car, cab companies abound. A proliferation of boarding houses and so-called hotels and outright whorehouses offer lodging of a sort, much of it at rates by the hour. Dutch Harbor is a place where the women haven't taken over (yet!), and so it's free of the dainty refinements of an overcivilized, self-indulgent town. Vegan dining, ballet, Frette linens, Junior League, sensitivity training, botox, bean sprout finger sandwiches, polenta scrubs, and aromatherapy, among similar feminine delights, have not yet found their way here, giving the place a certain appeal right off. High culture in Dutch Harbor means getting stoned while listening to Conway Twitty singing *Hello, Darlin'*. Any do-gooder who appeared in Dutch Harbor and announced that he was there seeking to ban cigarette smoking, or to promote sobriety or a low fat diet or sexual abstinence, or to campaign for animal rights or Hillary Clinton, would be unwelcome, to say the very least, keelhauled most likely.

On March 22, as the season for flathead sole was beginning, Captain Rundall, seated in his chair in the wheelhouse of the *Arctic Rose*, stared at the nautical charts on which he had plotted a course for the trip. Dotted lines across the paper chart ran from Dutch Harbor, north across the frigid Bering Sea, to the fishing grounds near the Pribilof Islands, a lonely place he must reach if the boat was to have a chance at earning a profit this year. After transposing into the GPS unit the precise heading, Rundall slipped the transmission into gear and eased the vessel away from the dock. Its prop wash etched a white trail across the slick surface of the harbor as he steered out of the protected waters littered with moored vessels, past the base of Cape Kaleta, past the barren northeast headlands of Unalaska Bay, and finally past Priest Rock, a 204-foot stone pillar rising from the sea. Atop the pillar is a forty-foot high steel mast supporting a light that flashes every twelve seconds, marking the harbor channel for the many vessels that enter and leave Dutch Harbor each year. The *Arctic Rose* passed the outer sea buoy and made its way north.

~~~

If there is a saltwater purgatory anywhere on earth, it is the Bering Sea. Its basin is just 930 miles long, from the Aleutian Islands in the south to the Bering Straits in the north, and 1,240 miles across at its widest, from the Alaska coast to the Kamchatka Peninsula. Though the bottom of its deepest trench drops two and a half miles below the surface, for most of its area, the basin is comparatively shallow, averaging less than 600 feet deep. The sea floor is part of the Pacific plate, an active piece of earth's crust that presses hard up against the stolid North American plate. At the seam between the two, the rock that forms the Pacific plate is pushed below the crust of the denser North American plate where, under intense heat, it melts, loses density, and is forced upward under enormous pressure, resulting in more seismic activity than just about any other place in the world. Earthquakes shake this area routinely, volcanoes erupt with unsettling frequency,

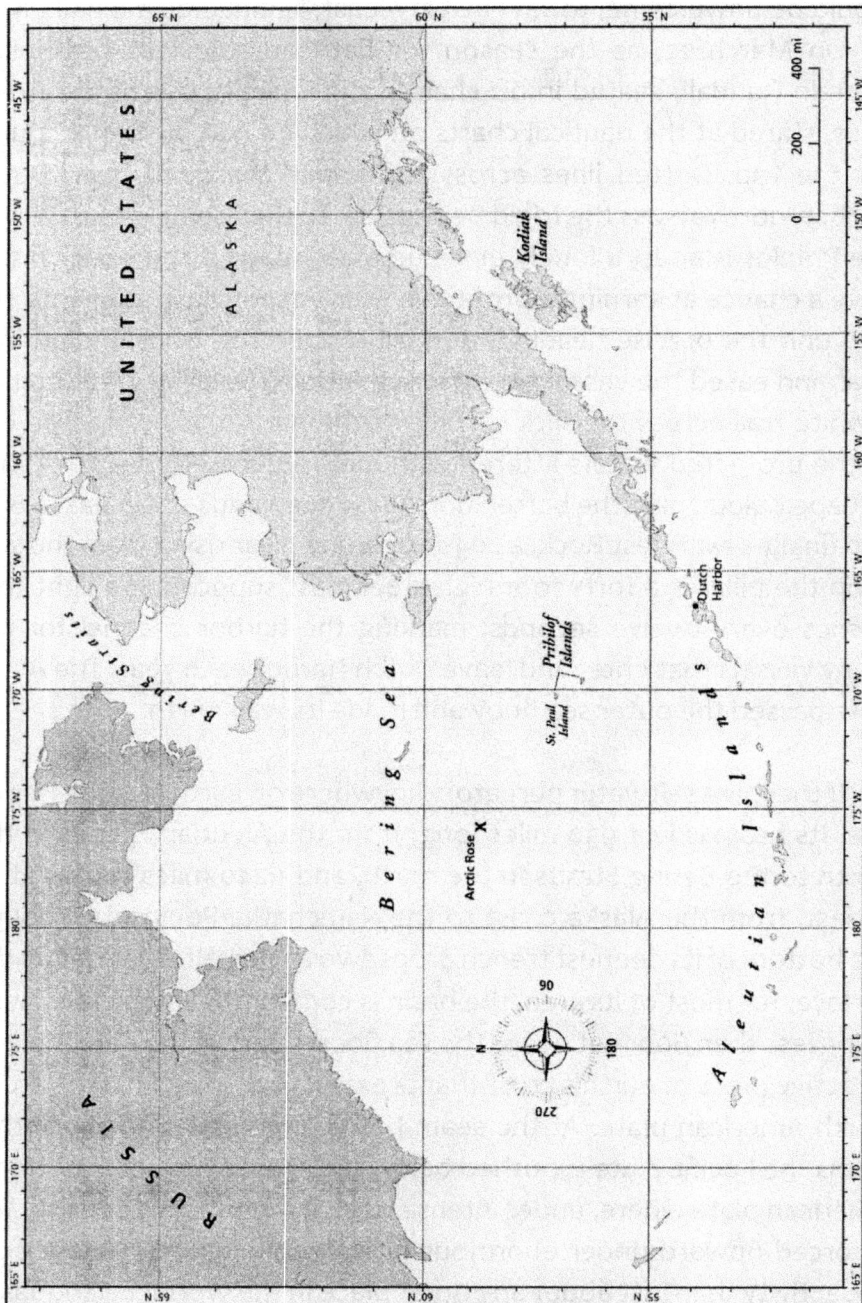

UNITED STATES

ALASKA

Kodiak
Island

Bering Strait

Bering Sea

Aleutian Islands

Dutch
Harbor

Pribilof
Islands

St. Paul
Island

Arctic Rose X

RUSSIA

65° N 60° N 55° N

145° W 150° W 155° W 160° W 165° W 170° W 175° W 180 175° E 170° E 165° E

N
90
180
270

400 mi
200
0

and new islands appear out of nowhere then as suddenly and mysteriously disappear or reduce to undersea pinnacles within just a month's time.

The weather in the Bering Sea is among the worst anywhere in the world. The warm Japanese Current runs clockwise along the continental shelf of Asia until it spills into the Bering Sea, where it encounters the counterclockwise flowing, extremely cold waters of the Bering Current. Where warm and cold currents meet, bad weather is sure to result. Adding spice to this concoction are the blasts of arctic winds that drive down from the polar ice cap over Siberia and Alaska, and south across the sea. These winds, and the brief explosive bursts of williwaws they generate, reach up to a hundred miles an hour as they drive over the shallow Bering Sea, pushing up tumultuous waves.

At high latitudes, the pull of the moon on the tides is accentuated. When the moon is full or new, tides in the Bering Sea run to thirty feet, sending billions of tons of seawater sloshing across the basin floor. When moon, sun, and earth are in alignment, the tides are magnified yet again. Running north on the flood and south on the ebb, these tides pressurize the water to 4,000 pounds per cubic foot and drive torrents running over fifteen knots, flushing the confined channels between the islands in the Aleutian chain.

Winter air temperatures on the Bering Sea are nearly always below zero, reaching down as far as sixty below, wind chill not included. As a boat moves north from the Aleutians, making for, say, the Pribilof Islands, it commonly is beating into a head sea. Its bow, plunging down off steep wave crests, sends billowing clouds of sea spray blowing back over the boat. As the spray freezes, ice soon begins to form on decks, railings, and standing rigging. In a short time, the ice thickens, the boat's speed slows, and it begins to wallow under the added weight.

Unless the ice is removed, the boat's center of gravity will slowly and imperceptibly begin to rise and its stability will become compromised. The boat will roll to port and starboard and back again, just as it always does: Ten degrees, then twenty, thirty degrees of roll, and the boat will right itself. On the next roll, it will heel to thirty-five, forty degrees, but this time, maybe bullied by a wave crashing into its beam, it will just keep rolling, pass its righting angle and never return. In that critical and unpredictable moment, upright turns to upended, life turns to death, and nobody sees the cataclysm coming until it's too late. For that reason, all boats operating in the Bering Sea carry as part of their standard gear baseball bats, ax handles, and sledge-hammers with which to break away the deadly shroud of ice and thus stave off otherwise certain death.

Were it not for the fish, the Bering Sea would be declared an unnavigable disaster area, but fish it has aplenty. The colliding forces of wind, current, and tide that make life so miserable, even deadly, on the surface, well up water from the deep and send it back down in a constant vertical cycle and recycle. This process of stirring the pot means the sea is always filled with the oxygen, light, and nutri-ents essential to breeding and sustaining enormous fish populations. The result is that the Bering Sea is the world's greatest cornucopia of edible fish. Shrimp, crab, halibut, cod, herring, pollock, sole, rockfish, mackerel, hake, and salmon from this sea lure thousands of boats and fishermen each year—spread over the regulated seasons—seeking profit from gathering up these riches in nets and traps. All those fish in these waters for the profitable taking also lure men to their deaths.

The *Arctic Rose* headed first to St. Paul Island in the Pribilof chain, 300 miles off the Alaska coast. From there, it moved on to a grim spot another 200 miles farther northwest, a place of frozen winds and icy waters set under perpetually bleak skies. Early on the morning of April 1, if the *Arctic Rose* operated like other boats, the crew was awakened by Kerry Egan, the mate, pounding on cabin doors. Still groggy from lack of sleep, the men dressed in their warmest clothes and slid on stinking oilskins stained with weeks of fish slime and entrails. As the boat's narrow beam rocked in the eight-foot seas, the men had to hold an arm against a bulkhead to avoid crashing into their fellow crew members. After a hot breakfast and coffee prepared by the cook, Ken Kivlin, at fifty the oldest crewman, the deckhands, Jeff Meincke, at nineteen years old the youngest man on board, and Ed Haynes, thirty-five, reported to the trawl deck. There they received orders from thirty-four-year-old Angel Mendez, the deck boss and only Hispanic and only Texan on board.

The big trawl net, left wound around the aft storage reel the night before, was prepared for setting. When the captain told the deck boss the boat was in position, the reel was unwound and the net lowered into the sea using hydraulic winches and cable. It was a high-opening bottom trawl net made from stretched-mesh polyethylene web with a cone-like front opening, a narrowing throat, and a cod-end, where the caught fish accumulate. When the net was in position on the sea floor, Mendez gave the order to open it, an instruction that his deckhands carried out by spreading the otter boards, big steel doors with lines attached to the net's corners.

On the *Arctic Rose*, the wheelhouse is mounted forward, and there Captain Rundall, using the GPS unit, color video fish-finder, recording fathometer, and autopilot, managed the trawl, keeping it over level bottom and on a desired course and depth. After a few hours, the net was closed and hauled aboard by Meincke and Haynes using the hydraulic winches. As the cod-end came aboard, it was emptied into the deck bin where the catch was sorted. Discards were tossed over, except for the pollock and cod that Amendment Forty-nine required they keep, and the keepers were sluiced into the factory for processing.

Aaron Broderick, age unknown, and his assistant, twenty-two year old Jimmy Conrad, headed up the five men who comprised the processing and freezing crew, called slimers: Robert Foreman and David Whitten, both thirty; Shawn Bouchard, twenty-five; James Mills, twenty-four; and Michael Nevreiter, thirty-seven. The slimers, all first-timers, got the scut work of twelve to sixteen hour days, standing at the factory line, elbow to elbow, beheading and gutting fish—relentless, tiresome, mind-numbing work. When processed, the fish went below to the freezer crew, who stored the finished product in the freezer hold only a few minutes after the fish had died and before they began to deteriorate.

At 4:50 p.m. on April 1, Captain Rundall sent an e-mail to his wife, Kari, mother of their three boys, ages four, twelve, and fourteen: "We are catching a few fish here, but the weather is rough again .... I love you and I miss ... your pretty face." Ten miles away, the *Arctic Rose*'s larger sister boat, the *Alaskan Rose*, heard from Rundall when he reported taking in a full ten-ton net of fish, a catch big enough to keep the processing factory busy through most of the night. We will never know exactly what happened next, but, given what is known of the *Arctic Rose*, a probable chain of seemingly innocuous events, and their consequences can be reconstructed.

That night, as the crew finished gutting, beheading, and storing fish in the freezer, they were exhausted. Working in extreme cold, jammed together in the tiny factory, the monotony of processing the fish, after the hard labor of hauling in the net and sorting the catch, had depleted any reserves of energy they may have had. As they cleaned up the processing area and washed down the stainless steel preparation tables, they were bleary-eyed from working nearly eighteen hours straight. They had the "Aleutian stare," that rheumy look of mindless trance when, robbed of volition, the body moves without apparent forethought. The alert mind needed to survive the Bering Sea had deserted them hours ago.

Captain Rundall slipped the transmission into neutral. As the ship's props stopped churning and the *Arctic Rose* came to rest, the vessel was no longer controlled by man. In that moment when the clutch disengaged the props, modern yielded to primitive, machine surrendered to nature. No longer motor-powered through the seas, the *Arctic Rose* traveled back across time more than a hundred years and became wind driven. Grabbed by the wind, the bow fell away downwind until the beam was fully exposed broadside to the weather. In nautical terms, the boat lay ahull. As waves struck, the boat's natural buoyancy dissipated the energy of each wave by rising up the crest and dropping into its trough, as well as by rolling, first to port then to starboard and back again, with the boat's superstructure and rigging swinging to and fro, a pendulum describing a wide arc. With each roll, it approached, but did not exceed, its righting arm.

The *Arctic Rose* didn't fish at night, so thirteen of the fifteen crew collapsed in their bunks. In their weary delirium, they failed to notice that the always troublesome steel watertight door leading from the factory onto the aft deck had not been closed securely. The door had always been difficult to close and leaked badly. Yet this barrier was all that separated the boat's secure interior from the pounding seas outside. The heavy door was the castle wall that kept out the invading sea, and now it was badly compromised.

Captain Rundall and his mate, Kerry Egan, were in the wheelhouse, where they too fell into a heavy sleep. Its freezer hold brimming with newly processed fish adding weight to its ballast, the boat, always heavy in the stern, was riding low. Todd Wheeler had seen that low stern completely awash a few years before when the boat was loaded, its net on deck and its hold full of fish. That heavy stern, caused in part by the addition of the steel-enclosed factory area, was what had led to the stability letter's strict loading requirements.

Seas at the time were running eight to twelve feet in winds of thirty knots, comparatively calm for the Bering Sea. A few hours later, as the crew slept, conditions worsened considerably when the leading edge of a storm intercepted the *Arctic Rose* at almost exactly 3:30 a.m. Seas were now running to twenty-four feet driven by winds of forty-five knots. With the boat already heavy in the stem, it was now poised for disaster as roaring winds turned angry seas into relentless mounds of energy that began to pound the *Arctic Rose*. The sleeping Captain Rundall had been through weather like this many times in his brief career, and this was certainly not the worst he had seen. But on this early morning in treacherous waters, events were accumulating all around him, cascading out of control. Mistakes he may not even have known about, could not see, were added to the inherent dangers of the Bering Sea.

The narrow beam, stable for a sixty-foot boat, now stretched to ninety-two feet, offered too little resistance to rolling. The shallow, rounded bottom, unlike the far more common deep keel, also was less resistant to rolling. An upswept stern meant that when it was hoisted by heavy seas to the crest of a wave, the underside of the stern, right where the factory had been added, could be attacked by the billowing sea, further upsetting the precarious balance. And then there was that heavy stern and that troublesome, not so watertight door. With the accumulation of events already working against the boat and its crew, there was little room for more error and no room at all for bad luck. It was on the edge of this dark abyss, we can reasonably surmise, that the last ruinous event was added to the concatenation, the event that may have sealed the terrible destiny of the *Arctic Rose*.

In the heavy seas, waves began to break over the low-riding stern bulwarks, flooding the aft deck. As the stern sank still lower under the added weight, sea water flushed by the rolling hull washed across the deck in waves. At first, only streaming rivulets gently stroked the seal where watertight door and bulkhead met. As the seas steepened, though, and bigger waves crashed onto the aft deck, as the stern slipped lower into the sea, the rivulets became a river. The seal that had always leaked weakened more, and water began to stream into the factory, though it was easily pumped overboard by the boat's automatic pumps. With each roll of the boat, the river of seawater continued to sweep back and forth past the heavy steel door, grasping at it like the malicious hands of an invader seeking to pry open a weakness in the boat's defenses, searching out a way to penetrate the wall of steel.

The stiff steel structure of the factory walls moved ever so slightly as it reacted to stresses from the deck waves and the stormy sea. Barely detectable torqueing and wracking of the factory walls loosened the grip of the steel door's locking pinions, already just barely engaged in the jamb. As the steel walls continued to flex and the waves continued their assault, the seal around the door leaked still more—until the leak became a flood. The high water alarm sounded, but captain and crew, nearly comatose in exhausted sleep, did not comprehend the meaning of the sound.

In a tragic moment, wave pressure on the door's leaking seal finally dislodged the locking pinions from the jamb. The aft watertight door, the wall designed to keep the deadly cold sea from encroaching, sprang open. Water poured in, quickly overwhelming the automatic pumps and flooding the factory; waves sloshed across the factory deck just as they also washed over the trawl deck outside and the stern sank lower still. Soon the water inside found its way down a hatch and began filling the freezer hold. The stern sank still more.

As the cold steel hulk of the *Arctic Rose* continued to slip into the sea, water rose around its hull. It rose above the Plimsoll line, the painted stripe around the hull that marked the maximum height of its waterline fully loaded. It climbed the freeboard and poured over what little of the aft bulwarks were not already underwater. As the hull continued to sink deeper and deeper, the weight of the sea pressing down on the stern forced the bow into the air. Rising up out of the sea, the boat seemed to be desperately gasping for a final breath of fresh arctic air and vainly attempting to escape the Bering Sea's death grip.

As the *Arctic Rose* sank by the stern, water climbed and flooded the main deck until the deck was submerged, then climbed toward the wheelhouse. Air pockets trapped inside the hull caused the doomed hulk to hesitate for a few moments, suspended in macabre equilibrium until the pressurized air escaped—once it did, the boat continued to sink. When the sea reached the wheelhouse, it encountered a metal bracket attached to an outer bulkhead in which was mounted an Emergency Position Indicating Radio Beacon, or EPIRB, the size of a shoe box.

In the crew quarters below decks, where spent men just moments before had slept in silent relief from their labors, now stunned men confronted sudden calamity and the flood of cold water. Quiet exhaustion turned to stark terror, illuminated decks turned to black, upended chaos, and chilled stinking air turned to unbearably cold and suffocating seawater. They could not escape.

The cataclysm happened so quickly that neither Captain Rundall nor Kerry Egan, who slept in the wheelhouse where the VHF and single-side band radios were located, were able to send a mayday call for help. Instead they struggled desperately in the sinking tomb, first to locate their survival suits and then to don them in the terrifying confines of the wheelhouse. Both men knew that to be in the Bering Sea without a suit meant certain death. In timed practice drills, each man could remove his suit from its orange bag, spread it on the deck, clamber into it with the hood over his head down to his eyes, the front zipped to his chin and both neck flaps closed, in a minute's time. But that was in the calm setting of a drill, a place with fellow crewmen around, a warm, well-lit, dry place, without impending death just outside the door and rising.

Now the heavy steel mass of the *Arctic Rose* was sinking fast, with most of its hull below the surface, its crew engulfed, and the deadly water rising around the wheelhouse. What had once been the deck beneath the feet of Egan and Rundall was now a vertical bulkhead. They stood, or tried to stand, on steeply slanted steel walls that had once kept them warm and dry and now provided their only footing. Commonplace, loose items of the wheelhouse were strewn about their feet: paper charts and a clipboard, a frayed and stained log, catch records, and coffee cups still dark streaked from the last cup either man would taste. Putting on a survival suit and zipping it tight in these conditions was just not possible.

The sea already filled the engine room, swallowing the new diesel engine Dave Olney had installed, shorting out the main electrical system and the backup, battery-powered emergency system. The wheelhouse, once lit by incandescent light, suddenly turned perfectly black. Somehow they managed to open the outer wheelhouse door before water pressure sealed them inside forever. Rundall had not yet fully donned his survival suit, unable to get it zipped tightly to his chin, and Egan had not gotten his on at all. Both men struggled out into frigid winds that tore at their faces, into the cold black water that would soon swallow them. As the boat dropped into the sea, Rundall's suit quickly filled with deadly thirty-eight degree water, and though he fought to close up the suit, it was too late. Egan, without a suit, never had a chance. Within minutes, the effects of hypothermia began to set in on the two men.

Cold water saps the human body of heat at a rate twenty-five times faster than cold air. At first, body temperature spikes, then plummets, setting off violent shaking. Blood that had circulated to the arms and hands, feet and legs, retreats from these extremities and concentrates its life-giving warmth around the most vital organs. Coordination begins to fail and consciousness wanes. When the core temperature drops below ninety degrees, shaking stops and the body joints and limbs grow stiff, nearly immovable. The skin turns pale blue, breathing becomes labored and shallow, the heart rate plummets sharply and soon the will to survive is overcome. As body temperature drops below eighty degrees, the instinctive ability to tread water is lost, and all physical and mental function shuts down completely, followed by death.

As the *Arctic Rose* continued to sink, plunging toward the bottom 428 feet below, the EPIRB unit, still in its bracket, reached a depth of ten feet. There, hydrostatic pressure and buoyancy caused the unit to release from its bracket and quickly pop to the surface where it began transmitting a radio signal at a frequency of 406 megahertz using a built-in antenna no longer than a common ruler. Its integral battery provided enough power to continue transmitting for forty-eight hours.

The signal, sent on an internationally recognized distress frequency, is monitored by a system of geostationary satellites operated by the National Oceanic and Atmospheric Administration, each carrying an instrument package that is the electronic heart of the Search and Rescue Satellite Aided Tracking (SARSAT) system. When received by an orbiting satellite, the signal is sent back to earth to land-based tracking stations located all over the world, called Local

User Terminals. From there, the signal is sent to a Mission Control Center, which for the United States is an office of NOAA located in Suitland, Maryland, outside Washington, D.C. There, on large wall-mounted screens, the position and status of all active EPIRB signals is monitored.

When a signal is intercepted by MCC, it is routed automatically to the command center for the area from which the signal is received. For the Bering Sea, that's the U.S. Coast Guard Rescue Coordination Center (RCC) in Juneau, Alaska. The RCC begins tracking the signal and gets a fix on the EPIRB unit's location, computed by the satellite using Doppler technology. Simultaneously, the RCC notifies the Coast Guard Communications Station in Kodiak, which then broadcasts over all VHF and single-side band emergency frequencies and sends to all public media an Urgent Marine Information Broadcast, describing what is then known about the EPIRB signal and its location.

Kodiak Comsta, nerve center of Coast Guard operations in the Bering Sea and coastal Alaska, is the oldest communications center of its kind in the U.S. It is responsible for a 6,000-mile, crescent-shaped coast from Attu Island at the western tip of the Aleutians, south and east along the crescent to the Canadian border, an area encompassing 900,000 square miles of ocean, twice the land mass of the entire continental U.S. At all times, at least twelve people at Comsta are on watch monitoring multiple radio channels from soundproof workstations. Radio signals they overhear come from possible drug traffickers, trespassing foreign fishing vessels, weather reports, and calls for assistance including the dreaded mayday calls.

Comsta picks up more than 300 EPIRB signals each year, but because EPIRB devices are mechanical/electrical and operated by error-prone humans, two-thirds of these turn out to be false alarms. The manual switch gets accidentally tripped, somebody's kid thinks it's a play toy and flips the switch, the unit's owner turns it on for testing without following the directions imprinted on the unit, or it gets dropped overboard and starts transmitting automatically. These and other false alarms come into Comsta regularly, but none is known to be false when received, so the Coast Guard treats each as a real alarm. In the harsh conditions of Alaska, where life turns on how fast a survivor can be plucked from the sea, the Coast Guard has no time to doubt a signal's authenticity. Nearly every 406 EPIRB signal received at Comsta results in the costly dispatch of a C-130 Search and Rescue plane.

Each 406 EPIRB signal has imbedded in it a code specially assigned to that unit, registered with NOAA and used to identify the vessel to which the EPIRB is registered. The registration form each EPIRB owner completes and files with NOAA contains phone numbers of the people to be notified in the event a signal is detected. These numbers are called to make certain the signal was not accidentally set off and to verify that the vessel is expected to be in the area indicated by the fix.

At 3:38 a.m. on April 2, 2001, the 406 EPIRB unit registered to the *Arctic Rose*, the unit that once sat idle in a bracket attached to the boat's wheelhouse, began transmitting its signal to satellites overhead. When it was received by MCC, the signal was relayed to the U.S. Coast Guard, Seventeenth District, Rescue Coordination Center in Juneau, and an Urgent Marine Information Broadcast was issued from Kodiak Comsta. Soon a C-130 Hercules Search and Rescue plane was dispatched from the Coast Guard Air Station on Kodiak Island.

When the EPIRB signal from the *Arctic Rose* was received and the C-130 launched in the darkest hours of a frigid night, the Coast Guard promptly slammed into the impenetrable wall of misfortune that would doom the boat and its crew of fifteen. The signal placed the ill-fated boat nearly 1,000 miles from the air station in Kodiak, a distance that would take the dependable but ponderous search and rescue plane precious hours to cover, hours that would give the cold waters more than enough time to sap the life from any survivor not fully protected by a survival suit.

The four-engine C-130 sent aloft on this mission banked low over the mountains of Kodiak Island and headed north. With a full load of fuel, the C-130 can stay aloft up to twelve hours on a level flight path, but add fuel-consuming turns and climbs and that time is cut to only eight hours. Normally, the plane carries a crew of seven: pilot, copilot, radioman, and four crewmen, sitting two on each side of the plane with eyes glued to the ocean below. The searchers look for any sign that might lead them to survivors, like life rafts, survival suits, strobe lights, oil slicks... anything. When an object is spotted, the searcher punches smoke, launching a smoke signal flare to illuminate and mark the spot for closer inspection. After two hours of peering at trackless ocean, fatigue sets in, and the searchers begin to spot objects that really aren't there. The work is grueling.

Five hours after the EPIRB signal was received at Comsta, the C-130 arrived at the precise location from which the signal was then still being broadcast: latitude 58 degrees, 56.22 minutes north, longitude 175 degrees, 53.10 minutes west, or 200 miles northwest of St. Paul Island in the Pribilofs. Down there, bobbing in the cauldron, was an EPIRB unit sending signals received and relayed by satellite to a Mission Control Center, that relayed the signals to a Coast Guard Rescue Coordination Center, which relayed them to the C-130, a marvel of telecommunications technology. But technology couldn't save the crew of the *Arctic Rose*. The C-130 arrived at least four hours too late. Dave Rundall, floating in a water-filled survival suit, and Kerry Egan, with no suit, surely died within less than an hour of the vessel's sinking. The rest of the crew went to the bottom with the boat, trapped forever in a steel coffin.

At the same time the C-130 was dispatched, the Coast Guard high endurance cutter **Boutwell**, based in Alameda, California, and carrying one Dolphin helicopter, and the icebreaker *Polar Star*, based in Seattle and carrying two Dolphins, were directed to proceed to the site fixed by the EPIRB signal and assist in a search for survivors. An HH-60 Jayhawk helicopter was sent to St. Paul Island to assist in recovery operations. Though it was 250 miles from the scene on a science mission when it got the call, the 399-foot *Polar Star*: with its crew of 130, arrived at the site of the sinking within twenty-four hours and became commander of the search operation.

Inexplicably, the *Alaskan Rose*, fishing just seven miles away, was not notified until four hours after the EPIRB signal was received. It arrived at the scene an hour later. At 10:00 a.m., a full six and a half hours after the EPIRB signal was first received by the Coast Guard, its crew found and recovered Captain Dave Rundall floating on the surface, his frozen body held buoyant by a bright orange, water-filled survival suit. The crew spotted one other body, probably Kerry Egan's, but had to abandon recovery efforts in heavy seas.

A three-day search, covering 2,500 square miles, turned up an empty life raft, trace debris, a small oil slick, and sadly, empty survival suits. Had the *Alaskan Rose* been promptly notified when the EPIRB began transmitting, Rundall and Egan might have been rescued. With survival times of up to thirty-six hours in a timely and properly donned suit, and the earliest rescue boat on the scene in just over five hours, every man who could have escaped from the boat might have survived the frigid seas had he only been able to put on his suit. Instead, all fifteen men on board perished together, including Mike Olney, the boat's engineer, brother of Dave Olney. It was the worst disaster among Alaskan fishermen in fifty years.

Dutch Harbor, Aleutian Islands, Alaska.

The Arctic Rose.

Unalaska Bay.

Chapter Eight

Giving money and power to
government is like giving whiskey
and car keys to teenage boys.
                              - P. J. O'Rourke

WHEN CONFRONTED BY the loss of innocent life, such as those lost in the sinking of the *Arctic Rose*, we want to know how it happened. What went wrong? How can we prevent such calamities from occurring again? At the most superficial level—generally the level at which investigative news reports, tort lawyers, and inquiry panels of the Coast Guard operate—we, or they, search for a culprit, someone to blame, someone who was negligent.

Based upon what little is known about events surrounding the *Arctic Rose*, we might conclude—at least from the speculative reconstruction of events described in this book—that culpability lies with the person responsible for securing the watertight door. That person, whether the deck boss, the first mate or, ultimately, the captain, we can say had a duty to perform a task, failed to perform it properly, and thereby caused the tragedy. Tort lawyers, looking for a person with access to lots of money, usually in the form of an insurance policy, on whom they can pin some degree of responsibility, will claim it was Dave Olney's fault because he had the factory installed on the aft deck and failed to assure that its door could be easily secured, or whatever other theory might produce a large damage award.

The great deficiency in this effort is that it fails to examine the underlying cause, or series of causal connections, without which the sinking never would have happened. It fails to ask what influenced owner, captain, and crew to behave as they did. Why, for example, did Olney buy a too-small, poorly built boat? Why did he retrofit it by welding a processing factory to the aft deck? What caused him to send this, of all boats, into the far frozen reaches of the deadly Bering Sea and with his brother on board? Why did his crew work to exhaustion? Why were they so utterly inexperienced, nine having never before set foot on a boat?

If we go one step beyond the superficial, we find that a possible, and compelling, answer to these important questions can be summed up in a single expression: government regulation. The Byzantine regime of commercial fishery regulations that Dave Olney faced, the set of laws, rules, regulations, permits, licenses, and fees, shaped and directed, mandated and coerced virtually every decision he and Dave Rundall and the crew members themselves made. Those decisions, so choreographed by government, led indirectly, to be sure, but inexorably to the tragic sinking of the *Arctic Rose*. And those same regulations, still in force today, are the inevitable result of a solitary political choice made nearly 300 years ago. Let's now explore, not the superficial, but the ultimate underlying reason why the *Arctic Rose* went down.

=================================

At this country's inception, the political principles under which it would be governed were debated and, when resolved, became part of the body of laws that formed the very foundation of today's America. One of those principles, one that was adopted with comparatively little debate because it was so universally accepted, concerned the question of who should own the country's wildlife. The men who engaged in the debate had just come through the crucible of war with England and were determined that America would have a vastly different government than the Mother Country. The new version of rule would be a republican form of democracy, based on a contract between the government and the people, on the consent of the governed. It would be the antithesis of a monarchy with its absolute power and its preening aristocracy whose wealth and status came not from personal achievement but from birthright and crown-granted privilege. America would be egalitarian; this new land would make life, liberty, and the pursuit of happiness the ideals for all the people, not just the highborn few.

So, when the time came to decide the issue of who should own the wildlife, the result was easily predictable. Back in England, wildlife was owned by the owner of the land where it was found, and the land was, of course, owned in sprawling estates by the aristocracy. Whether deer or red grouse, rabbit or duck, if the animal was found on the land of the earl of this or the duke of that, it was his deer or his grouse, his rabbit or duck, and anyone who hunted them without his lordship's permission was a poacher, a very serious offense indeed. Even the rainbow trout swimming in a stream were owned by the man who owned the land on both sides of the streambed.

The early statesmen of America wanted nothing in the new law that smacked of granted privilege. How could God's creatures that had roamed wild and free since the beginning of time be owned by a few men to the exclusion of all others? It seemed, well, blatantly undemocratic. Wildlife in a country founded on the ideas of Locke and Hume and Rousseau could only be owned by the people. Deer and red grouse in America would be the property of all the people of America, held by them in common with all other Americans for their mutual benefit. Landowners could certainly hunt wild game on their own estates, but so could anyone else, unless the landowner erected signs saying, Posted, No Hunting. Even when land was posted, if the game wandered off, it could be hunted by others. You could own land, but not the wildlife that lived on it.

This one essential principle, later known as open access, under-girds nearly all wildlife management in America today. It is a principle that enjoys wide popular acceptance and is so deeply ingrained in our culture that few give it much thought. Over time, government, first at the state and only lately at the federal level, became a proxy for the people, passing laws and making rules and regulations and erecting vast bureaucracies to regulate, but not own, the people's wildlife. Open access based on the founders' original principle, writ on the tabula rasa of the new country, became the little freshet that became the stream that became the torrent. So-called open access would flow across time through the cluttered offices of state and federal senators and representatives, committees, staffs, lobbyists, interest groups, governors, and even presidents. It would course through the winding corridors of bureaucracy where hearings would be held, experts would be heard, where even the common man could appear. Bills would pass and become law, regulations would issue. Rules and permits and fees would follow, as day the night. All of it, the whole lot, just assumed the founders were correct when they decided that wildlife should be owned by the people—open access—and its taking regulated by the government.

The goal of this growing and costly body of regulation is what has come to be called sustainability, that is, limiting the harvesting of wildlife to assure its continued propagation in adequate quantities to supply future demand. The word is an eco-chic, earth-love expression from the '90s, intended to convey in shorthand a set of errant ideas brought to us by modern, the-end-of-the-earth-is-near Malthusians. Applied to marine fisheries, the essence of these ideas is that glutton-ous demand from an exponentially growing human population will soon outstrip fish propagation, and extinctions (of fish, not humans) will be the almost certain result. Only edicts from a beneficent gov-ernment commanding greedy capitalist fishermen to rein in their wanton habits can change the outcome.

In achieving the goal of sustainability, regulators have been spec-tacularly unsuccessful. Prior to the early '70s, the marine fishery was small and its regulation a backwater of government. But in the after-math of the revelation that beef contains high levels of saturated fats and may contribute to heart disease and thus the untimely demise of

Baby Boomers, the demand for fish soared. Fast food outlets serving fish sandwiches, restaurants serving fish filets, farmers and ranchers using fish products as additives in livestock feed, all contributed to increased demand for the bounty of the ocean.

Within this rare environment of hyperdemand and soaring prices, many new fishermen entered the U.S. fishing industry with the hope of high profits from a seemingly inexhaustible natural resource. Like labor, capital too flowed in to meet demand. Larger and more sophisticated boats laden with newly developed fish-finding electronics hit the high seas. In response to this exhilarating new world, the regulators, with their bedrock policy of open access, instead of promoting sustainability, promoted intensely competitive, for-profit fishing. In no time at all, the industry was flooded with labor, capital, and technology, all employed to harvest a limited dynamic resource. As if to underscore its incompetence at regulating marine fisheries, the federal government began subsidizing the fishing fleet with low interest loans and incentive tax credits. As a result, more and still bigger boats were built, with still better technology, which depleted limited fish stocks even faster.

As they awoke to the disrupting effects on the fish population of inept regulations and government subsidies, regulators began to tighten the rules, hoping to cut back on overfishing, or the catching of a species beyond its level of sustainability. After first actively promoting, encouraging through its regulatory policies, and even subsidizing the entry into the market of labor and capital—more new fishermen with new boats, larger nets, and more advanced electronics—now the government, without warning, reversed itself. Acting solely in the best interests of the fish, not the fishermen, and certainly not the consumer, the regulators began to choke off the fishermen's economic life blood and the consumer's supply. All those new fishermen, who had taken substantial risks investing millions in new boats and equipment, just as government regulations and incentives had persuaded and subsidized them to do, found themselves betrayed. Almost overnight, the regulators changed the very foundation of their policies and began to limit sharply the number of fish caught. Or at least they tried to.

Traditionally, the government regulated by limiting the length of the season for each species. Where overfishing occurred, all they had to do was shorten the season. With less time to fish, fewer fish would be caught, overfishing would disappear, and the stocks would replenish themselves. The regulators also could place limitations on gear. If larger boats could trawl larger nets, simply limiting the size of the boats would result in smaller nets yielding smaller catches. If too many boats were going after too few fish—the much discussed problem of overcapitalization—the government had only to buy the excess boats and the problem would be solved. And so it went. The solutions were so simple and so obvious—and so wrong.

Without the faintest grasp of what effect their rules might have on a competitive market like commercial fishing, and, of far greater importance, what effect they would have on the dynamic behavior of human competitors within that market, regulators imposed rules, more rules, and still more rules. And the regulated reacted, as they should, to preserve the vocation that government policies and sub-sidies had persuaded them to take on in the first place, and to repay the debts those policies and subsidies had encouraged them to incur. In the ensuing battle between regulators and the regulated, it was no contest.

Government attempts at regulating marine fisheries have been, with a few notable and uncharacteristic exceptions, an utter and costly failure. For some species, like salmon, the cost of government regulation is so great that, when it is added to the cost of catching, processing, and marketing, the total cost of a fish exceeds its market value. Society would be better off, enjoy a higher living standard, if all salmon in the oceans simply disappeared. Yet, despite all the costly regulation, most salmon stocks continue to deplete, and where they are plentiful, the majority of that supply is due not to regulation but to the flood of high-quality farm raised salmon and to natural cyclical variations in salmon populations.

The fisherman's reaction to regulation was predictable. As a self-interested entrepreneur fulfilling his proper role in a capitalist economy, trying to wrest a living from the sea, he used his street-smart cunning to minimize the impact of each rule. If a rule limited the size of a boat as a means of limiting the size net it could trawl, he installed an overly powerful motor in the smaller boat and still trawled the bigger net. If the government offered to buy excess boats in an overfished area, the fisherman sold out and used the money to buy another boat cheaply from a second overfished area, retrofitted it, and continued fishing in the area of the buyout. A congressional study found that fully half of bought-out fishermen were back in business within two years. What did the regulators expect when they provided new liquid capital to men whose only skill was fishing? Were these men supposed to become real estate agents?

When regulators in open access fisheries exercise their police power to control the catch, without comprehending the effect a rule will have on the free choices available to competitors within that market, they promote an alarmingly inefficient use of labor and capital. They also needlessly endanger the lives of fishermen. When a fishing season is implemented, shortened, then shortened again, a fisherman's costs do not reduce accordingly. The loans on his boat and other fixed overhead continue. His kids still need the same amount of money for school. His home mortgage still must be paid every month. A fisherman, if he is to catch enough fish to cover his daily business costs, repay his loans, and provide an income on which to support his family, must fish during every possible moment and in all weather to make up for the shortened season. To comply with boat size limits, he may take on the risk of fishing in rough waters, like the Bering Sea, in a boat that is too small and ill-suited to the task; or to get his costs into line with lower revenues resulting from a shortened season, he may buy a lower cost, poorly built boat, like the *Arctic Rose*, thus shouldering a deadly personal risk in an attempt at economic survival.

The traditional method of paying the crew based on a share of a boat's profits makes things worse. It is in the crew's economic interest to work sixteen to eighteen hour shifts during the shortened season, even though their constant state of exhaustion, seen on their faces in the "Aleutian stare," invites death or injury and causes mistakes that imperil boat and crew, as we saw with the *Arctic Rose*.

So not just the rough weather, or the badly built boat, or the undersize boat, or the guy who while in a stupor of exhaustion fails to secure a watertight door causes boats to sink and people to die at sea. These are only the superficial causes, the choreographed consequences of behavior shaped by incentives, disincentives, reward, and punishment. It is largely government regulation that severely and abruptly changes market economics, increases financial risks, lowers financial rewards and, ultimately and most importantly, alters behavior, forcing people to accept greater risk.

The result is a long, sorrowful string of disastrous consequences, such as the sinking of the *Arctic Rose* and the loss of its crew. Hundreds of other boats have gone down and hundreds of other men and women have died in Alaskan waters due in some part to well-meaning but deadly federal regulation. The failure of regulators to grasp the effects of their edicts on human behavior—the law of unintended consequences—is an unmeasurable but significant cause of vessel loss and death in commercial fishing, and it all results from that one seemingly irreproachable decision by the founders that wildlife should be common property, not private.

~~~

In a now famous article, Garrett Hardin, a philosopher and environmentalist, described the inevitable results of owning wildlife as common property. Using an allegory, he described a village green owned by the village people in common, and thus owned by no one. The green is a lush parkland available for use by all the people, some of whom own cattle. Acting in his rational self-interest, a village cattle owner grazes as many cattle as he can on the green and continues to add new animals to his herd, because the cost of feeding the animals on the commons, unlike the cost of using his private pasture, is near zero. But this conclusion is also reached by every other rational cattle owner in the village until, alas, the overgrazed commons is finally destroyed by too many herdsmen adding too many cattle to graze on the limited resources of the green.

Because nobody owns the commons, it is in nobody's interest to husband the scarce resource, to protect it from overuse, to invest in its maintenance and improvement, to conserve it for the future. This natural consequence of public ownership Hardin called the "tragedy of the commons." Each villager's self-interest drives him remorselessly, as it would every other rational person, to overexploit any resource owned as common property and thus not protected by a private owner's more far-sighted sense of vested self-interest. As the regulators have learned, despite a maze of laws, rules, and regulations, despite harsh penalties and enormous government expenditures, marine fisheries, like the village commons, continue to be overused with the attendant grossly inefficient use of labor and capital. As sadly brought to our attention by the *Arctic Rose*, fishery regulation also results in a shameful loss of life and property.

This doesn't apply just to fish. Other examples of the inevitable overexploitation of common-owned wildlife abound. Early Spanish explorers described buffalo herds as a limitless brown sea that once numbered twenty-five million common-owned beasts. Since nobody owned them, they were essentially free for the taking, so that by 1895 only 800 remained, mostly owned as private property on ranches. The passenger pigeon, once the most numerous species of bird on earth, numbering around three billion, became extinct by 1914 because of widespread and lucrative hunting of these common-owned birds. The same fate befell the great auk and the heath hen, among others.

In stark contrast to the depletion of common-owned wildlife are the fecund and flourishing populations of private-owned animals. Hereford, Angus and Jersey cattle; the Rhode Island red, longhorn, and barred rock chickens; farm-raised salmon, catfish and trout abound and propagate to feed millions of people. Beyond animal populations, we must also ask why cattle and sheep ranchers overgraze public land, but carefully cultivate lush private pastures. Why do logging companies overcut public forests, but keep well-tended plantations of their own timber? Why are public lakes and streams treated by the populace with such indifference, while private water bodies are clean, clear, and strictly managed? Wherever common-owned property is found, we discover waste and overexploitation, but private ownership results in achieving the goal of sustainability, and it does so at a far lower cost, without inept regulation.

But how can marine fisheries benefit from the salutary results of private ownership? How can fish at sea be owned by anybody? How will private ownership reduce the risks to fishermen and result in fewer sinkings and lost lives, fewer tragedies like the *Arctic Rose?* For many species, a workable but temporary answer to these questions comes not from some experimental program but from an idea that finds wide application all over the world, and for a few species even in the U.S. It is a rights-based management regime called individual transferable quotas (ITQ's). Fishery managers, with scientific advice, determine the total allowable catch for each species. This maximum quantity is then allocated (ideally it will be sold on an open market) among licensed fishermen as individual quotas freely transferable among licensees by sale or lease. In contrast to the breakneck and deadly race to catch as many fish as possible before the other guy— the so-called Olympic system—the ITQs set the volume of fish each licensee is allowed that particular season. This quota can be caught at such times and in such weather and with whatever boat and gear the licensee decides is best for him.

Since he has a private property like ownership interest in his ITQ, each fisherman has the right market incentive to behave in a way that is most consistent with sustainability, while operating his boat at lower cost and reduced risk to vessel and crew. Over time, the most able fishermen will operate at lower cost, earn higher profits, and eventually buy out the quotas of their competitors. With increased concentration comes reduced overfishing and increased efficiency. Lower consumer prices and sharply reduced regulatory costs and government intrusion into private life result. The ITQ is not, however, the ideal permanent solution, as the case of salmon vividly demonstrates.

~~~

Overfishing for salmon, as well as many other species, is a problem being rapidly solved with the unknowing and ironic aid of government regulation. As regulatory pressure squeezed the marine fishery at a time when demand for salmon was growing, supply was constrained and, of course, prices soared. Today, wild caught fresh salmon bring up to $9.00 a pound at the local fish market—if it's available at all. Over much of the U.S. it's not, and even where it is, it can't be bought all year long. As we've seen in the flesh trades of Ketchikan and Dutch Harbor, so we see in the fish trade: Demand will be supplied. It was into this enormous void in the marketplace that the all-powerful force of private property blended with modern technology surged. It did so under the name of aquaculture or, to use the more prosaic term, fish farming.

Using technology first developed in Norway in the '70s, salmon farms today produce over 500,000 tons annually and supply sixty percent of U.S. salmon demand. Beginning life as fertile eggs from hatcheries in Scandinavia or Scotland, the farm fish travel to British Columbia or the Maritime Provinces in Canada, Maine, Ireland, Chile, Britain, or other places where clear clean seawater is found. Fed a controlled diet of fish meal, the eggs become first smolts, then finger-lings, and finally, over a two-to three-year period, harvest-size salmon. So efficient is the process that a pound of meal produces a pound of salmon. Through careful selective breeding, only high-quality fish result, available year-round at a cost to the consumer less than a third that of wild fish. If you order salmon in a restaurant or buy it in a store almost anywhere in the U.S., it's most likely farm raised, and if you pay $3.00 a pound in a store, it's certainly farm raised (wild salmon at retail is about three times the price of farm raised). Throughout my travels in Alaska, where ninety-seven percent of all wild salmon are caught, I saw firsthand the devastating (for the fisherman) economic effects of this relentless competition. Fish that once brought the fisherman $4.00 a pound now bring $1.00 and will soon bring even less. I also heard all the complaints about farm-raised fish, some marginally valid but none persuasive, most just predictable sour grapes.

Private-owned salmon will very soon destroy the marine salmon fishery, except perhaps for a small niche in the market for high-quality, high-cost fish from the premium rivers of Alaska. As private-owned fish farms continue to improve their product with ever-advancing technology, even this market niche could disappear. It is perverse irony that government regulators will very soon see the oceans and rivers of Alaska teeming with wild salmon, more fish than they ever could have imagined, not because of their success as regulators, but because their sheer ineptitude resulted in unintended but knowable and predictable consequences. Prices were driven so high and supply became so unreliable that a gaping door was left standing open for private entrepreneurs who responded to the opportunity handed to them. Perhaps the ultimate irony will come on the day when, their services no longer needed, government fishery regulators are asked to find other work.

Fishermen of still marketable wild species like to claim that farms will never produce a fish competitive with theirs. Don't bet on it! Thus far, farm-raised fish include salmon, catfish, trout, sea bass, tilapia, shrimp, striped bass, abalone, oysters, mussels, largemouth bass, perch, red drum, and even halibut. More are on the way. As technology continues to improve, the day will soon come when virtually all marine fisheries will disappear, replaced by private-owned fish farms, and the mistake made by the founding fathers will be set right. Environmentalists concerned about sustainability will have to find other issues to worry about, government regulators will have to find other employment, and the consumer, who is the point of all this, will reap a bonanza of high-quality, low-cost readily available fish.

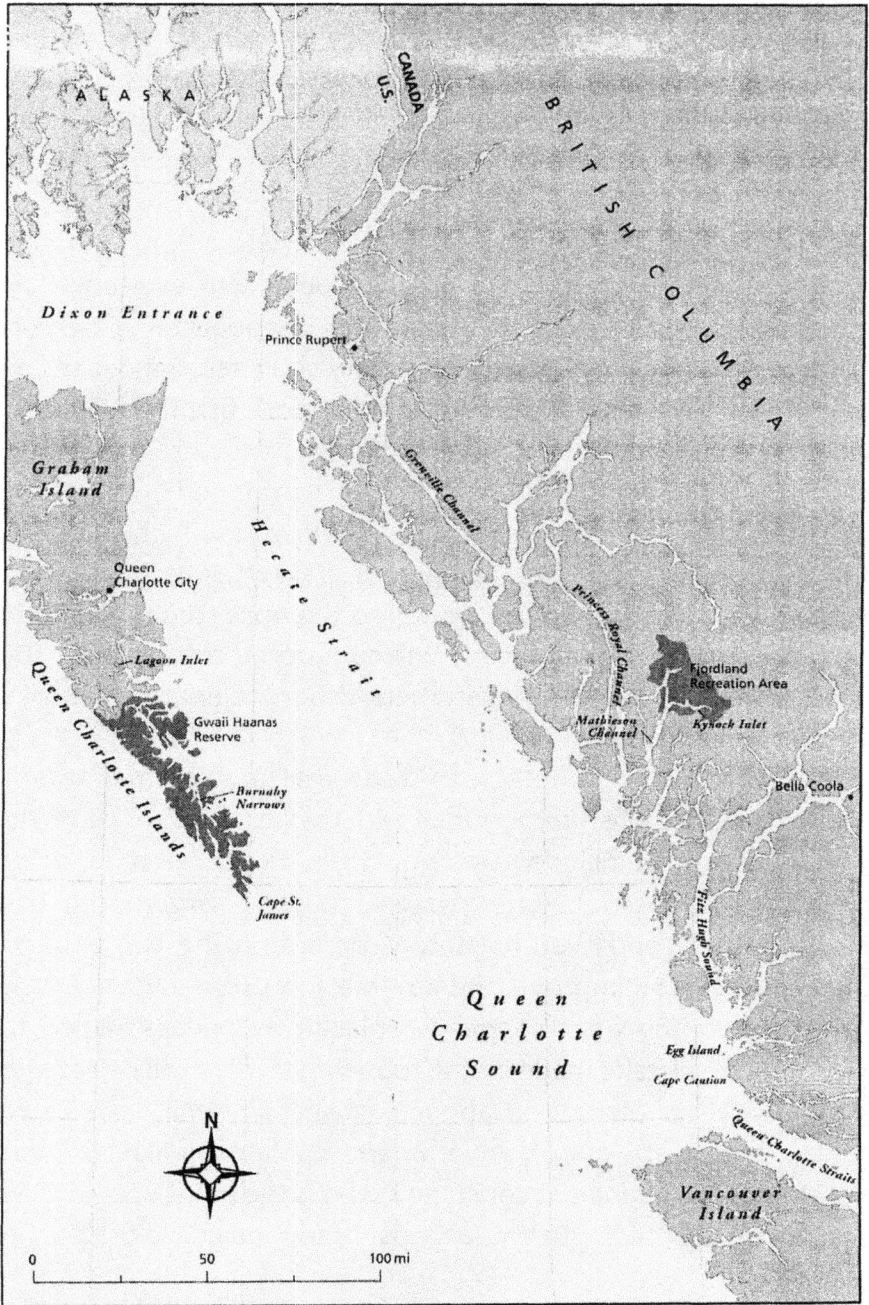

ALASKA

CANADA
U.S.

BRITISH COLUMBIA

Dixon Entrance

Prince Rupert

Graham
Island

Grenville Channel

Queen
Charlotte City

Hecate Strait

Princess Royal Channel

Lagoon Inlet

Fjordland
Recreation Area

Gwaii Haanas
Reserve

Queen Charlotte Islands

Mathieson
Channel

Kynoch Inlet

Burnaby
Narrows

Bella Coola

Cape St.
James

Fitz Hugh Sound

Queen
Charlotte
Sound

Egg Island

Cape Caution

N

Queen Charlotte Straits

Vancouver
Island

0   50   100 mi

Chapter Nine

There are two things a man can't
have too much of, and one of
them is horsepower.
                                    - Anonymous

HALF A MILE wide and a thousand feet deep, protected on both sides by mountain ridges, Grenville Channel is perhaps the world's most dramatic nautical corridor. Forest-coated, snow-patched mountains rise steeply from its shores, their upper reaches blurred most days by a veneer of low-slung, gray-curdled sky. Here and there, just back from the shore but a steep, bear-infested climb away, remote lakes serve as catch basins for the summer snow-melt. Betraying the presence of these lakes, tufts of gauzy cloud, frayed at the edges, hang low in the valleys. So narrow and high-sided is the channel that at a distance super-large cruise ships appear small as a child's bath toy. Even up close, the mountains, a stage backdrop hanging drip-wet and green, are of such scale that republic-size ships wither away, reduced by perspective to tiny floating intrusions.

Along this boulevard are a few openings in its enclosing walls through which a boat can enter the hidden lakes by way of narrow channels, unseen amid shoreline rocks and forest camouflage. With power enough to overcome tidal currents, a small boat, deftly piloted, can pick its way into the forest, winding among the trees and rocks, until it breaks free into a lake on whose black mirror surface a primal world is painted. It is at such a place that I gain entry into one of these lakes and, once inside, floating, motors off, on black sheen, I find myself centuries removed from the twenty-first, surrounded by a world with not the slightest suggestion of modernity or even of mankind. I have happened upon Baker Inlet, an inner sanctum, a place of tranquil beauty, of lonely serenity. After the drubbings I have recently endured, this place is nature's balm for the bruised spirit, so I linger here and savor the peace.

At the southern end of the Grenville Channel is another long, mountain-lined nautical boulevard, the Princess Royal Channel, both main thoroughfares for the many cruise ships that ply these waters during the summer months. Near the end of the Princess Royal, I travel by way of Sheep Passage to Mathieson Channel deep in the Fiordland Recreation Area, a park of 225,000 acres noted for its precipitous granite cliffs reaching over 3,000 feet from the water's edge. Up Kynock Inlet at Culpepper Lagoon are surrounding palisades of damp stone splotched with snowpack and streaked with dripping waterfalls that mimic the saturated sky. After winding through a maze of islands in stormy gloom, I arrive at a sport fishermen's resort, of a sort, where I stay the night in trailer park-like pre-fab housing.

Next morning, leaving through Lama Passage, I enter the miles-wide Fitz Hugh Sound in, surprising as it is, clear blue skies and calm waters. A lone orca feeds in the tide line, his dorsal fin oddly deformed by corrugations along its trailing edge. Unlike the timid humpback, the orca allows humans in boats—like me—to approach closely. But, mindful that they commonly drive out of the water onto rock shelves to snatch a hapless seal, I make sure not to get too close.

At the point where the waters of Fitz Hugh enter Queen Charlotte Sound, the morning's placid cruise over glass-smooth water is quite suddenly and dramatically shattered. A fierce wind arising from dead calm begins to blow on the bow. Nature allowed me to pass quietly one of the two most feared inlets, Dixon Entrance, but she will make me pay now as I enter the second. With trim tabs almost fully extended, her bow slicing into each onrushing wave, *Rascal* pounds through heavy seas on the way to Egg Island, fully exposed to north-westerly swells of the Pacific Ocean and the still strengthening wind.

The Canadian weather service, called Environment Canada, reports on the VHF that a ridge of high pressure is building along the western edge of the Queen Charlotte Islands, which eventually is expected to replace the prevailing low pressure system. In the meantime, as the high rushes into the relative vacuum vented by the low, winds result, howling through the tee-top in full gale force. A small craft warning is in effect as the wind velocity continues to rise and the seas to steepen. With trim tabs down and throttle reduced, *Rascal* makes only twenty-eight knots instead of the usual thirty-five to forty.

Well into the sound near Egg Island, I pass a small tug pulling an enormous ocean-going barge loaded with stacks of newly sawn timber strapped to the deck. A chain, called a tow bridle, with links thick as a leg, extends from one corner of the barge's flat bow to the other. Its midpoint, exactly in the center of the bow and well below the surface, is connected to a tow wire, a long arc of heavy steel cable extending from barge to tug. Half the length of its catenary lies underwater, where hydrostatic pressure keeps the wire from whip-ping wildly through the air as barge and tug are pushed about by the sea.

At the tug end, the many-stranded tow wire passes over the tran-som, across a flat length of an old rubber tire there to prevent chaf-ing, then through a pair of upright steel tow pins that keep the wire in lateral alignment. From the pins forward, the wire runs under a length of heavy chains, called hold-down chains, but known to tugmen as a gob rope, a simple device that keeps the tow wire from flailing about the deck and popping loose from the pins. Finally, the wire passes onto the hydraulically powered drum of the tow winch, where it is wound in or paid out as conditions warrant.

For the tug captain pulling a heavy load in a sea, a keen sense of rhythm is essential, much like the rhythm of a dance. As the enor-mous barge, with a displacement ten times that of the miniature tug, plows through stormy seas, it rises and falls to the tune of the waves that assault it. If the tug is singing a different tune, the tow wire is placed under enormous stress that even hydrostatic pressure on the catenary can't contain. The tow wire snaps taut, lashing off the deck and slamming into the gob rope in a bolt of violence. If the gob rope breaks and the tow wire is freed to find its way, the wire will get cross-wise to the tug's beam. Unless the captain acts quickly, the blundering mass of the barge will overpower the little tug, and the tow wire will easily jerk the tug over, sinking it. It has happened before. But if the captain has rhythm, if he can get barge and tug dancing in harmony, the tow wire does not flail at its containment, the gob rope sits idle, and tug and barge make headway safely through the seas.

Beyond the ominously named Cape Caution are the waters of Queen Charlotte Straits, now wind-whipped to a fury. Steep-faced waves pound *Rascal's* hull and toss me around at the helm. Very much wanting to get out of this mess, I hug the mainland coast of British Columbia, looking for lee protection. Off to starboard is the north end of the nearly 300-mile long Vancouver Island, a mountainous, tree-covered hogback running continuously along the length of the island's spine. To port are the soaring mountains and underlying hills of coastal British Columbia. In rain, wind, and cold, I venture up a desolate inlet, seeking quiet shelter, to no avail.

Then, as quickly as a light goes out when switched off, the sea becomes glassy smooth, a laminar field of tarnished silver under a sky still pewter gray. Behind the protecting wall of Vancouver Island, Queen Charlotte Strait is dead calm, while just a mile behind, unprotected from the gale force winds, the seas rage. Crossing the straits and passing through Blackfish Channel, I enter Johnstone Straits hard alongside the east shore of Vancouver Island, cruise through more winding channels, run turbulent tidal rapids, and at last find Blind Channel Resort in the failing light of day.

Blind Channel is neither the first nor the only fine resort the boater encounters moving south from Alaska into British Columbia, but it is representative of a subtle cultural change along the route. People from Seattle and Vancouver, in slow sailboats and motor yachts

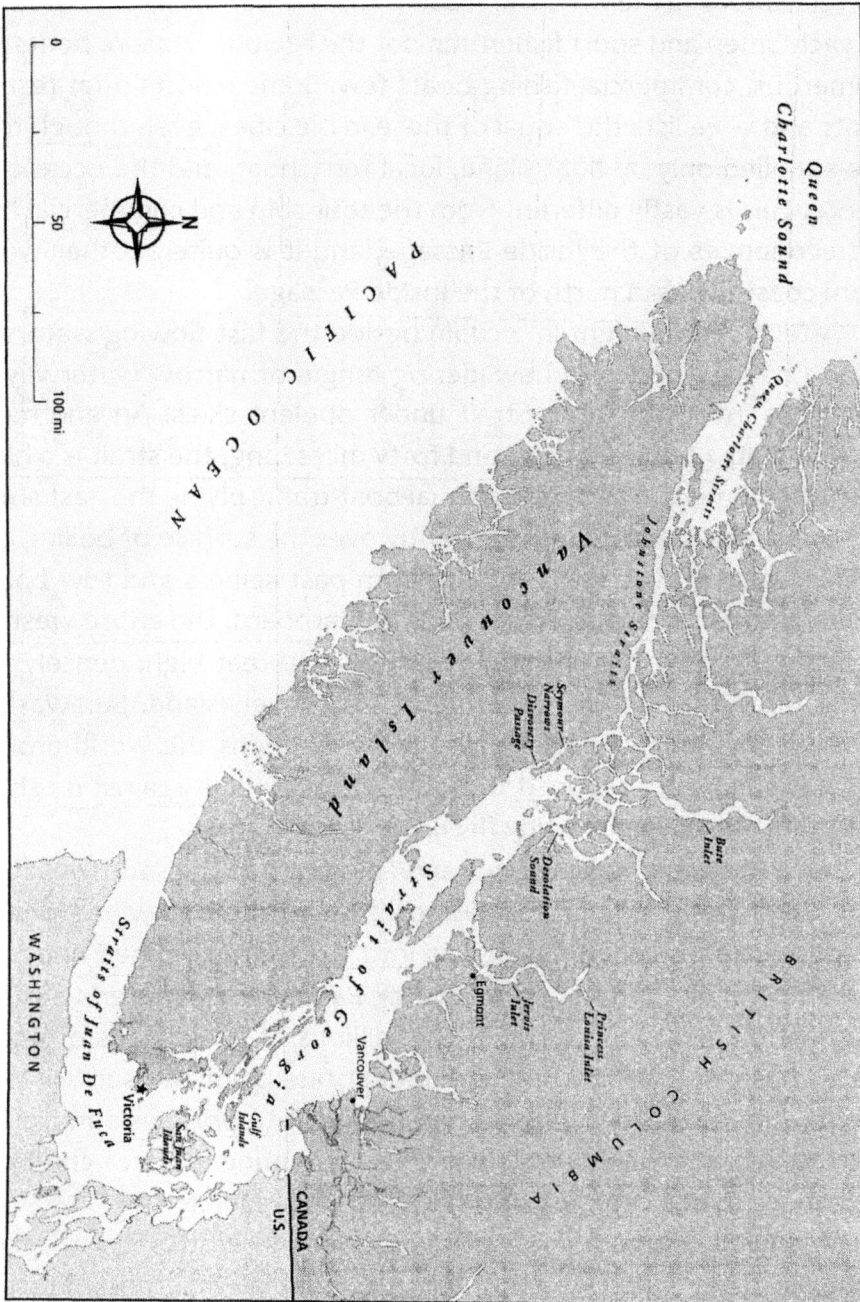

Queen
Charlotte Sound

PACIFIC OCEAN

Queen Charlotte Strait

Vancouver Island

Johnstone Strait

Seymour
Narrows
Discovery
Passage

Desolation Sound

Bute Inlet

Strait of Georgia

Egmont

Jervis Inlet

Princess
Louisa Inlet

BRITISH COLUMBIA

Straits of Juan De Fuca

WASHINGTON

Victoria

San Juan
Islands

Gulf
Islands

Vancouver

CANADA
U.S.

N

0
50
100 mi

heading north for a week, can easily reach this area, remaining in protected waters all the way. The result is that numerous resorts catering to yachtsmen and sport fishermen dot the region. Pleasure boats are numerous, commercial fishing boats few. Some resorts offer restaurants and wine lists the equal of those in big cities, even though they are supplied only by float plane, local ferry boat, and the occasional barge. This is vastly different from the tour ship and commercial fishing economies of the Inside Passage, and it is quite another world from coastal Alaska north of the Inside Passage.

After a restful night in a cabin beside the fast flowing waters of Blind Channel, part of a bewildering tangle of narrow waterways, I head out into Johnstone Strait under opulent skies. An enormous marine gully 1,000 feet deep and forty miles long, the strait is a highway of commercial and recreational boat traffic plying the east shore of Vancouver Island. Skimming lightly over the surface of boiling currents, *Rascal* moves in graceful rhythm past seiners and tow boats, sailing yachts, and sport fishermen. To starboard, the entire western sky is blocked by the Island. Towering 5,500-feet high, densely forested ridge that is the backbone of Vancouver Island. Sun-washed at this early hour, the long palisade overwhelms the world around it. Cruise ships are reduced to hobby shop models against its sheer walls, and *Rascal* is just a tiny fleck.

Soon the strait makes a wide sweeping turn to the southwest that takes ten miles to complete; at *Rascal's* speed, it is a slow-motion arabesque. Passing out of the straits into the more confined and thus more powerful currents of Discovery Passage, the water's surface is a blue membrane in turmoil. The millions of cubic yards of ocean water flushing through on the flooding tide paint the surface with scribbles and curlicues, pillows and boils. Off to port lies a miniature archipelago of small islands riven by a serpentine maze of channels, little more than a complex of spillways for Bute Inlet.

This inlet, a 2,000-foot deep gouge in the earth's crust, reaching back thirty miles into the British Columbia wilderness, fills and drains twice each day and, when it does—through the Arran Rapids, a 250-yard gap poorly suited to the purpose—violent whitewater, enormous whirlpools, and boiling cauldrons of sea result. Converging with the flow through Arran are the waters draining virtually all of the Desolation Sound complex that funnel through the nearby Yuculta Rapids. The two merged torrents, now become a seething clash of energies, then shoot through the Dent Rapids into the broader reaches of Johnstone Straight, where their power dissipates.

Soon enough, I come upon the infamous Seymour Narrows, a place where tidal flows reach fifteen knots, erupting in foaming cataracts, whirlpools, rips, and overfalls. Here the channel narrows to a keyhole that, until 1958, was divided into the even narrower east and west channels. Between the two sat Ripple Rock, the peak of an undersea mountain which at low tide lurked just beneath the surface where it caused many years of deadly shipwrecks. More than 120 vessels were sunk or damaged and 114 lives were lost as a consequence of this unfortunate geology. To remove the thing, engineers sank a vertical mine shaft on the east shore at Maude Island 570 feet straight down, then dug a horizontal shaft 2,400 feet into the base of the seamount under Ripple Rock. From there, they dug two vertical shafts 300 feet up into its twin pinnacles, and near the top of these shafts they set 2.75 million pounds of dynamite. When ignited, the result was the greatest non-nuclear explosion in the world to that time. Poof! No more Ripple Rock.

After running the now obstacle-free narrows, I set course across the Strait of Georgia for Jervis Inlet, another ragged fjord cut into the mainland shore of British Columbia. Relieved of the grim weather I've left behind, this day is one of sensory delight. The fifteen-mile wide strait is a place of sun-spangled water, framed in frilly ornamentation by distant mountains chiseled from the landscape. No hint of cloud mars the resplendent sky, and only gentle breaths ruffle the sea. Without the chilled and dripping air of recent days past, the pungent aroma of the sea returns to embellish the already alluring pleasures of a fast boat on calm water. After too much time under cold, rain-laden skies, I now, for the first time on this adventure, feel the warm rays of luxuriant sun. Also for the first time I begin to shed layers of wool.

Somewhere just north of the Strait of Georgia, the forests begin to change. Farther north, the Inside Passage is lined in vast swaths of evergreens—mostly the salt-hardy Sitka spruce mixed with red cedar, fir, and pine. But here in a comparatively milder climate, deciduous trees begin to appear. Madrona, birch, apple, and alder, big-leafed and stout, grow from hillside to shore, clustered in copses as if to fend off invasion from the evergreen horde.

At the village of Egmont, a short way up the Jervis Inlet, a modest cafe sits atop a steep bank, where from its outdoor deck, diners watch boats of every description run the Sechelt Rapids at the entrance to the Skookumchuk Narrows. These rapids, like all those around here, are the result of powerful ebb tides rushing over rock-strewn narrows causing overfalls and standing waves. The Canadian pilot book describes the "furious and dangerous Sechelt Rapids, the roar of which is audible for many miles." What the pilot book fails to say, though, is that in a fast seaworthy boat with plenty of power these rapids aren't so dangerous, and they are lots of fun. I wait for the rapids to reach their peak, then run them easily, *Rascal* sending up exploded geysers of white spray as she blasts through the waves. It's a welcome relief from the dispiriting days of misting rain under sludge-gray skies.

Far up Jervis Inlet, at the picture postcard-beautiful cascading waterfalls of Princess Louisa Inlet, the water is aswarm with boats on this fine summer day. A popular camp nearby supplies the vacation tableau with hundreds of shrieking teens who loll about on inflated tubes and rafts or splash in the frigid water. Fairly forewarned, I have passed from the hardscrabble environment of the Alaskan and northern British Columbia coast and reentered the genteel world of advanced civilization. It is a passage I am resigned to make—because it marks geographic progress toward my goal—but the transition is certainly not one I welcome. The closer I get to the territories of dense human habitation and their freedom-robbing array of laws, rules, and regulations (my encounter with the Park Service in Glacier Bay comes to mind), the more I yearn for the wilderness, at least on this getaway adventure.

Returning to the mouth of the inlet, I turn south down a long open fetch of the Georgia Strait, dead into a vicious chop that pummels *Rascal* continuously until I reach the protected harbor of Vancouver, B.C., where I spend a few days in needed rest in one of the world's most cosmopolitan urban centers.

~~~

Handsome and flower-festooned, the charming city of Victoria lies at the southern tip of 200-mile long Vancouver Island and on the northeast shore of Juan de Fuca Strait. A boat leaving the Victoria docks in front of the grand old Empress Hotel, passing by the British Columbia's Parliament Buildings and the Provincial Museum (since renamed the Royal British Columbia Museum), and exiting the outer harbor could turn to port and, after rounding a point and heading due east, would in ten miles encounter an archipelago of islands that are among the most delightful places anywhere on earth. The San Juan Islands, as they are called, number 750 at low tide, counting exposed rocks, reefs, and islets, 450 at high tide, and 172 important enough to bear names. They are a constellation of low granite slabs, jagged peaks and hills, verdant fields, sandy beaches and rocky cliffs. Here visitors are said to become afflicted with a condition that combines felicity and insouciance with a dose of Chamber of Commerce boosterism to produce an intoxicant locally called the Magic of the Islands.

The place is oddly quiet. Tides flush through its narrow rocky corridors twice daily, sending thousands of tons of pure clean seawater rushing about with nary a sound save the faint gurgle of freshet on granite. A lone seagull yowls, a distant sailboat's motor chugs, pine-scented zephyrs mix with salt air and gently ruffle boughs of spruce and fir and pine. But for these, all around is languid silence.

And so it has always been among the San Juans. Always, that is, except when the islands, or more specifically San Juan Island became the site of a war—and a most unusual war it was—between Britain and its upstart sibling, the nascent and acquisitive United States. This war was America's briefest, lasting less than six months, its most comically named: the Pig War, and it's the war with the fewest casualties: none, if you don't count the pig.

To grasp fully the humor of what happened here, some background is required. At the start of the nineteenth century, four nations—Spain, Russia, England, and the United States—laid claim to a vast and potentially lucrative area that today includes Washington, Oregon, Idaho, and parts of Montana, Wyoming, and British Columbia, then called Oregon Country. Through a series of treaties, cessions, and deals, the Oregon Country's claimants were reduced to two: Britain and the U.S. Fueled by the fire of Manifest Destiny and intense nationalism left over from the Jacksonian era, the U.S. wanted everything south of the forty-ninth parallel—that's the line that today separates the lower forty-eight states of the U.S. from Canada— while Britain wanted to move the line south to the Columbia River, which would give her water access to the interior fur trade.

After a two-year standoff full of hot-headed recriminations and bluster, the parties signed the Oregon Treaty of June 1846, which gave the U.S. all the lands lying south of the forty-ninth parallel, a total diplomatic victory. But in a portentous phrase, the result either of negligent draftsmanship or an incomplete grasp of geography, the treaty said the parallel should be extended west"... to the middle of said channel, and to Fuca's Strait to the Pacific Ocean." Trouble was, two such channels were implied: Haro Strait, between the San Juan Islands and Vancouver Island, and Rosario Strait, between the islands and the mainland. The San Juan Islands lay smack between the two, and whoever controlled the San Juans also controlled the harbor at Victoria and the approaches to the resource-rich Fraser River. Thus was the stage set for porcine pugnacity.

Of the twenty-five Americas living on San Juan Island, none held a land title recognized as valid by the British. Some Americans even claimed to own land that had earlier been staked out by the British Hudson's Bay Company. Each side regarded the claims of the other as obviously fraudulent and the presence on the island of the other as nothing short of common trespass. With both parties defiantly recalcitrant— and armed, by the way—only the slightest offense would be needed to ignite a war.

The transgression came in a most unlikely form. An American— and a particularly truculent American he was— named Lyman Cutler, spied a pig rooting up the potatoes in his garden. Not a man to take such affronts lightly, Mr. Cutler promptly fetched his rifle took careful aim, and killed the foraging beast. Turned out this was no ordinary pig but one owned by Mr. Griffin, the manager of the local outpost of Hudson's Bay Company, and a pig of which Mr. Griffin was particularly fond. Events, it seemed, were beginning to spiral out of control.

Lyman Cutler, in what he considered a magnanimous gesture of goodwill, offered to pay ten dollars as compensation for the deceased animal. Unsaid was the likely fact that Cutler had dressed, cooked, and eaten the evidence and so was the better off for his action. The irate pig owner demanded one hundred dollars, however, and to mediate the dispute called in a Mr. Dallas, the head of Hudson's Bay Company for all of North America. Dallas, an imperiously self-important, priggish sort, promptly offended Mr. Cutler with his arrogant manner and abusive language.

As if to underscore his talent for bad judgment, Mr. Dallas threatened to drag Mr. Cutler off to Victoria for trial in a British court. The obstreperous Mr. Cutler curtly reminded Mr. Dallas, in colorful backwoods vernacular one imagines, that he was an American citizen living on American soil and, consequently, not subject to British jurisdiction. Indeed, Mr. Cutler may have uttered to Mr. Dallas something on the order of "f*** you." Lines thus drawn deeply in the dirt, the Pig War had begun.

Acting precipitously, Brigadier General William S. Harvey, veteran of the War with Mexico, commander of the Department of Oregon, and an ardent Anglophobe, saw an opportunity to clarify, in America's favor, the ambiguous wording of the Oregon Treaty using force of arms. He ordered the always exuberant and bellicose Captain George

E. Pickett (later famed as the leader of a courageous but disastrous charge at Gettysburg) to occupy San Juan Island and protect the American citizens residing there, all twenty-five of them, including the now famous and central figure of Lyman Cutler.

Pickett's contingent, together with subsequent reinforcements, numbered 461 men with fourteen cannon. They occupied high ground that we can be reasonably certain was not called Pork Chop Hill, though perhaps it should have been. The Brits, meanwhile, indignant at the affront to the King's honor occasioned by the wanton murder of one of his majesty's citizen's prized porkers, sent to the island five warships mounting 167 guns and carrying 2,140 men, including Royal Marines. This was, indeed, an important pig, its demise having now provoked an international incident approaching all-out war.

Finally, seeing the folly if not the humor of the standoff, both sides backed away and eventually agreed to a joint occupation of the island, which lasted twelve years. Kaiser Wilhelm I of Germany, acting as mediator, later decided the dispute in favor of the U.S. Today, the old barracks, redoubts, and earthworks of the former British and American positions on the island have been restored and serve as minor tourist attractions. No memorial has been erected to the pig that started it all.

~~~

Today's forecast calls for gale force westerly winds in the frequently troublesome Straits of Juan de Fuca, the fifteen-mile-wide, sixty-mile-long body of water separating the state of Washington from Canada's Vancouver Island. To the south, hanging low over the Washington shore, is a black wall of dense storm clouds. The air is crisp, and the wind has freshened to twenty knots, both consistent with the dropping air pressure that signals a storm's approach.

Leaving the harbor of Lopez Island, I run a few miles to a cape protected by the lee of San Juan Island, then have only a fifteen-mile run across Haro Strait into a head sea to reach Victoria Harbor, a nasty passage, but short. Entering Victoria Harbor at midday, I dock in the heart of town at the Empress Hotel alongside the *Robertson II*, the last

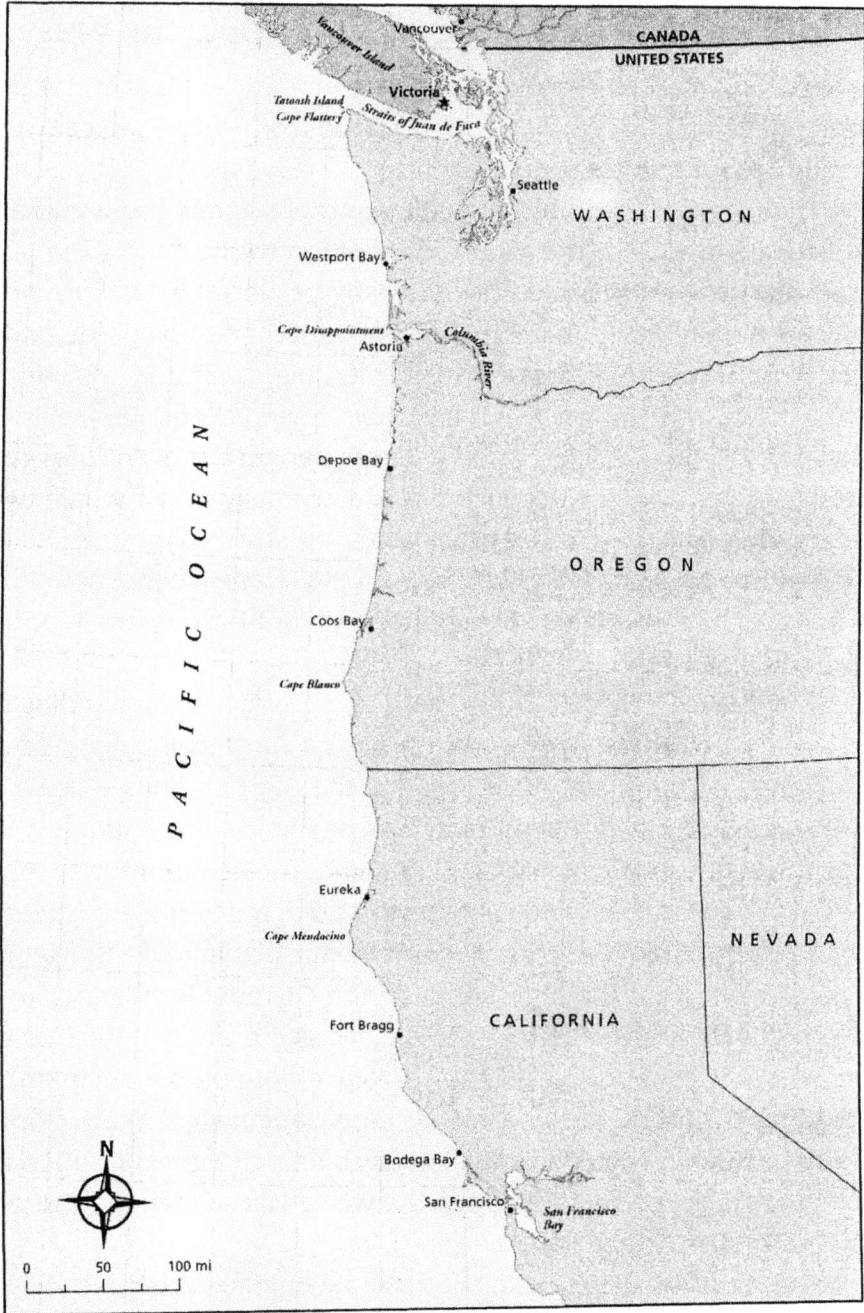

CANADA

UNITED STATES

Vancouver

Vancouver Island

Victoria

Tatoosh Island

Cape Flattery

Straits of Juan de Fuca

Seattle

WASHINGTON

Westport Bay

Cape Disappointment

Astoria

Columbia River

PACIFIC OCEAN

Depoe Bay

OREGON

Coos Bay

Cape Blanco

Eureka

Cape Mendocino

NEVADA

Fort Bragg

CALIFORNIA

Bodega Bay

San Francisco

San Francisco Bay

N

0   50   100 mi

sailing schooner built in Canada to fish the Atlantic Ocean's Georges Banks, now out to pasture as a tourist attraction. The two vessels make an unlikely pair, the one constructed of fiberglass and stainless steel, sleek and fast, the other fabricated from wood and canvas and oakum, stout and paint-dryingly slow.

The forecast next morning calls for more gale force winds at the western entrance to the straits. In addition to the winds, the task of transiting the straits is complicated by powerful tides common to this area. Small craft heading west encounter an ebbing tide draining much of the interior coast of British Columbia, setting against westerly to northwesterly ocean swells and their driving winds. The collision of these results in massive standing waves dangerous even to large vessels. Only last year, in just such a sea, a normally stable whale watching boat with large inflated tubes around a sturdy aluminum hull, the kind of boat the Coast Guard uses for rescue operations, flipped with a full load of passengers, killing one. I will not hit the straits until the flood tide has begun.

As I leave Victoria's outer harbor, the skies are sparkling blue and without clouds; the warming rays of sun recall childhood days on Florida's Gulf Coast. After crossing the bay that links Victoria with the straits, rounding Race Point, and heading west, suddenly, without the slightest hint of what is to come, the temperature drops by twenty degrees, the wind calms, and a cold, misty fog embraces me. Off to port, a hundred-foot thick alabaster blanket of sea fog partly shields from view the high peaks of the Olympia Range gracing the south shore. Above the blanket is clear sky, grandly detached from and describing in bold relief the cottony gloom below. A commercial ship just departing Victoria for perhaps Japan, slips easily from the clarity of sun-washed blue into a gauzy blur, her highest ramparts and exhaust stacks projecting above the white veil suspended there as if separated from the earth.

The weather service said the straits would experience patches of fog; it should have said patches of clear sky. With each change of tide, cold inland waters encounter warm tidal currents rushing in from the ocean and the winds that come with them, so that a dense blanket of fog results. Where eddies of cold water run alongside warmer ocean waters, the fog is intermittent, a jumble of gray patch and lucent sky.

At the northwest corner of Washington's Olympia Peninsula, also the northwest corner of the lower forty-eight states, sits Cape Flattery, a nautical landmark of sorts. Because it's actually a corner of little Tatoosh Island, sitting just offshore, it's not technically a true cape. But cape or not, it's my next destination, and it marks an important milestone of this voyage. From the initial launch at Homer, Alaska, the first 800 nautical miles to the Kenai Fjords, Prince William Sound, Kayak Island, Icy Bay, Yakutat Bay, and Cape Spencer, were mostly exposed to the Gulf of Alaska. Once around Cape Spencer, the next 800 miles to Cape Flattery were in the protected waters of the Inside Passage over predominantly flat seas, with the notable exceptions of Hecate Strait and Queen Charlotte Sound.

Upon reaching Cape Flattery, a third and final leg of this adventure will begin, one that for some 1,400 nautical miles will pass along the coasts of Washington, Oregon, and California to the Mexican border, with *Rascal* fully exposed to the Pacific Ocean. Quite unlike the first leg, this one will have numerous harbors, well-developed towns, a few large cities, easy telephone and VHF radio communications, numerous Coast Guard stations well-equipped for all emergencies, fine restaurants, and plenty of wine and cold beer. It also will have venti lattes, Pilates, Ferraris, line-caught fish on the menu (the better to protect the... whatever), earnest starlets out to cure world poverty or hunger or racism (while unknowingly contributing to world ignorance or at least humbug), and a galaxy of goofy ideas exhorted energetically as though the San Andreas Fault may give way at any moment without such things having been said.

This segment of the coast will not have 200 inches of annual bone-chilling rainfall, williwaws, icebergs, glaciers, roaming bears, orcas, Republicans (not many anyway), hundreds of peopleless square miles, a hardy kick-ass population, and snow-clothed coastal mountain ranges, features whose absence I regret. Most of all, life on the southern range of my adventure will be too easy, without challenge or risk, and consequently, much less fun.

================================

For the sixty miles to Cape Flattery, I move through fog, some thin with visibility of a mile, some soupy with visibility reduced to only a few hundred feet. The radar, set to a two-mile range, shows two large ships in the outbound traffic lane of the straits. Avoiding them requires heading for the south shore fifteen miles away, crossing both outbound and inbound lanes along the way. Thanks to the radar, I can accomplish this easily, like using a seeing eye dog to avoid trucks when crossing the highway though here the dog is electronic. At the seaward end of the straits, I have two options: heading out to a sea buoy offshore and rounding Cape Flattery or passing between the mainland and the cape. I choose the latter, because this route is both closer to shore and the more interesting.

In cold, wet fog, I pass around the corner from the straits into the Pacific Ocean close along the shore, winding among rock pinnacles rising from the sea and a gnarled, storm-carved shore. When the motors are turned off and *Rascal* is adrift, unearthly stillness resounds, broken only by the discordant shrieks of gulls. Fog imperfectly shields the coast from view. Gray air envelopes in gloom cathedrals of rock spires, dense thickets of cake-top islets, forests of bare outcrops, and grotesquely carved stone sculptures. A bald granite shelf appears, called Sea Lion Rocks, covered with a reeking colony of its namesake, some lying about indolently, others swimming near the boat, baying at my intrusion, heads periscoped to assess the invader.

Running among all these rocks would be nearly impossible without the GPS chart plotter; with it, the ride's a snap. The icon on the screen presents an instantly updated picture of the boat's relative position on the highly detailed charts. By simply zooming in as tight as the machine allows, the boat, and thus the icon, can be maneuvered easily, though I double-check constantly by visual reference and by radar to be certain the boat is actually where the chart plotter says it is. The day waning quickly, I set course for the outer buoy off the entrance channel at Westport, Washington, and arrive there in the gloaming, a cold fog enshrouding the harbor. Entering the harbor by way of radar, chart plotter, and occasional visual confirmation, I tie up for the night.

~~~

Unlike the East Coast, nearly the entire western shoreline of the lower forty-eight states is a long coastal escarpment, varying only in elevation and its proximity to the shore. For much of its distance, hills rise sharply from the sea, and the few towns, positioned precariously against the seaward slopes, are terraced up and away from the shore. At places, the sea over thousands of years has eroded what once was sedimentary shore leaving today only grand pillars, plump hat boxes, and contorted mounds of stone standing alone just off the shore, lined along their seaward edge by the white spray of dashed swells. At other places, a foreshore of sandy beaches is dotted with vacation cottages and fine homes.

Rivers that drain the miles of mountainous terrain east of the escarpment flow west and at a few places meet the ocean, where they form harbors for the towns and a few cities that have sprouted along their banks. Importantly to anyone entering or leaving these places by water, each river has an inlet to the ocean and a bar formed by river silt, littoral drift along the shore, and tidal action. Some inlets are bracketed by stone jetties, piles of rock extending out from the north and south shore of the inlet, there for the purpose of managing the accumulation of soil between them. It is at these inlets that dangerous forces collide to threaten marine traffic, even ships, and especially boats like *Rascal*. Sea conditions at the inlets are generally benign when the tide is flooding or slack, onshore wind is minimal, and ocean swells are modest. Seas are at their worst and become dangerous when the tide is ebbing strongly, an onshore (meaning westerly) wind is blowing, and swells are four feet or higher with a short period between.

As if to dramatize the dangers, the Coast Guard has stationed rescue units at all of the major inlets and established warning lights that tell offshore boats when the inlets can be safely entered. When conditions are dangerous, the warning lights are switched to red and the inlet closed. Better a boat circulate offshore in a holding pattern, even in grisly seas and black night, than enter an inlet in which onshore swells are breaking. When in doubt, any boat captain can contact the Coast Guard and receive a bar report that will tell him the height of seas at the bar as well as visibility. If a captain insists on entering an inlet in dangerous conditions, the Coast Guard will send out a patrol boat to escort the vessel through the treacherous seas, better this than a full-scale rescue operation.

One inlet stands out from all others along the Pacific Coast: the bar of the notorious Columbia River, the burial ground for more than 2,000 boats and ships wrecked there since records were first kept. As if to honor the dead and the wreckage, the Coast Guard has located on the river's north shore, correctly named Cape Disappointment (by Lewis and Clark), its small-boat handling school, where it teaches young men and women the fine art of piloting small rescue craft through the most horrific of coastal seas. Some of these craft are designed such that if they broach, they will right themselves. Crew and gear, harnessed in place, roll under and back upright as if in a simple kayak, and continue their mission. The Columbia River bar is a fine place to practice these skills.

I leave Westport in early morning, the hour of departure timed so that I will arrive at the Columbia River at late flood or slack tide. After crossing the Westport bar with ease on a flooding tide and mild northwesterly swells, I set course for the offshore sea buoy of the Columbia River, running five miles offshore. Wind-driven waves are three to four feet at a right angle to the swell making for a sloppy ride. After trying various trim and throttle settings to ease the discomfort, with no success, I begin to look around for calmer water. A curious fact of the open ocean is that, wherever you look, the water is, you are quite certain, calmer than where you are. This is so even though you also know you cannot accurately judge sea conditions at a distance. This illusion is simply the triumph of hope over reality, driven by an intense desire to escape unpleasant conditions and what the mind perceives as potential danger.

I set off toward shore, hoping the high headland of Cape Disappointment will block some of the southwest wind, an expectation based on reasonably sound calculation that actually works for a while, until mother nature, noting the stratagem, shifts her winds to westerly, cheating me of the cape's lee. Slogging unhappily ahead, I check the chart plotter hoping to discover some nearby refuge, and find one, an obscure harbor due east from here. Changing course, I head there until, a mile and a half offshore, the winds curiously abate and with them the seas.

Puzzled at this stroke of good fortune, I abandon the idea of seeking refuge, change course again, and head for the cape, now running close along the beach. This is a course I soon regret because it takes me into a nautical dead-end, trapped between the shore and the dreaded Peacock Spit Shoals, where most of the wrecks on the Columbia bar are interred. To escape requires that I either backtrack, giving up hard-won ground, or head due west directly out to sea and across the shoals, then south to the channel markers and into the inlet between the jetties. I can't bring myself to give up the ground so uncomfortably covered, believing the alternative route can't be any worse, an error of judgment, it soon turns out. Plotting a course on the electronic charts, I note numerous areas designated "wreck," where below the surface lurks the hull of some forlorn ship that wandered into these shoals and never left. This does nothing to ease my anxiety.

Leaving the shore and making for deeper water, I find the seas extremely rough, so rough that *Rascal* can't run on plane; the surface is too severely roiled. With standing waves and cross waves colliding, the long narrow hull of the boat is rotated, pitched, and yawed as the sea breaks into the boat over first one beam then the other. Water runs across the deck cascading in rivers over white fiberglass, collects at the stern scuppers, and pours into the bilge only to be returned to the sea by the bilge pumps. Pressing on, I head due west out to sea in search of calmer water, but off plane *Rascal* makes only ten to twelve knots. At times, the waves stall the boat, standing its hull straight up in the air as the engines growl in protest. By managing the throttles, adding power as steep walls of water threaten a stall, backing off over a crest to prevent the bow from burying into the face of the next wave, I try to ease the ride. At last, after more than two hours, the tormented seas begin to abate as *Rascal* passes safely out of Peacock Spit Shoals and into deeper water.

I've been heading toward the outermost sea buoy marking the entrance into the Columbia River channel, heeding the warnings of the *Coast Pilot* not to cut the entry short. At this moment, a small sport fishing boat runs across the bow a mile out, apparently heading for the bar. Speeding up, I catch the boat and pull in behind it. The seas are still pounding so badly I can't grasp the VHF mike while under way, so I come to a stop, grab the mike, adjust squelch and volume, and try to hail the boat by the name on its freeboard. No answer. Again catching up to the slower moving boat, I pull alongside and flag it down. Its captain stops and comes out of his all-weather enclosure onto the aft deck where I shout to him above the din of crashing seas. I ask if he's going into the Columbia River and, if so, can I follow him in; he replies that he is and I'm welcome to follow. In short order, I have acquired a local guide through the roughest inlet on the Pacific Coast, an inlet now a boiling tempest.

Before moving ahead, I consult the chart plotter to determine the stage of the tide, and it brings very bad news. In running Pacific Coast inlets, or any inlet, the single most critical datum is the stage of the tides. Ideally, inlets are run at slack tide, either low or high; second best is any time on the flood. The inlets, and especially the Columbia River bar, are at their worst on the ebb. All guide books and the *Coast Pilot* say simply do not attempt to enter an inlet on the ebb tide and certainly not against a westerly wind. Because I took so much time trying to avoid rough seas along the coast and fighting at idle speed across the Peacock Spit Shoals, I have missed the high slack, and the tide is now running at its strongest ebb. This would be only bad news, but tolerable, if the winds were helping the tide. On this day the weather gods are against us.

The strong winds that started all this, winds that once blew from the southwest, are now coming directly out of the west, blowing dead against the ebbing tide at an alarming thirty knots. As if an ebb tide running into strong winds were not enough, it is a tide flushed from its channel out into the ocean by the fastest flowing river in North America. Add to this the northwesterly swells and this place has just become a raging maelstrom. As a Jimmy Buffett song goes,

> *"I wish I were somewhere other than here,*
> *Down in some honky-tonk, sippin' on a beer."*

Placing faith in the local fisherman, I pull in behind him. He's not going to the outer sea buoy as I'd intended; instead, he's headed for one of the inner channel markers, the shortcut the *Coast Pilot* cautions me not to take. Still I follow, but not easily. Although his is a fine outboard-powered offshore boat, he's running at a much slower speed than *Rascal*. If I back off the throttle to maintain a safe distance, *Rascal* comes off plane and bogs in the wild seas, and if I speed up, she threatens to run over the guide boat. I know why we're out of sync.

The captain of the lead boat is handling the huge seas of the inlet using a traditional technique. He has trimmed his bow high, sharply reduced throttle, and is riding the back of a wave rushing into the inlet. He doesn't intend to run over its crest and surf down the face, which, if done inexpertly or in a boat not designed for the task, can cause the boat to slew sideways as it speeds down the face out of control, then broach. His method is safe, but with the waves moving only at ten knots, it's slow.

I know from experience that *Rascal's* hull design performs well when running at speed down a wave face. So I pull out and around the lead boat, promptly pass over a high crest, and plummet down the other side like a roller coaster car, making sure to keep the bow square to the wave crest and thereby reduce slewing. With the trim tabs raised, the bow isn't likely to bury in the back side of the next wave, but to be sure it doesn't, I ease up on the throttle near the trough, then add power as she climbs the next wave. Passing over several waves and nearing the protection of the jetties, I am suddenly blindsided on the starboard beam by a stout breaker that slams into the boat and engulfs me in a dense flume of cold sea. Just as I clear the water from my eyes, drenched and shivering from the cold shock, another wave hits, then another, and another. These are cross waves that have rebounded off the south jetty, attacking at right angles to the main wave train. A red light on the instrument panel comes on to indicate the bilge pumps are at work to rid the boat of the invading sea.

Finally, just minutes after it began, I am between the jetties, cruising along over placid water in schizophrenic contrast to my recent struggles, making for Astoria a few miles up the channel. Cold and soaked through, I'm relieved to have crossed safely, under the worst possible conditions, the nastiest bar on the West Coast.

~~~

In stark contrast to yesterday, this day dawns brightly with calm winds and a warm sun. The Columbia River bar, having humbled me a dozen hours ago, is now table-flat with gentle swells and a flooding tide. In ideal conditions, I pass along the magnificent Oregon coast just a few hundred yards off the beach, altering course to avoid rocks here and there or to pass around some minor capes. Crenellated black stone topped with shaggy dripping verdure, or billiard table-flat nude mesas, or convoluted shards jutting incongruously from the open sea are flamboyant ornaments adorning the shore. When he traveled along this coast on the third and last of his epic voyages of discovery (1776-1780), Captain James Cook said about the Oregon coast: "There was nothing remarkable about it." He must have become jaded by then or, more likely, the coast was hidden in fog.

What is truly remarkable about Oregon, though, is that it is home to a menagerie of Looney Tune characters and their zany ideas. Take the survivalists, for example, the one-day-the-Cuisinart-will-break-down-and-you'd-better-know-how-to-dice-carrots-with-a-Bowie-knife types. These guys (women, not as prone to lunacy, will go for home appliances until the bitter end) keep a lot of canned goods in the cellar and portable generators on hand, and they're good at fixing stuff too. They are also mostly harmless.

But then Oregon has more than its share of the not-so-harmless Earth First! crowd and their far more sinister guerrilla associates, the Earth Liberation Front. The principal aim of the Firsters is to return us all to the wiggy world of Jean-Jacques Rousseau's state of nature—primitivism, in a word—and the goal of the Liberationists is to blow us up (the bombs homemade, of course) if we don't go along eagerly.

John Davis, editor of *Earth First!* magazine (the exclamation point in its official title says a lot), has said, "Many of us in the Earth First! movement would like to see human beings live much more the way they did fifteen thousand years ago as opposed to what we see now." I could go for maybe thirty years ago, before my hair turned white and my Adonis-like physique became manateelike, but fifteen thousand seems a bit much. I prefer *Rascal* and her five hundred horsepower to a dugout canoe propelled only by me with a paddle; I don't think the family would much care for raw mastodon either.

Oregon is a principal home also to the animal rights types, like Roderick Nash, author of *The Rights of Nature*, a guy who actually worries himself over things like "the denial of natural rights to exploited and oppressed members of the American ecological community," and "enslavement of nonhuman species and of the environment." Stop Killing Innocent Roaches. Wharf Rats Have Feelings Too. Bring Back the Typhus Bacteria. Somehow, I don't think this flapdoodle will attract a large following, at least not outside Oregon.

Depoe Bay on Oregon's north coast is known as Hole in the Wall because its inner harbor is entered from the bay through a fifty-foot gap in the sheer rock precipice that shields and defines it. Floating in the outer bay a hundred feet from the gap and staring right at it,

I can't make out the opening. I see only a solid line of white foaming breakers washing the lower face of an unbroken cliff. Just as I start to think the GPS has failed me this time, a skiff appears magically as if disgorged from the cliff into the sea. Edging closer to the wall and following the skiff's trailing wake, I find and enter the well-disguised hole. Its entry channel angles off at its mouth, revealing only the rock wall beyond, thus hiding its inner reaches. Inside, steep walls encircle a tiny harbor with room only for a small marina, where the commercial fishing fleet docks alongside the all-important Coast Guard boats there to rescue the hapless souls who attempt to enter the bay in poor conditions.

From Depoe Bay, I travel along the coast to Newport, cruising easily several miles offshore over a smooth, sunlit ocean with air temperature in the mid-sixties. Waking me from this blissful world, the surface a mile off to starboard erupts in soft white splashes as a humpback whale cow and her calf, moving north, roll through the calm seas. I head in their direction and manage to get close before they sound, frightened I guess by the low drone of *Rascal's* idling motors. Moving off a few hundred yards in the direction they were headed when they last submerged, I bring the boat to a stop and stand on the aft deck, hoping to get a last sight of the pair, the boat rocking gently in the swells. Suddenly, the enormous cow, twice *Rascal's* length and weighing twenty to thirty tons, explodes from the water, breaching not more than a hundred feet away. Her huge body rises into the air as though she were a nimble sport fish hooked on a line, twists to her right, fins flailing the air, then crashes to the surface with an explosion of sea spray and a loud splash before disappearing beneath the roiled surface. This from the usually docile mammal I take to be a warning sign that I've gotten too close to her calf and had best keep my distance. Knowing that with one flip of her flukes or butt of her head she could easily crush and sink my boat, I promptly slip the motors in gear and get the hell out of there. It's on to Coos Bay for the night.

~~~

When I leave the logging center and mill town of Coos Bay in late morning, the winds are blowing out of the northwest at a stiff fifteen knots under an overcast sky, this the price for the fine weather of yesterday. From many days of experience under menacing skies along the coasts of New Hampshire, Maine, Nova Scotia, New Brunswick, Quebec, Alaska, and British Columbia, I've learned how profoundly the weather of the moment affects my mood. Under glorious blue skies and sunshine, I am elated, buoyant, an eager explorer of the new and exciting world around me. But gray skies or damp fog or unrelenting drizzle depress the spirits, and I become cautious, even anxious, and filled with longing for a warm dry place, like a nice dark bar for example.

Running close to shore in a white capped following sea, I pass Cape Blanco, a prominent headland where its infamous winds increase to thirty knots, and the seas grow steeper. Unless I back off the throttle, the bow sprit, jutting several feet forward of the bow stem, stabs into the back of the next wave, sending a blast of green water crashing into the windscreen and causing the boat to slew off to one side as it deflects from the wave. A partial solution to this problem is throttle control, but I can't man the helm, watch the water ahead and the various display screens on the electronics, and manage the throttles successfully all at the same time. So usually I fix the throttles at a power setting that seems best under the circumstances and focus on the other jobs, knowing this to be a necessary compromise.

The compromise would not be required if the autopilot worked as I wish it would. In milder following seas, the pilot can be set to hold a course, freeing me of the need to focus on the helm and allowing me to vary the throttle as the boat travels up and down the waves. In heavy following seas, this tactic won't work. The autopilot has sensors built into its computer that detect forces trying to move the boat off course. When these forces become severe, the pilot allows the boat to move off the designated course to a greater degree than in calm water, partially accommodating rather than fighting the rough seas, but this also allows the boat to get off square with the waves, increasing the chance of a broach. Were the autopilot not designed to make this accommodation, however, the violent waves would cause something to fail. An autopilot I once had on another boat had a means of overriding the accommodation. This I employed during a rough passage in the Bahamas, with the result that steel brackets that fasten the pilot's servo unit to the steering rams of the motors twisted like Play-Doh; lesson learned. The helm of a small fast boat in rough seas is better managed by the captain than by the autopilot.

Charts for today's travel reveal no rocks or other hazards to navigation and no shallow depths along the chosen course just off the coast. Thus relieved from watching the boat's display screens closely, I can devote attention to managing helm and throttle, and a somewhat smoother, but still not smooth, ride results. The only thing truly smooth out here on this wind-ripped sea is the reassuring drone of the motors, a source of order and constancy amid watery turmoil.

As suddenly as they began, the winds abate for the final leg to another mill town. Eureka, my first stop in California. To remind me that I've left the stalwart blue-collar logging towns of coastal Oregon and passed into a hyperhip, gentrified world, I must now watch, not for icebergs or for floating logs escaped from the inventory of a nearby mill, but for sea kayakers paddling along in colorful craft, their occupants clad in the very latest designer outfits, complete with oddly contoured plastic helmets shaped very much like a puffin's head.

Ten miles out from Eureka's offshore sea buoy, another surface disturbance erupts, this one a frantic boil of white water that churns the sea. Thousands of Dall's porpoises are rolling, jumping, tail dancing, streaking under the boat, bolting this way and that in utter delighted confusion and chaotic delirium. A confetti of white sea spray blankets an area at least a mile square as they feed in mass pandemonium on schools of bait fish. After taking in this wild display of mammalian abandon, reminding me vaguely of a New Orleans Mardi Gras on Bourbon Street, I head into Eureka for the night.

Vancouver, British Columbia, Canada.
Log boom, British Columbia coast.

Blind Channel, Canada.

Discovery Passage.

Blue Inlet, British Columbia.

Straits of Juan de Fuca.

Cape Flattery, Washington.

Cape Disappointment, Washington.

Washington coast.

Oregon coast.

Oregon coast.

Depoe Bay, Oregon.
Hole in the Wall, Oregon.

Coos Bay, Oregon.

Coos Bay, Oregon.
Cape Blanco, Oregon.

Astoria, Oregon.

Chapter Ten

Experience teaches you to recognize
a mistake when you've made it again.
- Anonymous

FLYING ALONG OVER the calm Pacific, graced by a radiant sun, I am this morning making my way toward the logging, fishing, and evolving tourist town of Fort Bragg. This would be just another transcendent day were it not for a curious hydrologic phenomenon that has chosen this opportunity to appear. Every now and again, for reasons not fully understood but related to the vagaries of the north-flowing California Current (also called the Japan or Kuroshio Current), cold, deep water wells upward, replacing the warmer sun-drenched surface water; an inversion it's called. The temperature difference between the surface and deeper water—according to my water temperature gauge the difference is twelve degrees, one at fifty-seven, the other forty-five—is quite a lot as these things go, enough, as it turns out, to disrupt the ever-precarious climatic harmony.

The result, in addition to bringing the nutrient rich cold water to the surface and with it lots of fish to the delight of local fishermen, is a dense bolster of sea fog squatting low over the ocean and blocking the approach to Cape Mendocino. I could escape it and run in clear open seas simply by heading offshore five to ten miles, but there I would have a price to pay. Offshore seas are usually (almost always) rougher than those close to the beach. The winds blow harder out there, unhindered by the numerous capes and points, caprices of geology whose lees protect the beach. The sun-warmed land creates its own breezes that blow out toward the colder sea, flattening the waves near shore. So the choice is shrouds of fog and calm water near shore or vivid skies and rough water farther out to sea. After being pounded by turbulent seas for too many miles, I reach up and turn on the radar, setting its range at one-half mile.

When I enter the cold wet fog bank, visibility drops to thirty yards, at times extending to sixty, and droplets of water form on the wind-screen that with no windshield wiper further reduce vision. To see ahead, I stand out to one side of the blurred windscreen, frequently looking up at the blank expressionless stare of the radar to be sure it shows no objects in my path. At a reduced speed of twenty-eight knots, I'm still going too fast for the limited visibility, but this is open ocean, just a mile or two off the beach where I'm not likely to encounter other vessels. If I do, they'll show on the radar in plenty of time to slow or alter course.

I can concentrate attention on the newly critical radar, thanks to yet more technology. The autopilot is wired into the GPS chart plotter; they "talk" back and forth, exchanging critical navigational data. By moving the cursor on the plotter's screen to a fixed point some twenty miles distant, I select a course on the electronic chart that ends just past Cape Mendocino, zoom in tight on the course to inspect its entire length, carefully check for potential hazards, then instruct the chart plotter to "go to cursor." A dotted line now appears on the screen, linking the vessel icon with the objective. On this and other pages, the machine informs me of how far away the objective is; whether I am off course, and, if so, how far; what speed and course I am making over the ground (which may be different from a speed and course through the water); several different graphic representations of the boat relative to the course; a graphic of the boat's directional attitude; and, at the current speed, the expected time of arrival. All of this data is continuously and instantly recalculated as the boat moves closer to the objective, and the results are displayed on the screen.

The GPS computes its output using radio signals from a minimum of four, up to a maximum of twelve, out of a group of twenty-four satellites encircling the globe on different orbits. One page displays a graphic showing which satellites it is using, where they are located above the earth relative to the boat, the strength of the signal received from each, and the calculated accuracy of the boat's position shown on the screen. *Rascal's* GPS unit is extremely accurate, giving position readings, or fixes, within six feet of actual.

If I wished to plan a long trip precisely, I could establish on the GPS up to 1,000 electronic destinations, called waypoints, and up to 500 legs, the course and distance between two waypoints. Using this method, combined with the interfaced autopilot, I could just sit back and let technology be the chauffeur. I prefer, however, to use the more spontaneous go-to-cursor technique, partly because, in a small boat, sea and weather conditions of the moment affect the route chosen and partly, perhaps primarily, because the less programmed approach, the free form, is more adventuresome and exhilarating. The rigid, preselected route—like railroad tracks over the water—is the polar opposite of the spontaneity I cherish.

Using either the go-to-cursor method or a series of waypoints, the course heading to the objective is fed automatically into the autopilot, which locks on to the proper heading and takes over the steering function, automatically adjusting for sea state. If the boat gets knocked off course by wave action, as it constantly does, the pilot adds rudder and brings it back to course. These two magnificent machines vastly simplify the job of the helmsman, allowing increased focus on the radar screen and the sea ahead.

================================

Navigation has not always been so easy. In the far gone years of antiquity, long before GPS, before sextant and compass, the earliest mariners found their way by reading the signs of nature itself. Whether they were Homeric sailors in the Mediterranean or Polynesians in the

Pacific or Norsemen in the North Atlantic, they moved over the ocean, senses alert, noting the size and direction of swells, the water's color, and the presence of kelp or shorebirds. The sun, moon, and stars were also their guides, when these could be seen, but often it was the sea alone that led them to their destination, just as blazes on trees led them through the forest.

In the first century A.D., cartographers learned how to make nautical charts by enveloping the globe in a latticework of grid lines. Concentric circles around its perimeter east to west, from zero degrees at the equator to ninety degrees at each pole became parallels of latitude. Longer, looping lines encircling the earth north to south and passing through the poles became meridians of longitude. Because the earth is fattest at the equator, where the sun, moon, and planets pass most directly overhead, the zero degree of latitude is fixed there by the laws of nature. Not so the zero degree of longitude, which has been set variously at the Canary, Madeira, and Cape Verde Islands, the Azores, Rome, Copenhagen, Jerusalem, St. Petersburg, Pisa, Paris, and Philadelphia. Lately, it is set at the Naval Observatory in Greenwich, England, just outside London. No law of nature compels it to be set there, or at any other place; the choice is just a matter of politics.

For a skilled mariner, finding the way from one parallel of latitude to another is easy enough. The length of a day or the height above the horizon of the sun or a guide star is all a sailor needs to know. Once on the desired parallel, perhaps with the aid of an astrolabe (an early version of the sextant), all the mariner has to do is remain at that latitude, sailing east or west. The distance north or south is also easy to figure. Each parallel or degree of latitude is separated from the next by an identical distance of sixty nautical miles, and that distance remains the same no matter where we are on the earth's surface. Each degree is subdivided into sixty minutes, so each minute is a nautical mile (6,080 feet, or 1.15 times a statute mile). If you want to go from, say twenty-seven to twenty-eight degrees of north latitude, just turn north and keep going for sixty nautical miles and you're there.

Meridians of longitude are quite another matter. They are lines on the globe representing spans of time. Because the earth rotates 360 degrees every twenty-four hours, each hour represents one twenty-fourth of a spin, or fifteen degrees, and each degree equals four minutes of time. Thus, to know what longitude he is on, the mariner must know what time it is both on his ship and at his home port or other place of known longitude; the difference converts to the longitude where his ship is presently. Degrees of longitude also correspond to distance traveled, though with more complications than figuring distance using latitude. At the equator, where the earth's circumference is greatest, the length of a degree of longitude is the same as that of a degree of latitude, sixty nautical miles. Move north or south, however, and the distance between degrees of longitude decreases until, at the poles, where all those looping lines converge, the space between the linear representations becomes zero.

When a captain knows the parallel of latitude and the meridian of longitude on which his vessel rests, he can locate its position on a chart. Knowing he is at the intersection of, say, thirty degrees, twenty minutes north latitude, and eighty-seven degrees, nineteen minutes west longitude (expressed as 30 20 N; 87° 19 W), he will know he is at the entrance to Pensacola Bay in the Gulf of Mexico.

Measuring distance is simply a matter of calculating a vessel's speed over time. At first, speed was simply estimated. Then some clever guy figured out that any floating object tossed overboard on the lee side of the bow would pass to the stern, a known distance, over a measurable period of time. This "Dutchman's log" was commonplace until the end of the sixteenth century when the floating object, now called a ship log or common log, was attached to a line knotted at regular intervals. Speed was determined by the number of knots paid out over time, measured by the sand in an hour glass. To this day, nautical miles per hour are called knots.

At an unknown time in the last centuries of the pre-Christ millennium, the Chinese discovered the directional properties of magnetized iron, or lodestone. They used this knowledge not to find their way at sea but to point the way south, an imperial direction imbued with mystical qualities. Later, about 1040 A.D., the needle that pointed south came to be used by the Chinese in coastal navigation. Thus we can say without much exaggeration that the Chinese invented the magnetic compass, an invention that ranks right up there in the annals of civilization with fire, the wheel, and golf.

The trade-minded sailors of the miniature Italian city-state of Amalfi, however, were the ones who first placed the magnetized needle on a spindle inside a box with a wind rose set beneath it. The wind rose, a simple round card, or circle drawn on a chart, that divided the circle's 360 degrees pie like to describe the direction from which the winds blew, had been around a long time. When placed beneath a magnetic needle, it became a compass card that pointed the way. Now the helmsman steered as the needle and card directed. Soon, a system dividing the card into thirty-two points was devised. A captain could call out to his helmsman to steer north, or southeast, or south by southwest, and both men knew the heading. Much later, compass points were replaced by degrees: "Steer 175 degrees" became the captain's call to his helmsman.

By the eleventh century, Europeans had begun to use the magnetic compass, and the skills required for navigation changed abruptly. Instead of the ancient talents that joined sailor to the sea, now navigation required nautical charts and a careful eye on a needle. The needle lay inert, unsullied by human touch, beneath an enclosing glass bulb and set in a binnacle just below the helmsman's chin. Skills acquired over centuries and passed along, mentor to student, were replaced by a mere mechanical tool that pointed helm to course. The ancient expert had been replaced by a device, a theme that would be endlessly repeated in the relentless march of civilization.

With the widespread use of the magnetic compass came vastly improved charts drawn to scale with the wind rose, now become a compass rose, imprinted on their face. Soon enough, after so many voyages around the Mediterranean, ship owners began to compile books of critical information about routes and harbors, where good anchorage and fresh water could be found, where dangerous rocks were hidden. These pilot books, or sailing directions as they came to be called, vastly improved navigation and the trade routes that helped drive the European economies. (The nine-volume *United States Coast Pilot*, three of which I used extensively on this voyage, are the official government sailing directions for U.S. coastal waters). Cultures that exploited these new devices, that found and used pilot books, charts, and the compass, became global powers, those that did not, languished.

European seafarers in the eighteenth century, then the world's most advanced navigators, still had a lot of trouble finding longitude. The fact is difficult for us today to comprehend, but back then sailors had no reliable way to keep accurate time on board a ship. Pitching and rolling in heavy seas, corrosive salt air, and changing barometric pressure and ambient temperature all had adverse effects on a timepiece. The result often was disaster. Over many years of failed attempts, timepieces evolved to chronometers and these began to give more trustworthy readings.

At the same time, complex lunar tables were developed as a further aid in finding longitude. Charts continued to improve with better projections of an ovate earth onto flat paper, and the compass became more reliable as more was learned about the effects of the earth's magnetic field on compass direction. By the time of the last of Captain James Cook's voyages in 1779, modern navigation had dawned.

Now in the early years of the twenty-first century, all the complications of earlier navigation—the sextant, chronometer, protractors, parallel rulers, conversion tables, pole stars, sun, moon, planets, and mind-numbing calculations—are gone. Even knotmeter and compass are superfluous. A captain's sheer ignorance of where his ship was on the globe at a particular time, botched calculations that told him he was in one place when he was actually in another many miles away, and the inability due to weather to get an accurate sighting of the guiding planetary bodies had throughout the past wrecked thousands of ships and killed many more thousands of adventuresome men. Now these deadly factors, as an element of life at sea, are forever consigned to history. Even the hidebound U.S. Naval Academy has stopped teaching celestial navigation.

Today, anybody with a $200 basic GPS unit, and without any more training than an hour studying the unit's owner's manual, can know at the press of a button exactly where he is on the earth's surface within a certainty of a few feet. If he is concerned about mechanical/electrical failure, he can buy two, three, ten back-up units and piles of batteries at a cost still far below that of earlier tools and have nearly perfect reliability. The result of this technomarvel is that lives and property have been saved to the eternal benefit of us all.

==================================

After I pass Cape Mendocino in dense fog, just a long dark blur on the radar screen, Shelter Cove looms ahead still in fog. Small objects begin to appear on the radar, so at fast idle I weave among what I assume are fishing boats and a few rocks, without ever actually seeing them, and enter the cove. Through the shroud of gray air, sets of mooring buoys, some with tethered boats, appear. This cove, on California's Lost Coast, is too exposed to the stormy winds of fall and winter to have a fixed pier, and no harbor has been cut by nature into the high wall of its shoreline. Undeterred, residents make their way to the beach down a steeply sloping switchback set into the face of a straight-walled cliff looming a hundred feet above the sea. They launch and recover their small boats using a trailer backed right off the beach behind a puny stone breakwater.

From Shelter Cove, I make a fogbound run to Fort Bragg, where the harbor is entered through a narrow crevice in another high cliff, the crevice serving as the mouth of the creek-wide Noyo River. After a brief stop, I'm on to Bodega Bay over gently ruffled waters along treeless bluffs colored by the arid climate in shades of ochre and tawny brown. There, greeted by still more wool-thick fog, I maneuver around

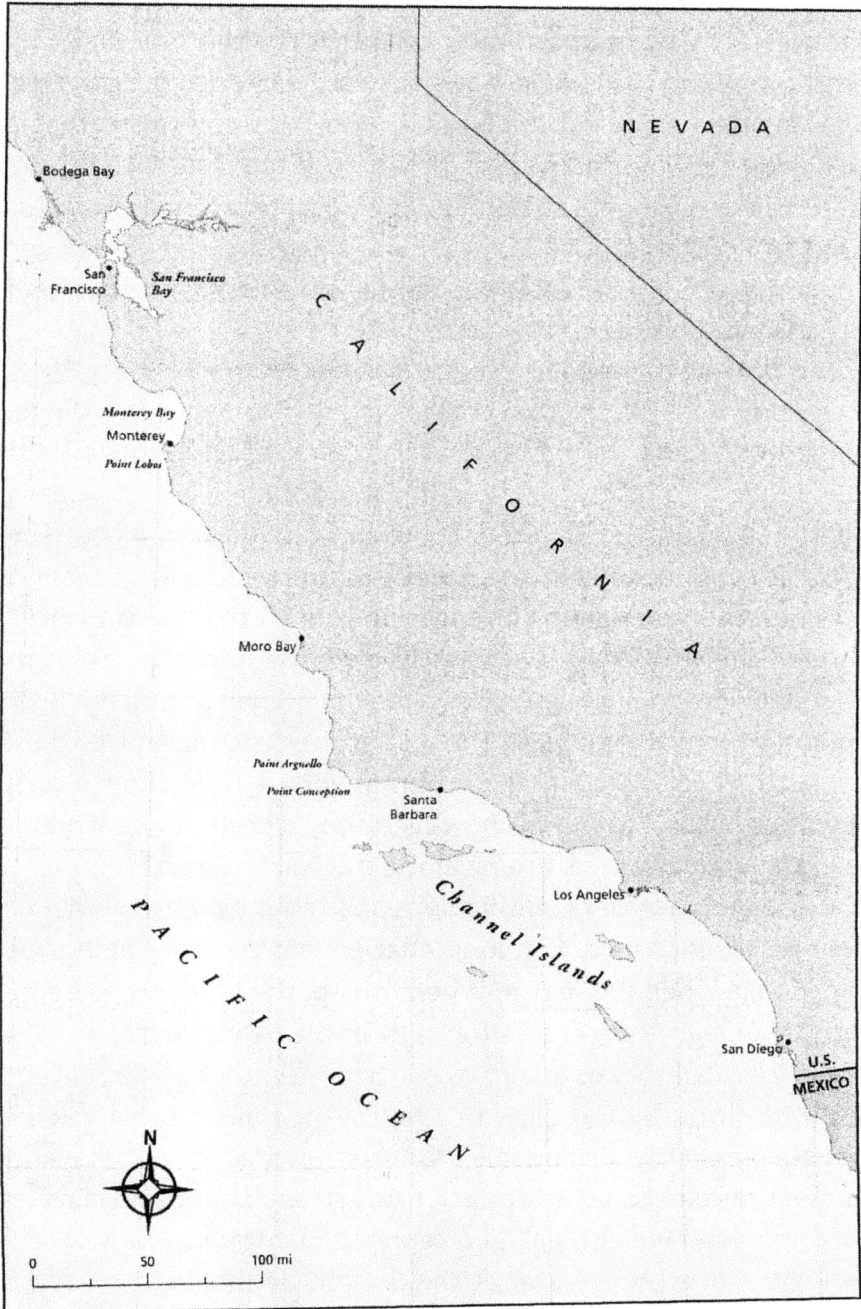

NEVADA

Bodega Bay

San Francisco

San Francisco Bay

C A L I F O R N I A

Monterey Bay

Monterey

Point Lobos

Moro Bay

Point Arguello

Point Conception

Santa Barbara

Channel Islands

Los Angeles

San Diego

U.S.

MEXICO

P A C I F I C   O C E A N

N

0   50   100 mi

Bodega Rock, through clusters of anchored boats and between channel markers, using only radar and chart plotter. Well into the bay, the miasma gives way to open water brightly lit by the sun. Gray fingers of fog caress the tops of the bay's seaward hills and cover the higher ridges in opaque gloom but do not invade this sunny, peaceful place.

Making my way around the bay, I arrive at the wharf of a fish house and restaurant, where I am kindly allowed to tie up against the *Ingot*, a forty-five foot salmon trailer. Its owners, Kim and Gary Brown, greet me warmly and, foolishly, invite me to join them for a cold beer or two, an invitation I eagerly accept.

The two of them have fished together for many years, ranging up and down the West Coast from Cordova, Alaska, to San Diego. As they got older and wanted to simplify their lives a bit, they sold their much larger and more complex fifty-six foot steel-hulled seiner and bought the *Ingot*. The Browns lament the state of commercial fishing, though it continues to provide them a comfortable but modest living.

Government regulation intended to protect the salmon stock limits their fishing to about four months a year. Add to that a month on either end of the season for repairs and maintenance, and the Browns work only six months a year. The rest of the time they have to themselves, to travel, take other part-time work if they choose, or just enjoy their leisure. Above all, however, they'd prefer to be working at the job they clearly love, fishing along the Pacific Coast.

The *Ingot* is a trailer identifiable as such by the twin aluminum outrigger poles, each forty feet long, that extend vertically alongside its wheelhouse when not in use. When fishing, the poles are lowered to a forty-five-degree angle on either side of the beam. Attached to each pole at spaced intervals are up to five heavy synthetic lines, called tag lines, with clothespinlike clips attached at the trailing end of each. The main stainless steel fishing lines run from hydraulic winches, known as power gurdies, on the aft deck through the clothespin clips, each line with a lead weight, called a cannonball, attached at its end and holding the line underwater at the desired depth. Tied to each fishing line and spaced apart to work at different depths are up to ten sharpened hooks, each hidden within a fish-attracting artificial lure, or baited, usually with herring.

With lines deployed, Gary trolls the *Ingot* at slow speed, the bait and lures working their magic in the depths. The choice of how deep to fish, how fast to troll, and what bait and lures to use and when and where to use them, are matters of expert judgment born of many years of experience and no small degree of mysticism. With many years of trying every possible combination of these variables, Gary Brown simply knows.

Unlike the salmon caught by the Alaska fleets, those Gary catches are exclusively mature kings, called feeders, not yet old enough to begin their trek up the stream whence they came to spawn and die. Gary claims his line-caught fish are superior to those caught in nets, especially gill nets, which he says damages the fish. He claims the kings of the California coast are the best of all the salmon stock, but he grudgingly acknowledges the salmon of the Copper River Delta in Cordova, Alaska, are more cleverly marketed and, as a result, bring higher prices.

Of far more concern to the Browns is the incursion into their business of huge quantities of farm-raised fish that now have sixty percent of the market. These fish offer to their buyers a dependable year-round supply of a consistent size and quality the commercial fishermen cannot match with their, as one promotional sign put it, "wild and organic fish." Because the commercial fisherman is thus under severe competitive pressure to deliver a fish of superior quality, his line-and net-caught fish are processed far more quickly today than they were in the past.

The very moment a troll-caught fish is pulled from the ocean, it is opened, eviscerated, and bled, packed in ice for not more than a few hours, then delivered to a processing plant where it is flash frozen. The edible meat of a fish begins to deteriorate the moment it dies. Cleaning, bleeding, and packing the fish on ice slows the process, but only freezing stops it. The large fishing boats working in highly productive waters, like the Bering Sea, are also floating processing plants that flash freeze the fish just after they are pulled from the water and cleaned, eliminating the time on ice and producing a very high quality finished product. All of these improvements in fishing and fish processing are the result of intense competitive pressures that benefit the consumer, but make life a struggle for the small-scale commercial fishermen like Kim and Gary.

~~~

After sharing early morning coffee with the Browns in *Ingot's* warm, dry cabin, a place quite different from *Rascal's* open cold and wet decks, I wish them good fishing and head out of Bodega Bay in now ever-present fog, staying in the channel only with the aid of the chart plotter and radar. Once I'm out in the ocean, the fog is still thick as I work my way along the shore toward today's destination, San Francisco, just over a hundred miles away. Keeping a watchful eye on both radar and chart plotter, I stay a safe distance from shore, thus avoiding rock clusters perched a few hundred feet out to sea sitting there silently like mines in a minefield waiting to do me in. At the outer reaches of San Francisco Bay, west of the Golden Gate Bridge, visibility improves to a few miles and the ceiling lifts to several hundred feet.

Like every other inlet along the coast, San Francisco Bay has a bar that, if not respected, can be dangerous. It extends in a wide arc running from the north shore to the south with a deep ship channel cutting through its apex. Like all bars, it should be crossed at slack or flood tide, but what makes it especially difficult are the often ferocious winds that come howling through the narrow gap spanned by the Golden Gate, with Marin County and Sausalito on the north shore and the city on the south. This gap acts like a venturi, focusing and speeding any winds that pass through it. This morning, the tide across the bar is flooding and wind is pouring westward out of the gap at twenty-five knots, routine by local standards. The colliding forces of wind and tide produce a short, hard chop on the bow, the sea condition for which *Rascal* was designed, and her knifelike hull handles it easily. When I hug the north shore, close around Point Bonita, a terrific tide rip, running full in the face of the wind, creates a much larger chop that, still, the boat handles well. At last passing under the great bridge, I'm on to Sausalito's harbor for a tour then to Tiburon for a breakfast stop.

As with all two-cycle outboards. *Rascal's* burn fuel inefficiently at low RPMs, especially when cold. As a consequence, they emit thin clouds of blue-gray exhaust. After breakfast, I fire up the motors and while the harmless fumes drift over the dock, the voice of a man with apparently delicate sensibilities is heard above the motor noise: "Ooh, yuck, your motors are polluting the air. They're stinky too."

Technically he is right in the sense that a bird defecating pollutes the air or a human sneezing pollutes the air or a sailboat expelling diesel exhaust pollutes the air. Unburned hydrocarbons emitted by two-cycle outboards contribute to air pollution. No doubt about it. Here, in the automobile-dense Bay Area, where sailboats abound and outboards are few, the outboard contribution is minuscule. Though he's right, his remarks betray at least one of his unappealing qualities. Like all the environmentally obsessed, he is a fanatic, labeling any pollution from any source as bad, meaning evil. Air pollution is not a subject for balancing interests or weighing costs and benefits. Only quasi-religious purity will do. A quote from *Pudd'nhead Wilson's New Calendar*, by Mark Twain, comes to mind: "There are no people who are quite so vulgar as the over-refined ones." Not sufficiently riled to confront him, I throttle up the twin 250-horsepower motors, which respond by spewing forth a larger cloud of blue vapor that drifts back over the dock and engulfs the man. In a show of abhorrence, he covers his mouth and nose, feigns coughs, and retreats in utter disgust as *Rascal* eases out into the bay.

Past Alcatraz Island, along the city waterfront, I tour the west bay, cutting through sharp-edged chop and finally dock at the venerable St. Francis Yacht Club, sited on one of the most gracious bits of waterfront property anywhere in the country. Communism, that enticing and for millions of innocent people deadly set of truly dumb and corrupting ideas, is still idealized in five places in the world: the worker's paradises of China, Vietnam, North Korea, and Cuba, and just across San Francisco Bay at Berkeley, or the People's Republic of Berkeley, as it is known. Here is found what may be the world's finest university and what may also be the world's finest collection of colorful odd-balls, including aged radicals, time-warped, tie-dyed flower children, and dazed potheads. These are mostly harmless and generally amus-ing folks, some of whom are given to demonstrating noisily in favor of whatever daffy idea is in vogue at the moment. They keep life in the Bay Area pleasantly off balance.

The winds I encountered upon entering the bay are a predictable and, for sailboaters at least, a felicitous climatic event. Every after-noon in the summer months, beginning like clockwork just before noon, they begin to blow steadily out of the west at up to twenty-five knots. As the evening hours approach, they just as predictably die out to a wispy calm and in the morning begin to blow again but in the opposite direction. It is for this reason that each day, and especially on weekends and holidays, the Central Bay is a gleaming sea of blue, covered in whitecaps and stippled with hundreds of white mainsails and genoas and vividly colored spinnakers and bloopers. The raucous display can't be called a parade, a word that implies order; this is nau-tical chaos, splendid and colorful.

The great Central Valley, one of the world's most bountiful agricul-tural cornucopias, lying east of the city, is the engine that provides the power to run this smoothly and reliably functioning wind machine. There, the weather runs hot, sometimes very hot, and when it does, the intense heat siphons the cool coastal air into the bay through the Golden Gate. Wind speed in the bay is a direct function of heat in the valley. The relationship is so precise that wind speed is easily pre-dicted, varying from fifteen knots when it's ninety degrees in the val-ley to twenty-five knots when the thermometer there hits a hundred or more. By early morning when the valley has cooled, the process reverses and the winds blow out to sea.

This happy confluence of nature's forces remains mostly undis-turbed throughout the summer, thanks to the enormous Pacific High

Pressure Zone that every year moves into place about a thousand miles out to sea and just sits there all summer, blocking storms from entering the bay, storms that would otherwise interrupt the machine. It's as though nature planned for the Bay Area to be a sailor's paradise, and that it surely is.

~~~

The *Coast Pilot* has this to say about the bar at the entrance to San Francisco Bay:

"Warning.—Very dangerous conditions develop over the bar whenever large swells, generated by storms far out at sea, reach the coast. A natural condition called shoaling causes the large swells to be amplified and increase in height when they move over the shallow water shoals. This piling up of the water over the shoals is worsened during times when the tidal current is ebbing, flowing out of the Golden Gate. The outbound tidal current is strongest between the time of high tide and the next low tide. The incoming large swells are met by the outbound tidal current causing very rough and dangerous conditions over the bar. Steep waves to twenty to twenty-five feet have been reported over the bar. Mariners should exercise extreme caution as the bar conditions may change considerably in a relatively short period of time.

"The most dangerous part of the San Francisco Bar is considered to be Four Fathom Bank. Bonita Channel, between the shoal and the Marin coast, can also become very dangerous during large swell conditions. The safest part of the bar is the Main Ship Channel through the center of the bar. But even that area can be extremely dangerous when the tidal current is ebbing."

Confident of *Rascal's* seaworthiness and my own skills now well-honed from many weeks of recent experience and looking for new nautical fun, I decide to confront the San Francisco Bay bar at ebb tide, knowing that *Rascal's* sure-footed hull and reliable power are up to the occasion. In the dull light of predawn, I pass under the Golden Gate an hour before the ebb settles into the equilibrium of slack tide, when nature's opposing forces will lie in harmony. The ebb greets the incoming ocean swells just south and west of the bridge, where the waves pile up sharply as the *Coast Pilot* warned, their chiseled features etched across the foreground of this pale gray morning. They are too large, steep and widely spaced to run at speed, so at fast idle making just ten knots, *Rascal* climbs the face of one huge wave, drops down its backside then climbs another.

Off to port on the high bluffs of the city west of the Golden Gate, homes cover densely some of the world's most expensive residential real estate, where few lights are on at this early hour. Plowing ahead, easily climbing wave after wave, I pass safely over the shoals and into smoother water. After a brief stop in Santa Cruz, noted incongruously as a home of aging '60s-era hippies and the place with the country's highest average housing costs, I set course across Monterey Bay.

While I pass over the 10,000-foot depths of Monterey Canyon, an underwater equivalent of the Grand Canyon, a strange angst creeps to mind, a kind of nautical vertigo. It comes from knowing that I am separated from the sea floor, nearly two miles below, by just a thin sheet of fiberglass. Beneath that flimsy partition lies the abyss, an alien place without light, where fantastic creatures dwell, odious things with eyeballs atop antennae, wart-covered translucent skin, huge piercing teeth and poisonous spires. These are not the abominations of campfire scary stories but real, and only *Rascal's* thin hull keeps them at bay. Subconsciously, I grip the helm tighter and push the throttles ahead.

Around the end of the Monterey Peninsula, where Seventeen Mile Drive and, among others, the Cypress Point and Pebble Beach golf courses lie in sullen luminance, the offshore waters are a dense tangle of kelp beds. Zaftig sea lions luxuriate on rocky outcrops, while Barbie doll-cute sea otters float among the kelp, belly to the sky, dining on morsels of abalone. From Carmel and Point Lobos south, the coast is a high escarpment of pale desert tan, mostly treeless, etched along its length by the Cabrillo Highway. Tractor trucks leading sinuous strings of cars move across the barren face of this coastal ridgeline. Their occupants are surely awed by the panoramic vista before them, marred on this day by a tiny imperfection, a white splotch on the blue sea with a frothy scar of wake trailing behind *Rascal* and me.

The day is not without its problem. While cruising happily along, I am jolted from a dreamy reverie by the sharp wail of the overheat alarm for the starboard motor. As I shut down both motors, the hull settles heavily into the ocean and rolls on the ever-present swells. A quick check confirms my suspicion that small pieces of kelp have become lodged in the intake through which seawater flows to cool the motors. A piece of wire is all that's needed to scrape away the blockade and open the vital aqueduct. In short order, I'm on my way again, rolling past Big Sur and the Hearst Mansion at San Simeon, on to Morro Bay, where I stay the night and prepare for the important passage around Point Conception, the Cape Horn of the Pacific coast.

~~~

As I pass out of the harbor at Morro Bay, the predawn sky promptly turns to cold fog so dense I have no visibility at all beyond the bow. The radar screen flickers with the images of a few fishing boats and the nearby coastline, but it and the GPS reveal no obstacles along the planned route to Point Arguello. Responding to the growing heat of the morning and the warming sea temperature as I move south, the fog thins to a pale haze through which a bleak coast of high, desert-like cliffs appears. Outcrops of rocks and lone pinnacles, some a mile offshore, punctuate the coastal waters along San Luis Obispo Bay and Point Sal. I arrive at Point Arguello in yet another opaque thicket of fog.

The *Coast Pilot* warns that, "Point Arguello is considered by mariners to be one of the most dangerous areas along the coast." The point appears on the charts as an 800-foot long narrow peninsula jutting out into the sea. Up close, it is a magnificent contortion of hewn rock faces and grotesquely chiseled silhouettes dramatized by the sound of surf crashing onto its shores and the sight of exploding geysers of sea spray partly veiled by the gray air. All around me, thousands of sea birds float in densely packed swaths, stonily quiet until chased to flight by the roaring boat bearing down on them. Kelp beds, hundreds of acres of them, line the shore, their willowy leaves undulating in the surf, and behind these a parched coast rises to 2,000 feet. From Point Arguello to the bold headland of Point Conception, it is a glorious run of just twelve miles along a desolate shore of 400-foot-high, steeply cleaved rock cliffs.

At Conception, the climatic world changes abruptly. In Homer, Alaska, the water temperature was forty-two degrees, at Point Arguello it was just sixty, and here it jumps to seventy. The cool moist air I have lived in for many weeks has, in barely more than a heartbeat, turned to hot desert air. Point Conception marks a major geographic turn to due east from the generally southerly direction of the U.S. West Coast, a kind of geographic notch. That turn, together with the effects of the climatic changes, results in a high frequency of gale force winds that occur with no warning. I have the good fortune to arrive at the massive cliffs of the point in quiet fog and to pass on in a gentle breeze making for Santa Barbara, happy to have safely rounded the "horn."

Just past Point Conception, now in wispy fog, the ocean swells are inexplicably suppressed. The deck does not feel right underfoot, the hull is not rising and falling in the rhythmic cadence I have grown to expect. I sense the boat is moving over a field of thick syrup, not the Pacific Ocean. Something about the sea itself is odd. No glare reflects from the attenuated sun light, and the water's surface is not the deep black it should be in this scrim of fog. *Rascal's* bow wave and wake seem sluggish and too small. And now, as I begin to ease up on the throttle, wary of these puzzling conditions, a stench comes to me on the still air.

Alarmed, I bring the boat to a stop, and discover the cause of this strangeness: oil. As far as I can see in the fog, the water's surface is coated in brown viscous goo. Unlike the waters I have been passing over earlier this day, there are no noisy flotillas of yowling birds. It is a stunning realization that briny sea has turned to this slimy surface of rank crude oil which soils *Rascal's* hull at the waterline. Is this ugly slick the result of a massive oil spill from a wrecked tanker? Has an offshore drilling rig sprung a leak?

Later, in Santa Barbara, I learn that the many square miles of the stuff I encountered are the result of naturally occurring oil seeping into the ocean through subterranean faults and crevasses. It is lurid irony, and blaring testament to the lunacy of some environmental laws, that hundreds of gallons a day of a substance pour continuously into the sea *naturally*, while if a teaspoon of it were dropped into the sea accidentally by a human, stiff fines and criminal sanction could result. This inexplicable contradiction in the antipollution law makes my Glacier Bay experience all the more disturbing.

Out of fog and oily slime into a gloriously open and, for the first time, warm sea, I set course for one of North America's nearly perfect towns, Santa Barbara. There I arrive just as a sailboat race is about to begin, part of the weeklong annual celebration of La Fiesta. Sailboats of every imaginable description are jammed into or just easing out of every available slip, the foreground sky a madcap jumble of masts, stays, and spreaders. Half-raised mainsails and jibs flutter about wildly as crews scamper around the decks cranking on halyard winches and hauling in the jib sheets of back-winded sails. The plink of wire halyards on aluminum masts fills the air like a hundred flat, off-key wind chimes playing discordant tunes. Weaving among this happy chaos, I arrive at an assigned slip in ideal weather, a balmy condition that charms the area pretty much year-round.

~~~

From Santa Barbara, the coast runs south as it also falls away to the east, past Ventura, Oxnard, and Santa Monica. At Marina del Rey is the world's largest man-made marina, home to some 6,000 boats, where *Rascal* is a single white dot in an ocean of white dots. Hulls of fiberglass, wood, aluminum, steel, and even ferrocement, powered by wind and every imaginable variety of motor, move along broad water boulevards, avenues, and local streets, going to and from their assigned slips. Local police in launches, and the Coast Guard from a watch room on shore, fill the VHF airwaves with cautions to slow down. An unfortunate few are pulled over and ticketed.

After a few days of needed rest enjoying the gracious hospitality of good friends, Diane and Jack Burnell, I'm back to sea. Over the next few days, in stark contrast to my experience in Alaska, I cruise lazily over warm blue seas under warm blue skies, enveloped by the climatic bliss that has brought so many people to this coast. At Long Beach, I idle around the *Queen Mary*, permanently docked in her berth. Once among the greatest ships afloat, she is small by the standard of today's 2,000-passenger cruise ships, like those I saw in Alaska and B.C. In Newport Beach, the harbor, intricately woven with canals, is lined with fine homes jammed onto tiny lots barely larger than their foundations. The town's waterways are filled with vessels, mostly resting at anchor or secured to moorings or tied in slips or, on this fine day, promenading, their crews out for the nautical equivalent of a Sunday drive.

From Newport Beach south, the densely inhabited coast passes Laguna Beach, San Juan Capistrano, San Clemente, Oceanside, and Carlsbad. In short order, running smoothly over opulent seas, I reach San Diego, pass the red-roofed Hotel del Coronado, and avoid a U.S. Navy heavy cruiser exiting San Diego's harbor, its superstructure prickly with gun barrels and missile launchers.

As the ocean south of the harbor becomes shallower, its color changes from deep translucent blue to mouthwash green. Winds that earlier were just five to ten knots have increased to twenty, lathering the surface into a field of whitecaps. Plowing uncomfortably through the steepening seas, I reach Mexican waters just offshore of the tawdry border city of Tijuana, and the end of this voyage.

===============================

For six weeks, I've cruised south, mile upon mile, day following day, encountering whatever the moment held waiting. I journeyed under luminous skies, under feathery wisps of cloud, and under cheerless flint-gray skies. The sea fog I passed through came in endless variations: walls of talc-white, blankets of dead gray, and dense pea soup that obscured all vision. I passed through an enshrouded, sodden world where sky joined sea in dank gloom and drizzle. I experienced days of resplendent sea, brilliant sun, and elation, and days of punishing seas, bleak sky, and angst. *Rascal* passed gracefully over glossy sheens of flat water, punched and jabbed her way through the rumpled turmoil of choppy water, and slam-banged her way into storm-jagged seas. Through it all, she did her job without a single mishap. No part of her broke or misfired or cracked under the strain.

If the sea and sky brought sensory variety, so did the coastal scenery. The first 800 miles of the voyage, from Homer to Cape Spencer, is a place of such incomprehensible beauty that John Muir was moved to write: "Never before this had I been embosomed in scenery so hopelessly beyond description." The next 800 miles, from Cape Spencer to the Straits of Juan de Fuca, was a voyage through tortuous channels over mostly flat water, with the stark exception of Hecate Strait, amid mountainous islands blanketed by great forests and scabbed in blotches of granite and snowpack. Signs of man's conquest of nature began to appear, and the velvet touch of advancing civilization softened the rough edges.

The last 1,400 miles was a mostly beeline route just off the sheer-sided coasts of Washington, Oregon, and California that brought an ever-advancing wave of civilization. Rough, blue-collar towns became restored historic villages with gentrified collections of boutiques, turning their backs to the canneries and mills that had spawned them. Towns whose economies were once based on gathering and processing natural resources—fish and logs—now discovered the fickle tourist trade and painted themselves in contrivances suited to their new purpose.

On it went, this slowly gathering wave of refinement, growing inexorably as I moved south, town by town. From Westport, Washington, to Astoria, Depoe Bay, and Coos Bay, Oregon, the wave gathered and grew. From Eureka and Fort Bragg to Bodega Bay, California, each place became progressively sleeker and more comfortable, more painted and charming, and the wave grew still more. Beginning at San Francisco and rolling southward, this onrushing wash of luxury and refinement became a cultural tsunami finally reaching its crest at San Diego.

Just south of there, at Tijuana, the wave dashed itself against the squalor of Mexico, collapsing at the border. A country in which corruption and a long dismal history of bad economic ideas has suppressed the creation of wealth cannot sustain the great wave of higher living standards and a sweeter life. Tijuana is the end of the long metaphorical progression that began in Homer. From there south, it just gets worse.

Despite the increasingly affluent standard of living and the easy life that comes with it, on my way south I am overcome by a longing for the wilderness of coastal Alaska, a longing I have fought since Cape Mendocino. There, any pretense of raw, primitive nature I had mustered since leaving British Columbia finally succumbed to the drubbing of civilized reality. Marauding brown bear challenged manicured poodle, the towering snow-covered peaks of Mount Saint Elias faced off against the toney vineyards of Napa Valley, and wizened fishermen in stout forty-foot salmon trollers worked their lines in competition with spandexed yupsters "working out" in gaily striped kevlar kayaks.

The fragile facade of self-deception all comes crumbling down this day when I check into a small hotel in La Jolla. There, the desk clerk tells me, is a full-time staff psychologist on call—should my psyche need a tune-up—and a yoga instructor too—who, I suppose, is there to help me reach spiritual harmony. In my room is a copy of, not the usual Gideon Bible, but *The Seven Spiritual Laws of Success: A Practical Guide to the Fulfillment of Your Dreams,* by none other than Deepak Chopra. I have stumbled, it seems, into the place where Chopra devotees are housed while attending his various seminars held nearby.

What a stunning contrast for anyone who loves the precivilized world of coastal Alaska and its stalwart people. From a magical land magnificently clothed in feral mountains, a land of hardy men and their plain, tough women, where the main topic of conversation is the fish catch and too much government control, I have come to this, a place where mountebanks peddle vacuous knockoffs of Eastern mysticism blended with hip psychobabble about self-discovery and personal fulfillment. Chopra may not be among these, but his message, gleaned from the complimentary book, may as well be written in Sanskrit for all I get out of it.

It's enough to make my heart ache for the frigid waters, drenching rains, and glaciated mountains of Alaska. Still, the weather's nice, and I suppose that's really what attracts an apparently large share of the world's lost and gullible souls. I found no Deepak Chopra books, much less hotel staff psychologists, in Alaska, another of the place's many attractions.

<div align="center">~~~</div>

In the plane heading east, I reflect on what this journey has meant. I did not have as a purpose of the voyage the intention to discover anything at all about me. At my age, little remains to be found; I know myself well. My attributes and flaws don't need to be explored, and certainly not in a book for others to read. Nor did I set out to test myself in any meaningful way, to find the limits of endurance or courage or determination, these the province of younger men seeking self-definition. No, my hopes for this trip were far simpler: I sought fun and adventure, and these I found, though sometimes more adventure than I expected. I also wanted to see up close and at a leisurely pace what I knew to be some of the world's most spectacular landscape. Mountains of otherworldly dimensions, glaciers, rocky fjords, the Kenai Peninsula, Prince William Sound, the Dangerous Coast, and the Inside Passage. All of these I yearned to see and did.

I should confess that I also wanted to be for a time in a place that was not civilized in the modern way, not populated by humans, a place remote and primitive and desolate, away from the conveniences, the soft sweetness of living we take for granted. For that reason, the coasts of Washington and Oregon, especially that of California, were less appealing. The increasing presence as one moves south of a refined, rich, secure, risk-averse way of life I found unappealing, not edgy enough to qualify as the adventure I sought. Nice places to visit, and I was happy to have seen them, but in the end they were too tame.

The coasts of Alaska and British Columbia were all I could have hoped for. That secret thrill of happening upon new places that I had known as a young boy was rediscovered along these north coasts, where I found "scenery so hopelessly beyond description." A wild and flamboyant world revealed itself: seas once placid suddenly raging, winds zephyr-soft turned to gale, sky radiant become a blanket of gray and drizzle.

My senses blended with the scenery in perfect harmony. I spent blissful days of unrestrained exhilaration, dreary days of rain-fed gloom, and fearsome days of pounding seas. White-shrouded monoliths, steep-walled fjords, and lonely vistas of blue sea studded in colossal sculptures of ancient ice enchanted me.

Going new places, traveling fast in an open boat, seeing new and very different landscapes, meeting the challenges offered up by the seas and the weather, these in the end were everything this voyage meant. It was a fun-filled escapade, and a fine way to get nekkid.

Shelter Cove, California.
Cape Mendocino, California.

Bodega Bay, California.

Bodega Bay, California.

Alcatraz Island, San Franscisco Bay, California.
San Franscisco Bay, California.

Fog bank in San Francisco Bay.

Seal colony, Montery Bay, California.
Rascal *passing under the Golden Gate Bridge.*

Big Sur, California.

Morro Rock in Morro Bay, California.
Morro Bay, California.

Tijuana, Mexico.
San Luis Obispo Bay, California.

Attributions

IN WRITING THIS book, I have had the pleasure of reading, among others, the books listed below, all of which I commend to anyone interested in their subject. I have also borrowed from them shamelessly, secure in the knowledge that what they contribute has added texture to the story of my travels.

CHAPTER ONE:
The facts surrounding the true story of Roger Cashin's death, stuck in the mire of Cook Inlet, are taken from a story related in *Alaska: Tales of Adventure from the Frontier*, edited by Spike Walker (St. Martin's Griffin, 2002), who excerpted it from *Danger Stalks the Land*, by Larry Kaniut (Larry Kaniut, 1999, reprinted by St. Martin's Press).

CHAPTER FOUR:
For the story about the great tsunami wave that struck Lituya Bay, I am indebted to Francis E. Caldwell for his description and verbatim quotes from survivors contained in *Land of the Ocean Mists: The Wild Ocean Coast West of Glacier Bay* (Alaska Northwest Publishing Company, 1986).

CHAPTER FIVE:
The bear attack on Matheny and Bahnson is taken from a story by Anthony Acerrandini, *Sports Afield Magazine*, vol. 224, No. 3, March 2001. Though the attack it describes occurred in Montana, it could as easily have happened in Alaska. The battle between two sow Kodiak bears with cubs is taken from *Alaska: Tales of Adventure from the Frontier* (St. Martin's Griffin, 2002) edited by Spike Walker, who excerpted it from *Monarch of Deadman Bay*, by Roger Caras (Roger A. Caras, 1969).

CHAPTER SIX:
The whole of this chapter, except its brief introduction and conclusion, is an excerpt from *Working on the Edge*, by Spike Walker (St. Martin's Press, 1991).

CHAPTER SEVEN:
All of the known facts and quoted testimony concerning the sinking of the *Arctic Rose* were taken from the U.S. Coast Guard's web site and various news reports posted on the web. For many of the factual details concerning the Bering Sea, vessel construction and trimming, stability letters, and the like, and Coast Guard rescue operations, I borrowed from Patrick Dillon's excellent work in *Lost at Sea: An American Tragedy* (The Dial Press, 1998). From *Blue Latitudes* (Henry Holt, 2002) by Tony Horwitz, I learned more about the seedy side of Dutch Harbor than I already knew. Factual detail relating to the Alaskan fishing industry and its practices, vessels, trawl gear, and Amendment Forty-nine came from a variety of online sources, including: various articles on Alaska Fisheries at JobMonkey.com; numerous articles at the Groundfish Forum's website; and an article about Alaska fishing at About Seafood's website.

CHAPTER EIGHT:
Much of the material in this chapter benefited from *"Resolving the Tragedy of the Commons by Creating Private Property Rights in*

Wildlife" by Robert J. Smith, published online in the *Cato Journal,* vol. 1, No. 2. Also, *"Overcapitalization in the U. S. Commercial Fishing Industry"* by Eugene H. Back, published online in CRS Report for Congress; *"Environmentalism Refuted"* by George Reisman, published online at the Ludwig von Mises Institute website; *"A New Approach to Managing Fisheries"* by Robert Repetto, published online at Issues in Science and Technology Online; and *"The Tragedy of the Commons"* by Garrett Hardin, published online at dieoff.org.

CHAPTER TEN:
For the brief history of navigation and nautical charts, I was aided by Amir Aczel's *The Riddle of the Compass* (Harcourt, 2001), Dava Sobel's *Longitude* (Penguin Books, 1996), and *The Charting of the Oceans* (Pomegranate, 1996) by Peter Whitfield.

GENERALLY:
With much of what I have written, it is impossible to segregate what was learned from one book from that gleaned from many. At this level, the source of knowledge becomes a blur. Still, I should pay respects to Jonathan Raban's *Passage to Juneau* (Pantheon Books, 1999), for factual detail obscured by a morose frame of mind, and to the wildly funny and contentious *All the Trouble in the World* (Atlantic Monthly Press, 1994) by P. J. O'Rourke, for a truculent go-to-hell attitude and free market approach to the environment.

About the Author

PHIL PHILLIPS WAS born and spent most of his formative years in Pensacola, Florida, hard by the Gulf of Mexico and just a few miles from the Alabama line. After earning advanced degrees in business and law, he practiced law for a while and later formed a company that today develops suburban office parks in Florida. When he is not at their home on a tiny island in the Bahamas, he lives in Jacksonville, Florida, with Kitty, his wife of twenty-eight years, and their fifteen-year-old son Grant, aka Hot Rod, an adventurer in training.

www.ingramcontent.com/pod-product-compliance
Lightning Source LLC
Chambersburg PA
CBHW072047020426
42334CB00017B/1416